Gentlemanly Capitalism
and British Imperialism

D0147922

Gentlemanly Capitalism and British Imperialism

THE NEW DEBATE ON EMPIRE

edited by
Raymond E. Dumett

with an Afterword by
P.J. Cain and A.G. Hopkins

LONGMAN
London and New York

Addison Wesley Longman Limited
Edinburgh Gate,
Harlow, Essex CM20 2JE,
United Kingdom
and Associated Companies throughout the world

*Published in the United States of America
by Addison Wesley Longman Inc., New York*

© Addison Wesley Longman Limited 1999

All rights reserved; no part of the publication may be
reproduced, stored in a retrieval system, or transmitted
in any form or by any means, electronic, mechanical,
photocopying, recording, or otherwise, without either the
prior written permission of the Publishers or a licence
permitting restricted copying issued by the Copyright
Licensing Agency Ltd, 90 Tottenham Court Road,
London W1P 9HE.

First published 1999

ISBN 0 582 327822 PPR
ISBN 0 582 327814 CSD

Visit Addison Wesley Longman on the world wide web at
hhtp://www.awl-he.com

British Library Cataloguing in Publication Data

A catalogue record for this book is available from the British Library

Library of Congress Cataloging-in-Publication Data

A catalogue record for this book is available from the Library of Congress

Set by 35 in 10/12 pt Bembo
Produced by Addison Wesley Longman Singapore (Pte) Ltd.,
Printed in Singapore

Contents

Contents

List of tables

List of figures

Notes on contributors

SHIGERU AKITA is Associate Professor in the Department of Area Studies at Osaka University of Foreign Studies, Japan, where he specializes in the history of the British Empire and Commonwealth. His publications include 'Gentlemanly Capitalism, Inter-Asian Trade and Japanese Industrialization at the Turn of the Last Century', *Japan Forum*, 8–1 (1996) and, with N. Kagotani (eds.), *Order of Asia in the 1930s* (forthcoming). He also is involved in research on the deployment of the Army of India in the British Empire.

PETER J. CAIN is Research Professor in Economic and Social History at Sheffield Hallam University, where his specialties include political economy and the history of British financial institutions as well as imperialism. In addition to his co-authorship of the two volumes of *British Imperialism*, discussed in this collection, he has published *Free Trade and Protectionism* (1996), and *Economic Foundations of British Overseas Expansion* (1981). He is currently completing a book on the life and writings of J.A. Hobson.

LANCE E. DAVIS is Harkness Professor of Social Science, California Institute of Technology, where his main research area is United States economic history. An econometric historian, he is the author of numerous books and articles, including *Institutional Change and American Growth* (1971) (with Douglas North), *Mammon and the Pursuit of Empire: the Political Economy of British Imperialism* (1988) (with R. Huttenbach) and *International Capital Markets and American Economic Growth* (1994). He is Past President of the Economic History Association of the United States.

RAY E. DUMETT specializes in African economic and social history (with a focus on Ghana) at Purdue University, where he also teaches courses on British imperialism. His articles have appeared in the *Journal of African History*, *English Historical Review* and the *Journal of Interdisciplinary History*. He is the author of *El Dorado in West Africa: the Mining Frontier, African Labor and Colonial Capitalism* (1998) and (coed. with L.W. Brainerd), *Problems of Rural Development* (1975). He was a visiting senior member at Linacre College, Oxford in 1992.

BARRY GOUGH teaches Canadian and Commonwealth history at Wilfrid Laurier University, Ontario. With an additional concentration in maritime history, he is editor of *The American Neptune*, and the author of numerous publications on British naval power, including *The Royal Navy and the North-west Coast of North America, 1810–1914* (1971) and *The Falkland Islands/Malvinas: the Contest for Empire in the South Atlantic* (1992). He has been a visiting scholar at the Institute of Commonwealth Studies, London.

E.H.H. GREEN is Lecturer in Modern History at Oxford and a Fellow of Magdelen College. His research interests are politics and political economy in Britain from the late Victorian era to the present. Major publications include *The Crisis of Conservatism: the Politics, Economics and Ideology of the British Conservative Party, 1880–1914* (1995) and the edited collection *An Age of Transition: British Politics, 1880–1914* (1997). His recent article 'Thatcherism: an historical perspective' appeared in *Transactions of the Royal Historical Society* in 1999.

A.G. HOPKINS is the Smuts Professor of Commonwealth History in the University of Cambridge and a Fellow of Pembroke College. He has served as editor of both the *Journal of African History* and the *Economic History Review*. His numerous publications in the fields of imperial and African history include *An Economic History of West Africa* (1973) as well as the two volumes on *British Imperialism* discussed in the present study. He is currently writing a book on the conquest of Africa in the late nineteenth century.

ROBERT KUBICEK is Professor of History at the University of British Columbia, Vancouver, where he teaches Commonwealth history and has served as Associate Dean of the Faculty of Arts. With an emphasis on the administrative and economic history of the British Empire, he also has worked on South Africa. His publications include *The Administration of Imperialism: Joseph Chamberlain at the Colonial Office* (1969), and *Economic Imperialism in Theory and Practice: the Case of South African Gold Mining Finance* (1979).

MARIA MISRA is Lecturer in Modern History at the University of Oxford and a fellow of Keble College, Oxford. With a research concentration on the history of modern India, she is the author, most recently, of *Business, Race and Politics in British India, c.1860–1960* (1998). She is currently doing research for a comparative study of British and French colonialism in South and South-East Asia.

ANGELA REDISH is Professor of Economics at the University of British Columbia with a research focus on Canadian and European banking history and monetary policy. Her publications include 'The Evolution of the Gold Standard in England', *Journal of Economic History* (1990) and 'New Estimates of the Canadian Money Stock: 1871–1967', *Canadian Journal of Economics* (1998).

NICHOLAS J. WHITE is Lecturer in Economic and Social History at Liverpool John Moores University, where he specializes in British imperial history and the modern and contemporary history of South-East Asia. His publications include *Business, Government and the End of Empire: Malaya, 1942–1957* (1996) and *Decolonization: the British Experience* (Longman, forthcoming). He is currently engaged in research on Anglo-Japanese relations in South-East Asia.

British Imperial Territories – 1939

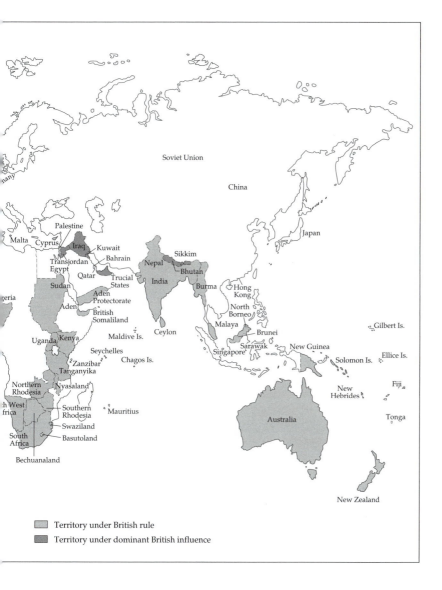

Soviet Union

China

Japan

Palestine
Malta Cyprus
Iraq Kuwait
Transjordan Bahrain Sikkim
Egypt Nepal
Qatar Trucial Bhutan
States India Burma Hong
Sudan Aden Kong
Aden Protectorate North
British Borneo
Somaliland Malaya
Ceylon Brunei
Maldive Is. Sarawak New Guinea
Uganda Kenya Singapore
Seychelles Gilbert Is.
Zanzibar Chagos Is. Solomon Is. Ellice Is.
Tanganyika
Northern New
Rhodesia Nyasaland Fiji
Southern Mauritius Hebrides
h West Rhodesia
frica Swaziland Australia Tonga
South
Africa Basutoland New Zealand
Bechuanaland

eria

nany

Territory under British rule

Territory under dominant British influence

INTRODUCTION

Exploring the Cain/Hopkins paradigm: issues for debate; critique and topics for new research

RAYMOND E. DUMETT

There is today ample evidence of a renewed popular, as well as scholarly, interest in the British Empire as a vital chapter in modern history. After nearly half a century that testified to the dominating preference for area studies (Africa, Asia, the Middle East and Latin America) in academic discourse, the late 1990s saw a return to more broadly based international surveys which found that the study of empires and imperialism had great relevance for global history and was a useful vehicle for integrating studies of diverse countries and cultures over the course of many centuries. Editors of important scholarly journals in both British history and general world history report a great upswing in the popularity of imperial and colonial topics in articles submitted and accepted and as ongoing research areas.[1] The flow of new monographs, biographies, general surveys and articles on the nations of the former British Empire has been unceasing.[2] And current interest in women's social history

1 Dr Margot Finn, editor of the *Journal of British Studies*, states that there has been a great renewal of interest in British imperial and colonial topics, both in terms of manuscripts submitted to and articles published in this prestigious journal (personal communication, Dec. 1997). She added that there is also evidence of an upsurge in popularity for imperial and colonial MA and PhD dissertation subjects in British studies, a trend further underscored by the increased use of the term 'topics in British history' rather than the older and more conventional 'English history'. In a recent issue of the *American Historical Review* (102/4, Oct. 1997), three out of the four main articles were devoted to imperial or colonial topics – one on women in Australia, a second on Hong Kong in the 1940s, and a third on Christian missionary activity in Madagascar.

2 A multi-volume *Oxford History of the British Empire*, under the general editorship of W.R. Louis, has already started to appear. For another recent survey see Peter J. Marshall, *The Cambridge Illustrated History of the British Empire* (Cambridge, 1996). Biographies of prominent imperialists have always been a popular genre and they continue to have wide appeal. See John A. Mackenzie, 'The bad, the indifferent and the excellent: a crop of imperial biographies', *Journal of Imperial and Commonwealth History*, 23/2 (May 1995), pp. 317–24. Added to this has been the continuous flow of articles on imperial and colonial topics in such well-known journals as the *Journal of Imperial and Commonwealth History*, *History*, *Historical Journal*, *African Affairs*, the *Economic History Review* and the *Journal of British Studies*. See Bibliography, this volume.

1

and post-modernist cultural history has undoubtedly enlivened the debate about empires and the imperial mentality. But the core of scholarly research and debate still centres on the structural and institutional features of the British imperial system. For students and scholars of the national histories of India, Canada, Australia, the West Indies, of anglophone Africa and a host of other countries and regions, there has been a reconsideration of the colonial experience and that perennially favourite topic, the causes of imperialism.

Among these recent studies the two-volume work *British Imperialism* by P.J. Cain and A.G. Hopkins stands at the head of the list in terms of its sweeping coverage of a broad range of countries and issues and its attempt to develop a unified paradigm or field theory of imperialism. Since its appearance in 1993, reviews in leading British newspapers and scholarly journals for the most part have been generous and affirmative in their acclaim for a study that set out both to redefine the social and economic foundations of British global hegemony in the nineteenth and twentieth centuries and, at the same time, to re-examine the nature of Great Britain's relations with colonies and nations in each of the major continents of the world, including North and South America, Africa, East Asia, Australasia and the Near East. Early praise in *The Guardian* and the *Times Literary Supplement*[3] appeared justified when in 1995 the American Historical Association awarded *British Imperialism* its Forkosch Prize for the best book on modern British or British Commonwealth history published in 1993–1994.

One of the central aims of Peter Cain and Antony Hopkins in writing *British Imperialism* was to reintegrate the story of Englishmen overseas with the domestic economic and social history – particularly the financial history – of the home islands.[4] Secondly, and over the long term, the two scholars also hoped that their study might play a part in reintroducing and popularizing the study of the British Empire and Commonwealth – after a long dormancy – among university undergraduates. Already there are strong signs of a revival of interest in imperial studies in new courses, postgraduate seminars,[5] and on programme panels at scholarly conferences and symposia on imperialism and

---

3 Examples of early reviews were by Will Hutton, 'Empire on which the sun should finally set', *The Guardian* (7 June 1993), p. 12; P.J. Marshall, *Times Literary Supplement* (20 Aug. 1993), p. 22; R.D. Long, *Choice*, 5/31 (Nov. 1993); Theo Barker, *History Today*, 5/44 (Nov. 1993), p. 49; M. Chamberlain, 'The causes of British imperialism: battle rejoined', *The Historian*, 39 (1993), pp. 10–12.s; and D.K. Fieldhouse, 'Gentlemen, capitalists and the British Empire', *Journal of Imperial and Commonwealth History*, 22 (1994), pp. 531–41. See also the bibliography at the end of this volume.
4 P.J. Cain and A.G. Hopkins, *British Imperialism*, Vol. I: *Innovation and Expansion, 1688–1914* (London, 1993) (hereafter C&H, I), p. 53. This idea of bringing the history of the empire closer to the study of mainstream English history and vice versa was also promoted very early on by Professor Peter J. Marshall, emeritus of King's College, London University.
5 Observers point to the surprising vigour of postgraduate seminars at both the imperial history seminar (Institute of Historical Research) and at the Institute of Commonwealth Studies, University of London. Both Oxford and Cambridge Universities also have flourishing imperial and Commonwealth history seminars. It is significant also that the University of London's School of Oriental and African Studies, a world centre for 'area studies' research from the 1960s onwards, now offers graduate history concentration entitled 'The Imperial World'.

empire in the United Kingdom, Commonwealth countries, and especially in North America.[6]

Because *British Imperialism* is an important work, perhaps a benchmark, in the historiography of the British Empire, it seemed desirable to publish a companion volume of representative and in-depth critical essays, both on broad features of British economic and imperial history, and also on specific regions and aspects of the former colonial empire, where specialists have either disagreed with the two authors and wish to challenge their inferences and conclusions, or have agreed with the essentials of the Cain/Hopkins paradigm but seek to enlarge or amend the model with more detailed references to topics and countries omitted from or underestimated in the original book. Our purpose in this volume is to stimulate student and scholarly discussion about the Cain/ Hopkins model (which is really a compound of many sub-theories, rather than a single hypothesis), its overall conceptualization and organization, interpretive slant and, above all, its impact on future research and teaching in British Empire and Commonwealth history. Students tend to take to historical subjects that involve problem-solving; and it is difficult to think of a major field that presents more sub-topics for controversy than the analysis of the causes, the functioning and the impact of British imperialism. As editor, I believe that the present set of critical essays – though far from exhausting all the possibilities – offers a window on a number of the substantive issues raised by Cain/ Hopkins in ways that will stimulate undergraduate and graduate student thinking about the canons and methodologies of historians, and at the same time suggest certain topics and directions which new research on British imperialism might take in the future. In line with this aim, the present Introduction extends beyond the conventional summary of the contents of the volume, to offer its own critical commentary on the new revisionist paradigm.

The two authors, who come from divergent academic backgrounds, first joined forces in the study of British imperial history while serving in the Department of Economic History at the University of Birmingham, England. Peter J. Cain, who has written extensively on the economic writings of J.A. Hobson, is now Research Professor at Sheffield Hallam University and is presently engaged in research on the history of banking and finance in the City of London. Antony G. Hopkins, who earned his early reputation writing on the economic history of West Africa and who has served as editor of both

6 Speaking of the organization of a recent programme for the annual meeting of the North American Conference on British Studies, Christopher Waters points out that there was a tremendous number of requests for historical panels on imperial topics, out of which just an unprecedented seven panels (each with three or four papers) was selected (personal communication, Jan. 1998). Further examples over the past few years were (1) a conference on the British Empire in relation to the history of South Africa, held at St Edmund Hall, Oxford, 28–30 March 1996; (2) a Roundtable held at the annual meeting of the American Historical Association, San Francisco, Jan. 1994 on the Cain/Hopkins model for British imperialism; (3) a symposium directed towards an analysis of the Cain/Hopkins hypothesis, held at the University of Cambridge in the spring of 1994; and (4) a panel on gentlemanly capitalism and imperialism, held at the annual meeting of the Association of British Studies, Vancouver, BC, Oct. 1994. This list could be extended.

the *Economic History Review* and the *Journal of African History*, is now Smuts Professor of Commonwealth History at the University of Cambridge.[7] In putting forward a new model for the causes of British imperialism the two scholars took on a Herculean task, attempting to explain the generating force behind British expansionism in a way that would take full account of the transformation of the English economy and its impact abroad, without ignoring the latest area studies research on British power in Africa, Asia, the Middle East and Latin America. After protracted study and discussion, the two colleagues found what they believed to be the key to unravelling this tangled skein of economic forces and political institutions in the concept of 'gentlemanly capitalism', a melange of attitudes, class affiliations and agencies which, they argue, not only represented great wealth but also carried enormous social prestige and exerted a powerful political influence in the carving out of new imperial domains and spheres of influence in both the nineteenth and the twentieth centuries.[8] Perhaps the strongest testament to the impact of this book is the way in which the words 'gentlemanly capitalism' have already entered into the permanent lexicon of British economic and imperial history. Not every scholar will agree that the concept has the logical coherence and all-encompassing historical force that Cain and Hopkins ascribe to it, but it is unlikely that any future study of the modern economic history of the United Kingdom or of Greater Britain will be able to ignore it. And few would deny that this phrase is useful as a tool for intricate historical enquiry and as a starting point for debate.

REFLECTIONS ON BRITISH IMPERIALISM VOL. I:
INNOVATION AND EXPANSION

It is impossible to summarize, let alone evaluate, all the merits of this ambitious work in its entirety; and it is hardly an exaggeration to say that each of the 15 chapters in volume I is worth a separate review essay. For ease of understanding, and at the risk of great oversimplification, the Cain/Hopkins paradigm is best perceived as an analytical tripod. The first leg consists of

---

7 Fuller biographies of the two authors and the rationale for their scholarly partnership are given in P.J. Cain and A.G. Hopkins, 'Reconstructing *British Imperialism*: the autobiography of a research project', *Itinerario*, 18 (1994), pp. 95–104.

8 In putting forward their model the authors take pains to point out that their approach differs markedly from the classic *Imperialism: A Study* by J.A. Hobson (London, 1902). Whereas Hobson viewed imperialism as a late nineteenth-century phenomenon engineered mainly by a small group of investors and concession-holders in the tropical world (especially the Randlords of South Africa), Cain and Hopkins see imperialism as a much more broadly based (and less conspiratorial) phenomenon emanating from the general mixed nature of the British economy and stretching back two and a half centuries. They contend that their ideas owe more to the social theories of Joseph Schumpeter and Thorsten Veblen than to Marx and Hobson (C&H, I, pp. 14–16). They also pay credit to the recent work of W.D. Rubenstein (see Bibliography, this volume). An example of the extreme complexity with which Cain and Hopkins argue their case is seen in the fact that they posit two phases in the evolution of gentlemanly capitalism – one covering the period from approximately 1688 to the early nineteenth century, the second which they say began about 1850 (C&H, I, p. 104).

the underlying economic structures – financial, commercial and industrial – of modern Britain which laid the base of imperial power. The second leg in the study is the English socio-political ruling elite, which, Cain and Hopkins argue, evolved from a synthesis between the older landed elite (aristocracy and gentry) and the *nouveaux riches* of the City of London controlling what they label 'the service sector' of the economy. The third leg of the tripod represents the 'periphery' of the imperial and quasi-imperial structures – the outer regions of political control and commercial penetration which Cain and Hopkins dub 'the wider world'. The degree to which the two writers have gone out of their way to master the literature and intricate details on diverse regions of the globe – South America and India are just two examples – that lie far outside their original fields of research expertise is really quite remarkable. They seldom take shortcuts or stint the reader on important information that they think is necessary for their arguments. Nor do they shy away from taking unpopular positions and challenging the conventional wisdom on such topics as Leninist and modern 'world systems' interpretations of capitalism and imperialism, multi-causal explanations of empire-building, the famous Robinson and Gallagher strategic thesis, related peripheral theories on the locus of imperial causation, balance of power interpretations, and (in a more recent critique) one of the current faddish favourites, post-colonial discourse theory.[9] If they probe deeply enough, readers can find in every chapter old facts presented in a new light and unorthodox reinterpretations of traditional themes to sink their teeth into.

The primacy of the London-based financial and service sector

From the start the authors probably anticipated that their icon-breaking approach would ignite serious discussion and possible rebuttal. We cannot, of course, take up the broad range of all the critical issues raised both by Cain and Hopkins in the accompanying essays and in the brief space allotted here: any introduction is bound to be selective. One point which catches nearly every reader's eye at the outset, however, is the proportion of space in the two volumes which the authors devote to an analysis of the social and economic history of England (approximately 55 per cent of volume I, as compared with about 27 per cent devoted to the formal empire and 18 per cent to 'informal imperialism' in independent countries). This is very different from most conventional histories of the British Empire and Commonwealth. Two of the major interpretive themes of the work lie in the extent to which the authors de-emphasize the force of the manufacturing industries of the Midlands and the north of England in Britain's overseas economic and imperial power and, concomitantly, the extent to which they hammer home the cardinal importance of what they call the 'financial and service sector' (including merchant

9 For a recent concise statement by Hopkins on post-modern colonial discourse theory, as well as on his general views on the historiography of imperialism, see A.G. Hopkins, *The Future of the Imperial Past: Inaugural Lecture, University of Cambridge* (Cambridge, 1997), pp. 13–14.

banking, arbitrage, insurance, bill discounting, shipping services and the like) – centred on the City of London and the south-east of England – as the focal point of both British domestic economic strength and British imperial power.

This ties in with the group or entity the authors see as the primary movers of British imperialism – the 'gentlemanly capitalists'. Who were these 'gentlemanly capitalists'? Initially, according to Cain and Hopkins, they arose from the association and merging of two distinct forces – the older landed aristocracy and the rising new commercial bourgeoisie of the City which bought its way into the upper class through wealth, ambition, bribery and intermarriage. In the late eighteenth, the nineteenth and twentieth centuries this group is said to have controlled the London-centred financial and service sector of the British economy. And more importantly, Cain and Hopkins aver, this group supplied the main originating and generating force behind imperialism over more than two centuries. Throughout the two volumes the authors are invariably very guarded in their analyses, supplying numerous caveats and qualifications, lest readers assume too readily that their interpretation is a reductionist or monistic one. Nonetheless, readers should question whether the construct 'gentlemanly capitalism' is asked to carry too much historical and sociological weight, and whether the 'gentlemanly capitalists' of the City of London (which could after all include such diverse people as discount bill brokers, insurance company executives, commodities merchants, even solicitors, investors in real estate, bank clerks, agents for shipping companies, as well as leading merchant bankers, gold bullion brokers and directors of the Bank of England) are made to appear too much as a homogeneous entity, as if all members thought and acted alike. One of the main thrusts of sociological research today is towards the investigation of 'subcultures' within larger classes and categories.[10] How far the landed/aristocratic families and City of London elements in the Cain/Hopkins model operated at various times separately, in tandem or in conflict during the eighteenth century, as well as in the nineteenth century, is seldom explored. Though the authors may issue disclaimers, the impression gained, nonetheless, is that of a monolithic entity. The exposition in volume I, though it commences in 1688, concentrates mainly on the nineteenth century – and especially the second half of that century – by which time, according to Cain and Hopkins, the merchant/financier class was clearly in the driver's seat, having absorbed some of the social graces, family connections and stature of the older landed classes. 'Our argument will be that aristocratic power was in clear decline but that power and prestige devolved more upon a new gentlemanly class arising from the service sector than it did upon the industrial bourgeoisie' (C&H, I, pp. 70, 117). In short, the financial and service sector is seen to have laid the foundations and provided the principal motive force behind imperialism.

---

10 Cain and Hopkins are certainly aware of the issue of conceptual sub-categories. One problem with the use of the term 'gentlemanly capitalist' is that it appears to mean different things at different times in the two volumes. Chiefly it means the great banking and investment houses, but sometimes it could be taken to mean 'City men' at large.

The corollary to this argument, which I shall call the 'industrial minimalist' approach, means that Cain and Hopkins must greatly downplay the industrial revolution as a factor in British imperial expansion – a factor which, they say, has been exaggerated in prior accounts and has received its strongest expression over the years from historians of the Marxist tradition (C&H, I, pp. 18–19, 22, 56–7). This line of interpretation is open to debate on several grounds. First, the writers whom Cain and Hopkins attack most heavily for exaggerating the industrial connection with imperialism are not mainly historians, but rather social scientists and economists who fall within the *dependencia* school of neo-Marxist critics of neocolonialism, most of whom began their work with the analysis of underdevelopment in the Third World during the twentieth century.[11] Distinguished members of the British school of Marxist historians who have written extensively on the industrial revolution as well as on imperialism receive little or no attention in this study.[12] Second, mainstream historians who have examined the industrial revolution in relation to the empire have not, for the most part, considered industrialization in isolation but, rather, have studied its relationship to imperialism in conjunction with a host of other complex factors,[13] such as the spread of technology in the widest sense, the opening of new markets and sources of supply overseas, the population explosion and emigration, the effects of the French wars, British business expertise, the spread of telegraphic communications and railway transportation, and especially British dominance in shipbuilding and world merchant shipping.[14]

A closely related area for research and debate concerns the very strong impression that Cain and Hopkins convey of a dichotomy or polarization between the alleged partnership of the older landed classes and their financier allies in the City of London – supposedly more avidly imperialistic – on the one hand, and the bourgeoisie industrialists of the provinces – said to have had less interest and leverage on foreign policy and the empire – on the other.

11 Key examples are Andre Gunder Frank, *Dependent Accumulation and Underdevelopment* (1978); Immanuel Wallerstein, *Modern World Systems* I (New York, 1974) and II (New York, 1980). See C&H, I, pp. 18, 57.

12 The best example is, of course, E.J. Hobsbawm. Among his excellent surveys are *The Age of Capital, 1848–1875* (1975, 1979), pp. 27–39, 43–7, 127–46; *The Age of Empire* (New York, 1987), pp. 34–93. See also Hobsbawm, *Industry and Empire: The Making of Modern English Society, 1750 to the Present Day* (New York, 1968).

13 For one of the best (and most neglected) scholarly essays which closely relates the impact of the Industrial Revolution, not only to colony-building, but also to the Napoleanic Wars, the Canadian timber industry and British shipbuilding, see J.H. Clapham, 'The Industrial Revolution and the colonies, 1783–1822', in J. Holland Rose, A.P. Newton and E.A. Benians, *The Cambridge History of the British Empire, Vol. II The Growth of the New Empire, 1783–1870* (Cambridge, 1940), pp. 217–40. Indeed, a number of the other chapters in this classic volume also have much that is pertinent to the relationship between the Industrial Revolution and the empire: see H.J. Habakkuk, 'Free trade and commercial expansion, 1853–1873', pp. 751–803.

14 Cain and Hopkins certainly touch on the importance of shipping and railways in the empire (see, for example, C&H, I, p. 230). But their references are brief and they do not relate these tentacles of imperial transport technology to the wider industrial revolution. For fuller discussions readers should consult Daniel Headrick, *Tools of Empire: Technology and European Imperialism in the Nineteenth Century* (New York, 1981); and *Tentacles of Progress: Technology Transfer in the Age of Imperialism* (New York, 1988).

Questions centre on whether or not these categories were so separate and distinct and whether there was not a great deal more interaction between landed (farming and real estate), financial, service sector and commercial and manufacturing interests than the authors are willing to concede.[15] It is a little-known fact that substantial members of powerful rural aristocratic and gentry families, whom Cain and Hopkins connect mainly with London financial interests, also had substantial holdings in British industry. This was demonstrated most notably in their ownership of mineral-bearing lands, especially coal, but also in their ownership and investments in factories (for example, iron and steel) and other forms of entrepreneurship. The most powerful man in the coal-mining lobby in late Victorian England was Lord Londonderry, a celebrated Anglo-Irish landowner; and other examples could be cited.[16] Furthermore, there was much middle-range manufacturing located in London and the south-east.

What is suggested here is that there was more of an overlap, and less of a clear-cut division, between northern/Midland industrial wealth and power and the combination of landed aristocratic and London-based financial power than Cain and Hopkins allow for. Is it not possible, as a separate point, that manufacturing interests exercised far more indirect leverage in the corridors of power in Westminster than is stated in *British Imperialism*? It did not necessarily require that representatives of British manufacturing to occupy high places in the ruling hierarchies of power at Westminster (which Cain and Hopkins say they did not) for members of Parliament, Cabinet ministers, civil servants and foreign service men abroad (even those from patrician backgrounds) to give British industrial exports the best promotional backing possible.

At a different level, certain reviewers have suggested that the Scottish factor is still a much neglected research area in the two-volume work and in studies of British expansionism generally.[17] What about the great explorers, soldiers of fortune and missionaries who were either born in Scotland or were of Scottish descent, such as MacKenzie, James Bruce, Mungo Park, Joseph Thomson, Livingstone, and scores of others? The same question may be asked about the myriad of Scotsmen who worked as traders, medical doctors, lawyers, politicians and administrators of the colonial empire – a number which, as every student of Britain overseas knows, was out of all proportion to the size, wealth and population of that mountainous, wind-swept country.[18] The

---

15 For a fuller criticism on this point see M. Daunton, 'Gentlemanly capitalism and British industry, 1820–1914', *Past and Present*, 122 (1989), pp. 137–40. Cain and Hopkins are cognizant of this issue of interdependence and overlap between the industrial and service sectors (C&H, I, pp. 21, 41 and *passim*).

16 One contemporary publication noted: 'As it is nearly one-half of the House of Peers are mineral owners, whilst a good many are also producers of mines, and work them in the ordinary way as traders [that is as businessmen]' (*The Mining Journal*, 9 Jan. 1986, p. 54). See also David Cannadine, *Aspects of Aristocracy* (New Haven, CN, 1994), pp. 14–16, 18.

17 See Andrew Porter, '"Gentlemanly capitalism" and the empire: the British experience since 1750', *Journal of Imperial and Commonwealth History*, 18/3 (Oct. 1990), pp. 277–8.

18 Consider just a few of the great builders of empire who were of Scottish or Scots-Canadian ancestry: William Balfour Baikie, George Brown, James Bruce, Verney L. Cameron, Hugh

well-known Anglo-Irish, as well as Scottish, component in the officer corps of the British Army and the Army of India opens up yet another category for analysis. Nor should Welshmen be left out of the story. Cain and Hopkins tend to respond that it was the pre-existing gentlemanly capitalist worldwide framework of finance and services that provided the arena that enabled these men of ideas and action to extend the bounds of empire and to find their own places in the sun. That certainly is a solid point for debate. A further response might be that these men of the Celtic fringe were in many cases the real creators of the empire, not simply its servants and beneficiaries.

The Mechanics of Control: How did the 'gentlemanly capitalists' affect imperial policy?

To complete the home islands thrust of their argument, Cain and Hopkins further claim that there was a definite link-up (brought about by common class, cultural and institutional allegiances) between the financial and service sector elite of the City and their counterparts among politicians, Cabinet ministers and higher civil service mandarins in Westminster and Whitehall. Interestingly though, for Cain and Hopkins the key determinant was less the desire for profit from overseas investments than an identity of interests between the City and Whitehall (represented by the Treasury) on the principles of governmental thrift or 'Gladstonian fiscal doctrine'. Here, surely, is one of the most solidly consistent themes in *British Imperialism,* and one on which some of its claims to originality and to logical coherence must stand or fall. According to this nuanced interpretation, the British Empire was held together mainly by the widely held concern for sound public finance and balanced budgets in both the metropole and the colonies and dominions. These common upper-class interests were cemented by aristocratic family connections, by 'old school ties' and by later membership of the same social and sporting clubs. It is by this clever stratagem that Cain and Hopkins try to justify their notion that 'gentlemanly capitalism' embraces much more than the mere financial manipulations by the moneyed men of the City. The concept embraces the 'decision-makers' who ran the imperial government from Whitehall and the 'men on the spot' who administered the possessions overseas – both the mandarins and the guardians of empire.[19]

Clapperton, Samuel Cunard, Donald Currie, James Douglas, Henry Dundas, Mountstuart Elphinstone, Simon Fraser, A.O. Hume, L.S. Jameson, Alexander Laing, David Livingstone, William Lyon Mackenzie, MacGregor Laird, Charles Gordon, William MacGregor, Patrick Manson, Roderick Murchison, John Murray, Mungo Park, Ronald Ross, Alexander Selkirk, David Thompson, Joseph Thomson. This does not, for the most part, include people of Scottish descent who made their names in Australia and New Zealand.

19 Cain and Hopkins have very good sections on the composition and attitudes of the colonial civil service and the Indian civil service (see, especially, II, pp. 24–30, 177–80). They tie these elite groups closely to the ideology and culture of what they call 'the gentlemanly order'. It is not always clear whether this is synonymous with the 'gentlemanly capitalists'. In fact the term 'gentlemanly order' appears to be a much wider and more amorphous socio-cultural category; and its connections with the 'capitalism' of the City of London are far from self-evident.

Two questions which emerge from this important sub-thesis are, first, whether this hypothesized 'bridge' or communications pathway depended primarily upon the ability of City of London 'worthies' to bring personal pressure and influence to bear on their counterparts in Whitehall or whether it rested more upon an automatic complementarity or identity of interests. A more important and related question focuses on whether Cain and Hopkins provide sufficient detailed evidence on precisely how the alleged City–Westminster connection influenced imperial and overseas economic, political and administrative actions. One can certainly find close ties between the Bank of England (a private corporate body under government charter) and the Treasury on domestic matters, owing to the need for close consultation on questions pertaining to the funding of the national debt and current interest rates. Whether one can find equally tight links between the Bank of England, Lloyd's of London or major merchant banks and the Foreign or Colonial Offices, Admiralty or War Office on a wide range of vital matters pertaining to foreign policy strategies or 'crisis responses' on the frontiers of empire or on matters of colonial administration is much more problematical. It is somewhat puzzling in this connection that an important branch of international relations research called 'decision-making theory'[20] has never attracted a wide response or emulation among historians of British imperial and colonial history, despite one or two forays in that direction.[21]

Cain and Hopkins make it clear that their main concern is with the general context within which actions took place.

This, however, leaves a good deal to be explained. Though at various points throughout the study they claim to be very much interested in the decision-making process behind imperialistic ventures,[22] when it comes to concrete cases they seem to avoid or minimize the detailed tracking of causal links between business, military/naval, or missionary and reformist pressure groups and government action from the record of directives within ministries

20 Examples from a considerable literature are Graham Allison, *Essence of Decision* (Boston, 1971); C.E. Lindblom, 'The science of muddling through', in F.A. Kramer (ed.), *Perspectives on Public Bureaucracy* (Cambridge, Mass., 1973); and David Vital, *The Making of British Foreign Policy* (New York, 1968). In contrast to the highly rationalistic approach of Cain and Hopkins, Vital notes: 'It is often difficult to trace the origin of a policy, as opposed to policy decisions.' He adds further that 'the possibility of randomness and the unique event should not be excluded' (pp. 44, 49, 105–6). Compare this dictum with the views of Cain and Hopkins on causation quoted in n. 22 below.
21 For one or two case-studies in British colonial and imperial policy that focus on the decision-making process, see Raymond E. Dumett, 'Pressure groups, bureaucracy and the decision-making process: slavery abolition and colonial expansion in the Gold Coast, 1874', *Journal of Imperial and Commonwealth History*, 9, 2 (Winter 1981), pp. 193–215; also idem, 'Joseph Chamberlain, imperial finance and railway policy in British West Africa in the late nineteenth century', *English Historical Review*, 90 (April 1975), pp. 287–321.
22 Cain and Hopkins devote considerable attention to denouncing what they call a 'chaotic view' of history that traces historical occurrences mainly to random actions with little or no purpose behind them. Eloquently they argue: 'The fact that individuals concerned had a wider sense of purpose which they shared with like-minded compatriots beached on other shores, itself casts doubt on the thesis that imperialism was a big accident caused by a "fit of absence of mind"' (C&H, I, p. 43, also p. 13). However, in passages like these Cain and Hopkins sometimes exaggerate the methods and conclusions of those whose interpretations run counter to their own.

and departments as rather meaningless searches for mere 'smoking guns' (C&H, I, p. 50). This, some critics might argue, is one of the jobs that historians are supposed to perform. The essential inference on causation that readers are apparently expected to take almost on faith from *British Imperialism* is that the 'gentlemanly elites' of the City and of Whitehall were united by a 'likemindedness' and a 'common view of the world' (C&H, I, pp. 28–30). In taking this line Cain and Hopkins come perilously close to what experts in decision-making theory long ago dismissed as the 'rational actor' (or national actor) approach to the history of foreign policy formulation, namely the tendency to speak of 'Great Britain', 'the USA' or the whole of 'the City of London' as if these were organic entities making a decision or advocating a particular line of action. Two alternative approaches which better reveal the conflicts and frictions within the decision-making process are the organizational process paradigm and the bureaucratic politics model.[23] Analysts of imperial history need to strive to identify the offices and voices in particular ministries and departments of government that carried the most weight in specific decision-making, whether for aggressive actions, retreats and withdrawals or for consolidation and maintenance of the status quo. This means a close examination of the interactions between the Foreign Office, the Colonial Office, the India Office, the War Office, the Admiralty and the Treasury – all under the overarching control of the Prime Minister and the Cabinet. It is only by this method that we can test whether the major causal processes at work in the empire were indeed financial/fiscal, industrial and commercial, political, strategic/military, or perhaps religious and humanitarian. It is not that readers would expect Cain and Hopkins, or any single work of history, to dissect imperial decision-making for the establishment and defence of *every* enclave, island base and corner of the empire from Halifax to Hong Kong, from Trinidad to Tristan de Cunha, or from Cyprus to Ceylon. It is rather that some may have hoped for a greater number of representative examples on precisely how the allegedly powerful financial/fiscal capitalism of the City of London directly influenced overseas political, military and naval operations, the building of new colonies and the extensions of empire.

'Gentlemanly capitalism' and the British economy, 1890–1914

In the first essay in this volume, Ewan Green tests the gentlemanly capitalist model in depth and detail with respect to his own very considerable knowledge of the London financial world, particularly during the controversies over bimetallism and protectionism in the late nineteenth and early twentieth centuries. At the outset, Green follows Cain and Hopkins in taking on the large question of whether the British economy really was in a state of decline relative to the other great nations of the world during the period 1870 to 1914.

23 David Welch, 'The organizational process and bureaucratic politics paradigms: retrospect and prospect', *International Security* (Fall, 1992), pp. 112–46; J. Bendor and T. Hammond, 'Rethinking Allison's model', *American Political Science Review* (1992), pp. 301–22.

Green notes that Sir John Clapham long ago documented the shift in wealth from the industrial north-east to London and the south-east that is central to the Cain and Hopkins model. He also cites D.M. McCloskey and Roderick Floud to demonstrate that the British economy was undergoing less of a general decline in the late Victorian age than a transformation away from dependence on industrial export earnings for its surpluses on the balance of payments ledger and more towards reliance on earnings from invisible exports.[24] Less well understood was the other side of the coin – that Britain's growing reliance on profits from overseas investment, sales of insurance and shipping earnings also required that she keep her ports open to an increasing volume of foreign manufactured *imports*, even though this angered domestic industrial interests.[25]

The value of Green's essay lies in its comprehension of both the financial and the manufacturing worlds in the late nineteenth century. In line with their industrial minimalist approach, Cain and Hopkins did not attempt to link the famous 'new imperialism' of the Rosebery/Chamberlain/Salisbury era (1890–1905) in any substantial way to pressures by frustrated British industrialists on successive Liberal and Tory governments to 'open up' new markets in Africa and Asia. Taking a different position, Green points out that the critical report of the Royal Commission on the Depression of Trade and Industry (1885) did, indeed, represent a broad consensus of discontent by British manufacturing interests over the closure or tightening of longstanding markets in Europe and the United States as a consequence of the movement towards protectionism. Without going into great detail, he suggests that industrial pressures to find new markets (expressed through organizations like the major chambers of commerce and the United Empire Trade League) were too vociferous for either Liberal or Conservative/Unionist Party leaders to ignore, and that this undoubtedly did play a part in the more aggressive imperial expansionism of the 1890s.

Clear understanding of the dissonances in the British domestic economy at the *fin de siècle* enables Green to link both the debate over bimetallism and the divisive controversy over Joseph Chamberlain's tariff reform campaign to the alleged cleavage between northern industrial interests and the service sector of the south-east which lies at the heart of the Cain/Hopkins paradigm. As in the United States of America at this same juncture, the strongest support for the free coinage of silver came from those agricultural and industrial interests

---

24 In their summation, Cain and Hopkins also touch on this question. It was McCloskey's conclusion that the economy of Victorian Britain 'did not fail', and that if there was a downturn, it did not begin until after 1900 (see D.N. McCloskey, 'Did Victorian Britain fail?', in McCloskey (ed.), *Enterprise and Trade in Victorian Britain: Essays in Historical Economics* (1981). In their summation, Cain and Hopkins try to bring about a synthesis between McCloskey and his critics when they write: 'If the most recent work on earlier periods is included, the picture that emerges is that of a steady acceleration in the growth of both productivity and output between the late eighteenth century and about 1870, at which point there is some evidence of deceleration, a partial upsurge in the 1890s and a more decisive fall after 1900' (C&H, I, p. 108).

25 This point is also well developed in C&H, I, p. 198.

(notably Manchester cotton producers) which hoped that the inflationary features of bimetallism would counteract the problem of falling prices. Meanwhile, major backing for maintenance of the gold standards came from leading financiers such as Bertram Currie, chairman of Glyn, Mills and Currie, merchant bankers of the City of London. Similarly, Green demonstrates that in the equally important arena of tariff reform debate, the strongest support for protectionism came from the farmers' lobby and the iron and steel barons of the Black Country and Midlands who were most affected by foreign imports in machinery and the metals trades. By the same token, a majority of City of London interests favoured the continuation of free trade. Green quotes effectively from the speeches and tracts of the time to show that the split between those (farmers and industrialists) who regarded themselves as the active producing classes of the realm and their adversaries (who lived off the profits from fixed capital investment and derivative service industries) was a very real one. At the same time he is careful to point out that these lobbying groups were not monolithic and that there was considerable deviation and diversity both within manufacturing interests and among various classes of City men on both the bimetallist/gold standard and protectionist/free trade questions.

All told, Green's paper, with important modifications and qualifications, appears to offer some of the most potent support in this volume for the historical validity of the Cain/Hopkins finance-cum-service sector model of economic and political dominance. As effective as this discussion is in helping general readers to understand two of the more complex and arcane debates in British *domestic* politics at the turn of the nineteenth century, serious students of the late Victorian and Edwardian periods may still wish to ask what this debate on the economic and political foundations of bimetallism and protectionism tells us about the major issues and movements of the day concerning *imperialism* and the effects of British domestic economic policies on her overseas possessions.

Military Force and the Annexation of New Territories

Two of the universally recognized criteria for measuring the strength of an empire are assessments of the instruments of physical force (land, sea and air power) and the extent of territorial conquest. Throughout the history of great world empires, including that of the British Empire, this force has taken the form of military and naval intimidation ('showing the flag'), treaties of trade and friendship, full-scale wars, the carving out of 'spheres of influence', domination (including enslavement and annihilation) of indigenous peoples and states, the crushing of rebellions and, finally, the annexation of new territory by the sovereign imperial power.[26] Such issues lie at the very heart of

26 For a recent article, see John Darwin, 'Imperialism and the Victorians: the dynamics of territorial expansion', *English Historical Review* (Jan. 1997), pp. 614–42. The present Introduction was completed before the writer became aware of Darwin's article. This territorial approach to British imperialism is also stressed in a recent survey by Lawrence James, *The Rise and Fall of the British Empire* (New York, 1994).

imperialism.[27] One specialist has estimated at least 75 small colonial wars, suppressions of rebellions and the launching of so-called 'punitive' and 'pacification' expeditions for the Victorian era alone.[28] Certainly military, naval and territorial factors are mentioned briefly at selected points throughout *British Imperialism* (C&H, I, pp. 12, 71–2, 91–4, 102, 203, 452, 321, 325, 457–8, 463–4; II, pp. 24–30); but some readers may find it surprising that these major elements do not figure prominently or centrally in the overall conceptual schema or detailed substantive analysis in the two-volume study.[29]

It would be difficult, of course, to formulate a single model for the *Pax Britannica* that would cover all imperial military and naval operations in the far corners of the globe, exploits which differed greatly as to background conditions, imperial motivations and outcomes. Each of the so-called 'frontier' or boundary wars between encroaching white settlers and indigenous peoples in such diverse temperate zone areas as British North America, New Zealand and South Africa present historians with their peculiar sets of causal problems. And numerous case-studies have tried to isolate the preponderant factors in the imperial decision-making process with reference to wars of hinterland conquest in such tropical possessions as Ceylon, Malaya, Fiji and elsewhere.[30] A brief survey of river engagements and up-country military expeditions between British forces and indigenous armies in the two disparate regions of Burma (not covered by Cain and Hopkins) and in West Africa suggests that the most common denominators were (1) demands by indigenous interior kingdoms for direct trade with coastal areas without the imposition of customs duties by European officials; (2) British demands for free and unrestricted access to interior producing regions without interference by indigenous rulers or rival European powers; (3) the invasion or military conquest by one indigenous state against another neighbouring indigenous entity over whom Britain maintained a responsibility of 'friendship', 'protection' or colonial control; and (4) the demands of expatriate merchants and administrators (where approval was given often only reluctantly by Whitehall) for armed force to be used to preserve security and stability against alleged 'civil disorder' in a

27 One theorist goes so far as to declare that no writer can afford to ignore armed force, warfare and conquest as central common denominators in the study of world empires: William Eckhardt, 'Civilizations, empire and wars', *Journal of Peace Research*, 27/1 (1990), pp. 9–24.

28 Brian Bond, *Victorian Military Campaigns* (London, 1967), pp. 309–11.

29 Limitations on space prevent this Introduction from examining a large number of interpretive statements in the depth they merit. One could, for example, take exception to the Cain/Hopkins conclusion on the East India Company's wars of annexation in India (1795–1850), that a majority of them were undertaken primarily for fiscal purposes – that is, to increase state revenues (C&H, I, pp. 323, 325). Other motives, such as the drive for political stability, law and order were also at work.

30 For a brief sampling of books on wars and territorial acquisitions, see Paul Mbaye, *British Military and Naval Forces in West African History, 1807–1874* (New York and London, 1978), pp. 1–3, 13–17, 112–54; John Flint, *Sir George Goldie and the Making of Nigeria* (London, 1960); W.D. McIntyre, *The Imperial Frontier in the Tropics, 1865–75* (London, 1967); J.D. Legge, *Britain in Fiji* (London, 1958); James Belich, *The New Zealand Wars and the Victorian Interpretation of Racial Conflict* (Auckland, 1986).

particular enclave.[31] This touches on questions raised above as to whether Cain and Hopkins – apart from the notable exception of their chapter on 'The Scramble for Africa' (I, ch. 11) – adequately investigate the ins and outs of decision-making by either leading merchant bankers and other wheeler-dealers of the City of London or by the bureaucratic mandarins of Whitehall with respect to overseas military and naval incursions or the annexations of new protectorates and colonies. As they stand, many of their most lucid interpretations on the supremacy of the City of London/Westminster financial and fiscal nexus – so far as the formal British Empire is concerned – have more to do with the maintenance of an existing system than with the causes of forceful interventions that would lead to the creation of new colonies and dominions and the territorial extension of old ones.

The role of the navy as an instrument of imperialism

At various points, Cain and Hopkins have put forward the disclaimer that they did not intend, and indeed could not, in the space available grapple with all of the instruments, departments of state and agencies that ran the empire. Against this some readers may respond (especially in view of the considerable amount of space devoted to a detailed analysis of the English domestic social order) that a survey of imperialism involves not only the delineation of lines of causation but also some elaboration on the methods and agencies by which influence, control and protection were carried out. As previously noted, when classic histories dealt with the foundations of the British Empire, they frequently discussed first and fundamentally the great components of land- and sea-based power – the productive might of the industrial revolution, trading companies and merchant shipping, the migration of peoples, and above all the roles of the army and navy. To cite one prominent example, it has long been recognized that Great Britain (or more accurately, the East India Company under Robert Clive) could never have ousted the French from the Carnatic and Bengal in 1750–63, nor have laid a base for territorial power in India, without the navy's temporary control of the main sea lanes.[32] The history of the empire is replete with other examples where British seamanship and naval power were decisive in the retention of spheres of influence and claims to new territory: British control of the St Lawrence prior to James Wolfe's victory over the French at Quebec in 1759; the voyages of James Cook in the Pacific, and resultant British claims to Australia and New Zealand; the map-making of George Vancouver for later colonial control over Vancouver Island and the

31 For a summary of the Burma wars, see Oliver B. Pollack, *Empires in Collision: Anglo-Burmese Relations in the Mid-Nineteenth Century* (Westport, Conn., 1979), pp. 39–111, 137–84; Vincent Smith and Percival Spear, *The Oxford History of India* (Oxford, 1958, 1964), pp. 586, 591–8, 693, 700. See also Gerald H. Larson, 'The three Anglo-Burmese wars of the nineteenth century' (unpublished PhD dissertation, Ohio University, Athens, Ohio, 1987).
32 See chapters by A. Martineau and H.H. Dodwell in *The Cambridge History of the British Empire*, Vol. IV, *British India* (London, 1929), pp. 125–80; also T.G.P. Spear et al., op. cit., pp. 465–80.

coast of future British Columbia; Admiral Rodney's victory at the Battle of the Saints (1782), vital for Great Britain's retention of power in the West Indies after the American Revolution; the annexation of Hong Kong as a consequence of the First China War, 1839–42; the occupation of Lagos in West Africa in 1851; and many more. To examine the full range of British sea power and to evaluate its effectiveness over the centuries would require far more space than is available here; but it seemed appropriate to include at least one contribution on the navy as the bulwark of the *Pax Britannica*.

In his paper, entitled 'Profit and Power: Informal Empire, the Navy and Latin America', Barry Gough focuses on the role of the Royal Navy in Latin America and the South Atlantic Ocean – two overlapping areas of operations within the orbit of informal commerce and investment during the nineteenth and twentieth centuries, and a sphere of influence that figures strongly in the Cain/Hopkins survey. As with most of the other contributors to this volume, Gough is impressed by the tremendous erudition and analytical range of the two authors; but he feels impelled to open up some neglected issues for invest-igation and critique, namely the contributions of sea power to the British hegemony. As the author of a recent book on the Malvinas (Falkland Islands) and the Anglo-Argentine confrontation of the early 1980s, as well as works on naval power in the North Pacific,[33] Professor Gough writes with the con-fidence of one who is familiar with how naval squadrons could be used as instruments of both 'peace-keeping' and coercion in the national interest. His paper also fills an important gap in our collection with its primary focus on problems and events in the *first half* of the nineteenth century, 'the age of revolutions' and the decades of so-called Liberal foreign policy under Can-ning, Castlereagh and Palmerston.

Whereas Cain and Hopkins throughout their two-volume study tend to regard explanations that trace great events in imperial history to more than one cause as the historian's 'easy way out' or as mere 'sleight of hand' (C&H, I, pp. 17, 51), a close reading of the Gough paper suggests multi-causal ex-planations for the exercise of naval power in numerous episodes in the far corners of empire. Obviously the pressures on naval commanders varied with the target of control. Thus, in the South Atlantic we see that Britain was driven in part by political and balance of power considerations to help South American republicanism emerge safely from the shell of the Spanish Empire, and also by a genuine humanitarianism, exemplified in the Admiralty's resolute efforts to stifle the South Atlantic slave trade. Gough sees naval actions in Latin America as being, in large part, responses by individual commanders to local crises. On the other hand, the Admiralty, as the strong right arm of the crown, often received direct orders from the Prime Minister in close conjunction with the Foreign Office. Thus, Britain's occupation of the Falkland Islands in 1832 (which

---

33 For one of Gough's accounts of the combined political, commercial, peace-keeping and human-itarian motives behind sea power in the north-west Pacific, see B.M. Gough, *Gunboat Frontier: British Maritime Authority and Northwest Coast Indians, 1846–90* (Vancouver, 1984), pp. 12–23, 204–13.

the Argentine government always viewed as an illegal act) was prompted primarily by the perceived strategic need for a way-station on the turbulent route around Cape Horn. In forcing Brazil to put a final end to the Atlantic slave trade, Viscount Palmerston was prompted in part by his own strong moral convictions as well as by humanitarian anti-slavery propagandists in the United Kingdom. One should note, when considering the nature of British imperialism in South America, that both of these operations involved the stringent use of armed force, such as landing parties and destructive actions by naval gunnery against merchant ships in the waters of independent sovereign nations.[34] At the same time, one finds in Gough's work considerable support for the Cain/Hopkins model of informal and 'pacifistic' economic imperialism, seen in the Royal Navy's efforts to protect Britain's expanding commercial interests in Argentina, Paraguay and elsewhere.

The essay on the navy and South America leads quite naturally into the next paper in the volume, by Lance Davis on informal empire.

The theory and practice of 'informal imperialism'

Two of the features that most distinguish *British Imperialism* from previous surveys of the British Empire and Commonwealth are, firstly, the amount of space which the authors allocate to regions and countries of the world outside the structure of the formal empire, and secondly, the lengths to which they stretch the concept of *informal imperialism*. Indeed, Cain and Hopkins devote more attention to British economic incursions into independent areas such as South America, China and the Ottoman Empire (treated in separate chapters) than they do to the Dominions of Canada, Australia and New Zealand (treated together as single chapters in each of the two volumes). Ever since the publication of the seminal article by Ronald Robinson and John Gallagher on 'The imperialism of free trade' in 1953, historians of British expansion have had to take cognizance of what is called the 'informal empire'.[35] This concept refers to the premise that Britain's hegemonic power 1783–1914 cannot be explained by the formal constitutional framework of the colonies and Dominions alone, and that any complete history must take into account her pre-eminence in world commerce, industry, shipping and finance as well. Attention in this debate has focused – as Cain and Hopkins do in volume I – on such countries as Argentina, Brazil, Chile, Peru, China and the Ottoman Empire, which were viewed both at the time and afterwards as economic satellites or 'almost colonies' as a consequence of economic penetration by British businessmen.

34 One is left wondering whether some of these acts of so-called 'gunboat diplomacy' should not fall into the category of direct and blatant *imperialism*, rather than acts of mere informal influence – the usual label for British enterprise in Latin America. For the Falklands, see F.L. Hoffman and O.M. Hoffman, *Sovereignty in Dispute: The Falklands/Malvinas, 1493–1982* (Boulder, Colo., and London, 1984), pp. 78–95; for naval actions against Brazil, see L. Bethel, *The Abolition of the Brazilian Slave Trade* (Cambridge, 1970), pp. 274–373.
35 Ronald Robinson and John Gallagher, 'The Imperialism of free trade 1815–1914', *Economic History Review*, 2nd ser., 6 (1953), pp. 1–15.

The essence of the system was control by informal influence and peaceful diplomacy when possible, but by force if necessary. The vast literature on this controversy, built up over the last 35 years and to which no end is in sight, is simply too voluminous to record here.[36]

Clearly Cain and Hopkins rest a substantial part of their case concerning the centrality of City of London finance and services to general world power on the activities of British banks, merchants and financiers in Latin America, the Middle East and the Far East. *British Imperialism* would not be the book it is without this concentration. Much of the debate in the past has turned on whether or not leading scholars (like Robinson and Gallagher) agree that the British home government itself lent substantial weight – through diplomacy or coercion – to the needs and requests of various classes of British business-men operating in foreign enclaves like Rio, Montevideo or Buenos Aires when they were in trouble, or whether, with D.C.M. Platt, they concur that, apart from maintenance of 'free trade' and open ports, the direct political assistance proffered by HM's government representatives to British merchants serving abroad was normally minimal. Cain and Hopkins neither accept nor reject the work of these pathbreaking scholars in their entirety, but cut a track that wends its way between these major poles of thought. Still, the opportunities for debate are enormous. In the present volume Lance Davis sets off a powerful intellectual charge, not only under the Cain/Hopkins edifice, but under pre-vious scholars who have dealt with the 'imperialism of free trade' question, by arguing in essence that a British 'informal empire' did not exist. Davis dislikes the notion of 'informal imperialism' and seeks to shake this intellectual con-struct to its very roots. By careful reading and dissection he arrives at the conclusion that Cain and Hopkins did not define crucial words or key concepts as well as they might have throughout the two 1993 volumes. The examples he singles out are the words 'imperialism', 'informal empire', 'coercion' and 'exploitation'. Taking a strict-constructionist view, Davis wonders how one can speak of any kind of imperialism, informal or formal, unless it can be demonstrated that (a) some type of coercion and (b) some kind of exploitation were also present. In their own extensive analysis, Cain and Hopkins rely on a broader and, some would say, 'softer' definition of imperialism than Davis, thereby contending that imperialism can include 'unequal' and disadvantage-ous relationships between countries in trade and investment and the exercise of undue *influence* through finance and diplomacy as well as through aggressive intervention in a foreign nation's political affairs.

Professor Davis counters that much of the leverage that Cain and Hopkins claim British lending institutions exerted on defaulting debtors in Latin America was, and is, typical of the kind of actions taken by most banks towards bad

---

36 Among the many works cited by Cain and Hopkins are D.C.M. Platt, *Finance, Trade and Politics in British Foreign Policy, 1815–1914* (Oxford, 1968); Richard Graham, 'Robinson and Gallagher in Latin America', in W.R. Louis (ed.), *Imperialism and the Gallagher and Robinson Controversy* (New York, 1976); John Mayo, *British Merchants and Chilean Development, 1851–1886* (Boulder, Colo., 1987).

credit risks in free market situations all over the world. He then raises the question whether large-scale investment by one country in the economy of another country must necessarily constitute imperialism. If so, he concludes, then a prime target for British capital investment and hence of British economic imperialism during the period 1865 to 1914 was the United States of America. Altogether, he notes, as much as one-quarter of all the funds raised through the auspices of the London Stock Exchange for investment abroad went to the USA. Furthermore, Davis notes examples of entire sectors of the US economy – railways, mines, public utilities and manufacturing – where British investment counted heavily. Why, he asks, do we not include the United States as a part of Britain's informal empire?

In response, Cain and Hopkins contend that, regardless of the size of the investment, the USA was too vast, too populous and too powerful a country, economically and politically, ever to have been regarded as a dependency or satellite of Great Britain (I, pp. 231–2). Furthermore, the capital supplied by Britain to the USA was but a small proportion of total American investment needs. In addition, here and in subsequent publications Hopkins distinguishes between 'informal imperialism', which he argues can be seen as an 'attempt' or an ongoing process of expanding economically and politically at the expense of a foreign country, and the existence of a fully fledged 'informal empire'.[37] All in all, the Davis versus Cain and Hopkins sub-debate is one of the most important in the present collection. It should induce student readers to re-examine basic definitions in history (particularly those surrounding imperialism), to call for clear-cut specification of issues, to make firm distinctions between various categories and sub-types[38] and, above all, to be cautious about accepting new or radical conceptual frameworks without solid grounding in the evidence.

Great Britain and the Dominions: Canada, Australia,
South Africa and New Zealand

For students in the United States of America, often woefully uninformed about the basic history of their northern neighbour, Canada, the Cain/Hopkins synoptic summary of the nineteenth-century histories of Canada, Australia and New Zealand in a single chapter (I, ch. 8) offers an insightful short guide to the struggles for Dominion self-government and nationhood within the context of imperial investment. Once again, readers cannot help but marvel at the great range of learning and masterful synthesis by which the authors manage to encapsulate the complexities surrounding the evolution of responsible

37 C&H, I, p. 43. See also A.G. Hopkins, 'Informal empire in Argentina: an alternative view', *Journal of Latin American Studies*, 26 (1994), pp. 469–84.
38 Useful conceptualizations of various types of imperialism and dominance relationships have appeared over the years in the *Journal of Peace Research*. For a pioneering treatment from the standpoint of the social sciences, see Johann Galtung, 'A structural theory of imperialism', *Journal of Peace Research*, 2 (1971), pp. 81–117, plus many subsequent articles and rejoinders in that journal.

government in Canada from 1837 to the 1840s and the achievement of Dominion status under the British North America Act in 1867, whilst highlighting, in their own inimitable way, the catalytic roles of British surplus capital, the London Stock Exchange and the irrepressible 'gentleman capitalists'. It has long been recognized that the British North America Act was the product of a congeries of forces emanating from both the Canadian colonies (in the form of a grass-roots desire for self-government and a fear of the United States if they remained disunited) and also from Britain, in the perceived need to maintain formal imperial authority whilst getting Canadians to shoulder the burden of their own defence budget.[39] What Cain and Hopkins highlight is Canada's continued – and, indeed, increased – need for large supplies of capital for her own internal development which, they argue, were supplied predominantly either directly by British investors or through the London Stock Exchange from a variety of other sources (see C&H, I, pp. 229–43). Cain and Hopkins assert that too much should not be made of Britain's allowance of representative and 'responsible government' under parliamentary systems in British North America and the (then) separate Australian colonies between 1840 and 1870, and further, that 'the economic bonds between metropole and colonies were, in fact, tightening, just as the political ones were slackening' (C&H, I, p. 241). Instead, what they see is less a radical shift 'from imperialism to colonial freedom' as a consequence of the evolution of 'responsible government' and the grant of Dominion status in 1867, than a transition 'from one form of imperialism to another' (C&H, I, pp. 235, 242) in which the dominating features were loans and investments by British banking houses and rentier investors.[40] By this method, continue Cain and Hopkins, in a cogent aside, Britain protected Canada from the embrace of the USA 'while supervising political and military withdrawal and tacitly recognising United States' hegemony on the American Continent' (C&H, I, p. 261). Readers should observe here Cain and Hopkins's remarkable extension of the concept of 'informal' or 'invisible' imperialism (normally reserved for Great Britain's relations with fully independent 'non-Anglo' regions of the world) to the very Dominions normally regarded as main bulwarks of the *formal* empire and Commonwealth.

Challenging this thesis of heavy domination by British capital, Robert Kubicek uses the comparative approach to analyse twentieth-century economic developments in the three Dominions of Canada, Australia and South

---

39 Donald Creighton, *The Road to Confederation: The Emergence of Canada, 1863–67* (Boston, 1965), pp. 7–8, 82–8, 276–83, 413–30; idem, *John A. Macdonald*, Vol. I, *The Young Politician* (Boston, 1953), pp. 384–97, 403–7, 420–65. See also the review article by Peter Burroughs, 'State formation and the imperial factor in nineteenth-century Canada', *Journal of Imperial and Commonwealth History*, 24/1 (Jan. 1996), pp. 118–31.

40 Thus by 1896 foreign capital totalling $1.2 billion had been invested in Canada, of which nearly one billion or 83 per cent was British. The bulk of this was invested in railway and government bonds and stocks: R.T. Naylor, *The History of Canadian Business*, Vol. I, *Banks and Finance Capital* (Toronto, 1975), pp. 228–9. It should also be noted that there had been a large build-up of British investment in Upper Canada before confederation – mainly for railways – particularly under the direction of the London houses of Baring Brothers and Glyn Mills (ibid., pp. 20–35).

Africa. In doing so he also attempts to answer another of the methodological questions raised by Cain and Hopkins – namely, are metropolitan-oriented theories of causation compatible with London-centred explanations?[41] At the outset, he asks whether it is not probable that local or endogenous Canadian forces for economic change counted for a good deal more than the Cain and Hopkins imperial/London-centred model comprehends. With economic development as his main focus of attention, Kubicek contends that it was more the ordinary local settlers and their later descendants (and much less the ruling eastern Canadian elites) who, in conjunction with British financial institutions, raised the capital necessary to extend farmlands and build the new railways, canals, mines and factories. In the creation of Canadian confederation and in the early economic expansion to the Pacific coast (epitomized by the construction of the Canadian-Pacific railroad), Kubicek points out that it was not only British investors but also Canadian-owned banks and, more importantly, the Canadian government itself who cooperated with one another in an interlocking network of potent investment activity. Again, comparison between Kubicek's interpretation and a close rereading of Cain and Hopkins shows that there are only limited disagreements over facts, but substantial differences in the weights allotted to internal versus external factor inputs. Whereas Cain and Hopkins invariably find tight British controls and hence 'imperialism', historians of a more neutral cast of mind tend to find interdependence and 'partnership' for mutual advantage in this investment relationship.

(Another point noted but not developed by Cain and Hopkins, nor by Kubicek, is the growing amount of United States investment in Canada, especially after the turn of the century.) Kubicek concedes that economic growth in the individual colonies of Australia – especially New South Wales and Victoria – was stimulated by substantial infusions of British capital; but he argues that the governments of these colonies 'managed to dictate to a surprising degree the terms on which they received capital, new immigrants and technology'. To measure statistically the force and effectiveness of imperial investment and entrepreneurship, as opposed to home-grown elements, in the economic development of the Dominions remains a formidable – and probably impossible – task for future historians. Nor should we forget that, as in the USA, there was much wasteful and unproductive expenditure (fraudulent land development deals, mining schemes and the like) in the opening of the Canadian and Australian frontiers. In reviewing Cain and Hopkins, Kubicek

---

41 At various points in volume I, Cain and Hopkins maintain that their own Anglocentric interpretation of imperialism is 'not in conflict' with alternative theories which trace the causes of expansion in forces emanating from the colonized areas (eccentric or peripheral interpretations) (C&H, I, p. 10). There may be some accuracy in this statement, particularly when applied to the history of nineteenth-century Canada and a topic like Canadian confederation. On the other hand, one can document examples for many other colonial territories, for example, where the fomenting of local wars and 'land grabbing' by avaricious white settlers against indigenous peoples did not set well with (and were often opposed by) officials in Whitehall. Therefore, the alleged compatibility between Cain/Hopkins-style metropolitan-centred interpretations and peripheral theories remains to be tested for many other parts of the empire.

underscores the limitations of a model for the history of international capitalistic development based mainly on the bi-polarities of a British metropolitan versus a dominion-centred relationship, and he suggests that we should re-examine the alternative potential of a more broadly based 'world systems' model. The work of Shigeru Akita in chapter 6 points in a similar direction. He raises the issue of whether it may be Eurocentric to view the political economy of Asia between the wars mainly in terms of a clash between East and West or between Great Britain and her satellites. Instead, he contends, there was a regional configuration of more balanced economic power relations in which all the Asian powers – India, as well as China, Japan, plus Britain and the USA, were leading actors.

The 'scramble for Africa': Cain and Hopkins versus Robinson and Gallagher

The Cain/Hopkins treatment of the 'Partition of Africa' (I, ch. 11), with its particular emphasis on British expansion in Egypt and South Africa, is both brilliant and lucid. They do not deal to any great extent with West, East or British Central Africa. In numerous review articles throughout the 1960s, 1970s and early 1980s, Hopkins, along with Colin W. Newbury, Hans Ulrich Wehler and other scholars, challenged the precepts of the then ruling modern interpretation – that presented by Ronald Robinson and John Gallagher in the classic *Africa and the Victorians* (1960), which focused on long-range strategic factors – particularly as perceived from the standpoint of the 'official mind' in London – as providing the common denominator for explaining the motivation, if not the causality, behind British annexations in the 'dark continent' between 1885 and 1905 and after. The revolt of a group of disgruntled younger Egyptian army officers, led by Urabi Pasha against the regime of the Khedive – presumably a threat to the Suez Canal – and the subsequent bombardment of Alexandria and occupation of the country by British troops in 1881–2 was analysed as absolutely central to the general 'scramble for Africa' because it supposedly triggered a reaction by France to expand her empire in the western Sudan (Haut Senegal-Niger) and subsequent activities by German and Italian expansionists as well.

Cain and Hopkins compel readers to refocus their attention away from the strategic considerations emphasized by Robinson and Gallagher, which had dominated scholarly discussions since 1960, and to re-examine the underlying economic (and especially financial) causes for imperialism in Egypt and the Sudan which, they contend, were central to the men who ran the empire. In 1880 Britain was Egypt's most important trading client, providing 44 per cent of her imports and purchasing 80 per cent of her exports. In addition, British investors owned more than half of Egypt's funded debt in the form of Suez Canal shares and bonds in the internationally funded Egyptian debt (C&H, I, p. 363). Relying on recent primary research by scholars such as J. Udelson, B.R. Johns and E.J.R. Owen, Cain and Hopkins make what is probably their strongest case in the entire two volumes for close prior involvement by lead-ing investors of the City – including the house of Rothschild (see C&H, I, p. 368) – in an about-to-be-occupied, overseas territory combined with intimate connections 'between those who formulated international policy and those who financed it'. One of the telling facts put forward by Cain and Hopkins to cement their 'gentlemanly capitalist' thesis with regard to Egypt is that when Prime Minister Gladstone ordered a combined military and naval strike against Egypt in 1882, some 37 per cent of his personal investments was in Egyptian stock.

Robert Kubicek is critical of Cain/Hopkins in their treatment of South Africa. He contends that *British Imperialism* is not as effective as it might have been in applying its overarching thesis to the decision-making that led to imperialistic wars and annexations at the periphery. It is generally recognized that one of the classic imperialist conflicts of the modern age was the Anglo-Boer War of 1899–1902. Even though they have obviously moved a long way from the older conspiratorial theories of the Hobsonian school – that the war stemmed mainly from the aggressive greed of the Randlords – Cain and Hopkins nonetheless argue that British-led diamond- and gold-mining im-perialism, and ultimately the war itself, served City of London financial and service sector interests (C&H, I, pp. 374–81). Kubicek, by contrast, suggests that Chamberlain (then Secretary of State for Colonies) and Alfred Milner (British High Commissioner to the Cape), in working up to a conflict with Paul Kruger (President of the Transvaal) over the Ouitlander question, acted *against* the dominant will of City financiers (as represented by the Rothschilds) who favoured a peaceful solution (Kubicek, pp. 121–2). This simplified sum-mary of Kubicek's comments merely demonstrates how difficult it is effect-ively to separate out the 'gentlemanly capitalist' financial/services element in imperialism from political and strategic considerations and (to cite another alternative theory of causation) the purely idiosyncratic acts of wilful poli-ticians and vainglorious 'men on the spot'.

Strong as they are in applying their gentlemanly capitalist service sector model to Egypt, the Nile Valley and to southern Africa, Cain and Hopkins are neither so rigorous nor relentless in their efforts to apply the City of London model to imperialism in other parts of Africa. Indeed, they concede that there is little evidence for strong 'gentlemanly capitalist' influence behind British territorial annexations in West and East Africa in the late Victorian age. They tend rather to argue that the absence of City interest in these regions of colonial annexations demonstrates (1) that these areas were not valuable enough to attract the profit-seeking propensities of the ruling financial elites of empire, and (2) that British territorial expansion in West and East Africa demonstrates *the very strength and resilience of City financial and service sector interests*, since they refused to become involved in a number of mere foreign policy sideshows that were not worth their while (C&H, I, pp. 282–3, 391). In passages like these, and at several other points in this fine work, however, it sometimes appears as if the authors have shifted focus, or lost sight of their prime target for analysis – the central causes of imperialism. Where financial and service sector interests were not prominent, the Cain and Hopkins account leaves room for alternative explanations. These merit further consideration.[42]

Despite the tendency of *British Imperialism*, volume I, to skim over their early colonial histories, the fact is that Great Britain did engage in extensive programmes of hinterland expansion and consolidation in West, East, and later in Central Africa – in the Gold Coast, Sierra Leone, Nigeria, Kenya, Zanzibar, Uganda, Zimbabwe, Zambia and Malawi. It is rather easy to minimize or dismiss a subject by arguing that the acquisition of a particular colony or protectorate in the tropical world did not matter so much in the total scheme of profit and power to the occupying power. The point is that the broadly based 'new imperialism' in British West Africa did matter to numerous important officials, regionally based commercial and shipping interests, mining conglomerates, colonial governors and pro-consuls, not to mention leading decision-makers in Whitehall.[43] The fact that such annexations did not figure strongly on the agendas of those London capitalists and financiers examined by Cain and Hopkins (presumably the great merchant bankers) is no test at all. Another mistake which a handful of historians have continued to make in analysing imperialism lies in assuming that this human phenomenon must have been based on *rational* motives. Since City of London financial determinants did not figure strongly in the movements to annex territories in southern Nigeria (1884–91), northern Nigeria (1895–1900), the Gold Coast and Asante (1895–1902) or the hinterlands of Sierra Leone during the *fin de siècle,* one obvious answer to the conundrum is that the dominant drive came from a complex of *other* elements, in which Anglo-West African business interests and a Europe-centred desire to pre-empt rivals for reasons of *prestige* figured most prominently.[44] Interestingly, the minimal emphasis in *British Imperialism* on the causes and force of British economic expansionism in West

42 Two other examples of what some would call a subtle shift of emphasis in Cain and Hopkins's attack, or circumventing the main issue – British imperialism – can be found in the chapter on British influence in the Ottoman Empire in volume I and in their very long discussion on British international banking and the Sterling Area in volume II, where their stress and focus are placed on the continued strength of high finance and currency controls centred on The City of London – as if this were the main thesis to be proved (C&H, I, pp. 397–421; II, pp. 92–105, 297–315).

43 Pro-imperialist pressures for colonial expansion and consolidation derived, not only from London, Liverpool and Manchester-centred trading and shipping associations, but also increasingly from mining companies. For a sampling of studies on shipping companies, see Peter N. Davies, *Sir Alfred Jones* (London, 1978); idem, *The Trade Makers: Elder Dempster in West Africa, 1852–1972* (London, 1973). For work on mining companies in West Africa, see R.E. Dumett, *El Dorado in West Africa: The Gold Mining Frontier, African Labor and Colonial Capitalism in the Gold Coast, 1875–1900* (Athens, Ohio, 1998); P. Greenhalgh, *West African Diamonds, 1919–83* (Manchester, 1985); Bill Freund, *Capital and Labour in the Nigerian Tin Mines* (Atlantic Highlands, NJ, 1981), pp. 201–35 and *passim*. Cain and Hopkins note that Anglo-West African commercial interests became more vociferous, but the implications of this for the Scramble for Africa and the new imperialism do not figure strongly in their model of imperialism (C&H, I, p. 384).

44 Support for this view comes in part from John D. Hargreaves, *West Africa Partitioned*, Vol. II: *The Elephants and the Grass* (Madison, Wisc., 1985), pp. 103–4, 105–7, 249 and other authoritative sources.

Africa differs somewhat from Hopkins's own exhaustive analysis of this topic in his earlier acclaimed economic history of that region.[45]

The Cain and Hopkins study of imperialism is so vast that its two volumes (which confront separate historical problems and time frames) have to be analysed separately. In volume II,[46] which contains twelve chapters, the two authors assess the question of Britain's status as a great power in the twentieth century. Did the British Empire expand or contract? Did it enter after 1919 into a slow and irreversible decline? Or did the empire exhibit surprising resilience, and even recovery, in the face of new international threats and dangers? What was the relationship, if any, between the continued existence of the British Empire and Commonwealth and Great Britain's overall rating as a world power? Each of these issues is tremendous in scope. The question is how far Cain and Hopkins address them effectively.

As in volume I, the range of subjects over which Cain and Hopkins exhibit a mastery, through exhaustive reading in the secondary sources, is most impressive. Sub-topics include: Britain's huge war debt and widespread unemployment after 1919; the fall-off in industrial productivity; the emphasis on balanced budgets and traditional laissez-faire economics; the disastrous effects of the return to the gold standard in 1925; the growing challenge from the United States of America; the Ottawa Conference and free trade versus protectionism; the Great Depression; colonial policy between the wars; and much more. Once again, Cain and Hopkins try to steer a course that analyses these questions at least as much, and probably more, from the standpoint of British economic history as from the standpoint of imperial history or the history of the Empire/Commonwealth. In an organizational schema similar to that in volume I, the authors devote nearly one-half of volume II to a discussion of the British domestic economy between the two world wars, particularly from the perspective of international finance.[47] We shall take that as our primary focus here, since it is impossible to do justice to the complex range of related topics raised in every chapter.

The British domestic economy, 1919–1939

What were the parameters of British global power in the twentieth century? Were the British Empire and Commonwealth strong or weak from 1900 to

45 A.G. Hopkins, *An Economic History of West Africa* (London and New York, 1973), pp. 124–86.
46 P.J. Cain and A.G. Hopkins, *British Imperialism*, Vol. II: *Crisis and Deconstruction, 1914–1990* (London, 1993). Hereafter referred to as C&H, II.
47 The proportions of space devoted to broad subjects in volume II are as follows: British economic and social history – 48%; the formal Empire – 33%; informal imperialism in independent countries (mainly East Asia and Latin America) – 18%. This means that the British economy and independent nations outside the formal Empire and Commonwealth account for 66% of volume II.

1990? What were the causes of decline and when did the end come? Most people would assume that these are moot points, since the British Empire came to an end during the independence revolutions of 1956–80 and the Commonwealth is but a shell of its former self. In evaluating Britain's role in the twentieth century, Cain and Hopkins make some provocative and unorthodox statements concerning the relative strength of Great Britain on the international scene during the 1920s and 1930s. While subscribing to the conventional wisdom concerning a general industrial output and export decline during the post-First World War era, they point out that Britain nonetheless gained new colonies at the expense of Germany, that some sectors of the British economy remained relatively healthy, and that British business and capital were extremely active in areas of informal imperialism such as South America, China and Canada; and they hazard the interpretation that Britain's so-called retreat from world wealth and power, at least up to 1940, was not so precipitous or so uniform in all sectors as some have supposed. Indeed, Cain and Hopkins insist that Britain experienced several upswings of resurgent power in the inter-war period and that she continued to be a major player in the world arena (C&H, II, pp. 3–7, 76–90). This is the heart of their thesis in volume II.

Though the Cain/Hopkins analysis of Britain's economic performance in the inter-war period is a model of synthesis and shaded generalizations, revealing many dips and swings, they do not depart in any substantial way in their broad assessments from most prior mainstream analyses of stagnation,[48] and the long-term negative implications of their data are unmistakable. Nothing is more revealing about Britain's diminished position in the international economy than the decline in her proportion of total world trade (exports and imports) from about a 32 per cent share in 1913 to 24 per cent in 1929 and 22 per cent by 1937.[49] This fall was paralleled by a commensurate reduction in the United Kingdom's portion of the world's ocean transport services – though on the positive side, this did not apply to the carrying trade between Britain and most parts of the empire, where the mother country enjoyed a near monopoly.[50] At the same time, despite the emergence of a number of important new industries – electrical, chemical, automotive, aircraft and others – and an upswing in domestic demand for manufactured goods to compensate for the loss of foreign markets, Britain certainly did experience a downward slide in exports, especially in the capital goods (coal, iron and steel) industries and in the major staple, cotton textiles. (On the displacement of British goods in

---

48 Actually Cain and Hopkins could have argued the case for domestic economic recovery between the wars even more strongly. It is interesting that despite their strong argument that Britain did not decline as a great power in the inter-war period, but rather consolidated its position and even experienced a resurgence in worldwide position, prosperity and power, Cain and Hopkins do not accept or take up any of the more positive and optimistic reinterpretations of the country's industrial and general economic performance in the 1920s and 1930s, as, for example, does H.W. Richardson, *Economic Recovery in Britain, 1932–39* (London, 1967), pp. 1–99; and S. Glynn and J. Oxborrow, *Inter-War Britain: A Social and Economic History* (London, 1976).
49 See R.C.O. Mathews, C.H. Feinstein and J.C. Odling-Smee, *British Economic Growth, 1865–1973* (Oxford, 1982), Table 14.5.
50 W. Ashworth, *Economic History of England, 1870–1914* (London, 1960), p. 346.

Asian markets by the Japanese see the article by Shigeru Akita in this volume.) During 1921–9, British unemployment figures averaged 8 per cent – a figure not as high as in some other industrialized countries. Despite the terrible aftermath of the Great War, as a result of which Britain became a net bor-rower and debtor, returns from foreign investments were still a relatively bright spot on the invisible earnings bill in the inter-war period. By 1927 Britain's accumulated total foreign investment had recovered to a plateau of £4,290 million, which yielded an annual income of about £299 million. But Britain never recaptured late Victorian levels of overseas investment; and Cain and Hopkins concede that there was a general and rapid decline in the coun-try's earnings from invisibles in the inter-war period (C&H, II, pp. 32, 40). After an extremely erudite synthesis of a vast array of statistical evidence (which is far more complex than can be summarized here), Cain and Hopkins, when it comes to purely economic indicators, tend to line up with what might be called the bright side pessimists. 'Measured against her European neighbours, Britain held her own between the wars in terms of productivity, but no more than that' (C&H, II, p. 12).

As long as Cain and Hopkins are content to describe and analyse the multi-plex problems facing the British national economy in the 1920s and 1930s, they are on safe ground. It is when they try to correlate the lacklustre record of Britain's inter-war economic performance with arguments about the main-tenance, and even the resurgence, of British overall global and imperial power in the twentieth century (II, pp. 3–7) that specification problems may arise in the mind of the reader. In spite of their recognition of Britain's clear-cut loss of industrial and commercial capacity, Cain and Hopkins argue that the country's relative position in the world should not be judged by conventional economic criteria alone, and that other less commonly recognized indicators of great power status must be taken into consideration. In the past, they argue, 'connections between economic performance and political strength [have been all too] often assumed rather than demonstrated' (C&H, II, p. 5). If other parameters of power – namely international banking, currency ex-change and finance – are included, they argue, then students and scholars will arrive at different, and more positive, conclusions regarding Britain's inter-national (and imperial) role in the twentieth century.

The question here is what are the criteria that Cain and Hopkins use for evaluating great power status. Do their conclusions with respect to British potency meet tests of specification and comparability with the might of other international powers? At various points in both volumes I and II, the authors appear to shift their ground and speak less of overall 'power' than of British 'influence', which is a far more amorphous, open-ended and difficult to test concept than 'power'. The authors themselves hint at the specification prob-lem when, further on, they state that 'A further hazard consists of discussing decline without defining the concept or specifying how it is to be measured' (C&H, II, p. 4). Cain and Hopkins attempt to deal with the problem of measuring a nation's power by recognizing that power in international relations is relative as well as absolute. Britain's economic power may have been less than it was in 1913, when judged by conventional measurements, but her political weight may still have increased in the 1920s because her rivals suffered even more as a consequence of World War I (which severely damaged Germany) and the world slump (which caused the United States of America to reduce many of her international commitments). Interesting though this approach is, it opens rather than settles the complex problems of differentiating between Great Britain's (and the Empire's) genuine capabilities and the actual exercise of British international power during the crucial periods under survey.

Great Britain and the international 'Sterling Bloc' countries

To shore up their main argument concerning a revival of British global power in the twentieth century, Cain and Hopkins devote primary attention to the central role of the Sterling Area as a mechanism for maintaining Britain's older financial supremacy in both the formal and informal empires. This is an extremely ambitious, and in many ways ingenious, piece of analysis of international banking; the exposition here is extremely detailed, intellectually dense and makes heavy demands upon the reader.[51] The attempt to relate this to a revival of British imperial power, however, as the essay by Angela Redish in this volume shows, is fraught with conceptual and empirical difficulties. In their predilection for bold hypotheses the two historians impute far greater significance to the basic data on banking and currency management in the Empire/Commonwealth than has been hazarded by most previous scholars. Not only were currency exchange rate controls and central banking policy bound up with the maintenance of the Empire/Commonwealth, but, they urge, evidence on the continued profits and power emanating from the London-centred financial and banking circles can be used to challenge and modify, if not to repudiate, the conventional wisdom on the supposed decline of British total world power in the twentieth century.

This is a very tall order indeed. To place volume II in the context of the entire two-volume study, Cain and Hopkins fasten on the presumed force of the twentieth-century sterling bloc as a way of demonstrating that Britain's international and imperial power was not always asserted in a direct or an orthodox way.[52] Cain and Hopkins endow the system with wide significance during the inter-war period. Indeed, viewed through their own distinctive prism the 'sterling area' becomes for Cain and Hopkins Britain's 'informal empire' of the twentieth century. 'The City of London retained its independence and its central position in British economic life, despite the fall in income from overseas investment' (C&H, II, p. 5). Few would dispute this. The questions which remain, however, are how is this power to be measured; and,

---

51 A.W.F. Plumptre, *Central Banking in the British Dominions* (Toronto, 1940).
52 The sterling bloc came into being during the 1930s. It was a less formal and less potent precursor of the Sterling Area that emerged in the 1940s.

more importantly, what does the point in the above quotation – heavily under-scored throughout volume II – have to do with *imperialism*? What about the impact on overall national income of invisible earnings outside of (1) trans-portation services and interest and (2) dividends from foreign loans and in-vestments? Such ancillary earnings, because they reflect the contributions of the service sector, would appear to be important for the Cain/Hopkins argu-ment; but they do not list them. These would have included profits from the financing of long- and short-term loans, the discounting of international bills of exchange, telegraphic credit transfers, and from serving as the chief deposit-ory for foreign sterling balances. According to one historian of the international economy, these earnings for *services*, though prestigious, 'could never have been more than a minor element in the balance-of-payments surplus'.[53] So where is the contribution of the City of London to Britain's overall prosperity and power in the twentieth-century world here? Is it possible even to speak of a 'holding pattern' or maintenance of the status quo? Cain and Hopkins con-cede that 'Britain's ability to supply capital for overseas investment was more restricted after World War I [and] and that her income from invisibles was less buoyant' (C&H, II, p. 312).

We also need to ask whether the continuing exercise of financial leverage, by virtue of London being at the centre of the sterling bloc, in the periods before and after the Second World War, was sufficiently important (in terms of bank and other service charge revenues, the ability to borrow on sterling deposits, or other intangible factors) to play a part in Britain's pretensions to great power status throughout the twentieth century. Cain and Hopkins con-tend that this was supremely important, and they delve at great length into negotiations by the directors of the Bank of England and the activities of British merchant bankers in Canada, South Africa, South America (until now virtually uncharted territory for imperial scholars) and China between the two world wars (C&H, II, pp. 146–70, 300, 306, 313–14). Added questions here are whether the City of London's control over the sterling area consistently and over the long haul conferred advantages and benefits that accrued mainly to Britain, or whether management of the sterling exchange system also con-tained burdens and ambiguities that could become a 'double-edged sword'? This is an important new area of research which scholars such as Gerold Krozewski have begun to explore in ways that promise to add greatly to our understanding of the final period of imperial hegemony.[54]

<hr>

53 Ashworth estimated that after subtracting the two largest items – income from foreign invest-ment and shipping earnings – from the total accounts that the annual income from service sector invisibles declined sharply during the period under consideration from an average of £77,000,000 in 1924–28 to £42,000,000 in 1934–38 (William Ashworth, *An Economic History of England, 1870–1914* (London, 1960), pp. 178, 347–8).

54 Gerold Krozewski, 'Sterling, the minor territories, and the end of formal empire, 1939–58', *Economic History Review*, 2nd ser., 46/2 (1993), pp. 239–65. That Britain's holding of her colonies' sterling balances in London could easily become a mixed blessing is discussed in Allister E. Hinds, 'Imperial policy and colonial sterling balances, 1943–56', *Journal of Imperial and Commonwealth History*, 19, 1 (Jan. 1991), pp. 24–41.

The Sterling Area and Canada

In her incisive contribution to this volume, Angela Redish takes on these issues and also raises a number of other tantalizing questions which cut to the nub of the Cain and Hopkins hypothesis concerning the City and the sterling bloc. To what extent can currency exchange systems and central banking be used as instruments of either direct or indirect domination by one nation over another? Are we really talking about 'imperialism' or 'exploitation' here, or are we talking about institutions and mechanisms that simply facilitated commercial transactions? As a specialist in Canadian as well as international banking and currency policy and history, Redish acknowledges that much of what Cain and Hopkins have to say about the history of central banking in the Commonwealth is correct; but she also argues that the emphasis on the decisive role played by London is overdrawn and that more attention needs to be given to the local roots of banking policy change within the Dominions themselves. Impressed though she is by the importance of the sterling exchange system and of the possible connections between international currency controls and the health of the British economy in the twentieth century, she nonetheless asks whether the relationships described in the chapters of volume II necessarily constitute 'imperialism'. For Redish, the word 'imperialism' of necessity means a situation in which one party to a transaction takes unfavourable advantage of a second party; it implies some kind of 'exploitation'. She wonders why Cain and Hopkins never raise the issue of exploitation at all in their two volumes. Second, as the central part of her paper, she re-examines the nature of central banking in Canada and the Cain/Hopkins argument concerning the role of the Bank of England in establishing its foundations. Third and finally, Professor Redish, like several other of the essayists in the present book, also questions whether Cain and Hopkins prove their estimate of the resurgence of British world economic power during the first three decades of the twentieth century, based as it is mainly on international finance, banking and currency exchange rate regulations. Rather, she counters that most of the evidence the authors provide on attempted currency and banking reforms in the Dominions and elsewhere following the Second World War tends to confirm the conventional view that Great Britain was slipping economically relative to other nations of the world and that most of the policies and actions which Cain and Hopkins describe in volume II of *British Imperialism* as demonstrating continued power suggest, in fact, rearguard 'defensive' actions.

British imperialism in China and Japan in the late nineteenth and twentieth centuries

Another of the scholarly regional essays in the present collection is that by Shigeru Akita, entitled 'British Informal Empire in East Asia: a Japanese Perspective'. Professor Akita shows where a knowledge of non-European and non-Western sources – in this case, the most up-to-date work by Chinese and Japanese historians – can enhance, modify or alter conceptions of East Asian history based mainly on Western sources and interpretations. Surveying both chapter 13 of volume I and chapter 10 of volume II of *British Imperialism*, Akita probes the nature of British imperialism in the Far East in both the nineteenth and twentieth centuries. He points out that Cain and Hopkins offer a number of useful new insights on relations between the two 'island empires' of Japan and Great Britain (which is, by the way, an extremely interesting suggestion for further comparative research). But he wonders whether the two authors might have paid far greater attention to the dynamics of change that emanated from within Japan, China and India, particularly in the economic realm, during the decades of Western-influenced modernization. This does not mean a simple return to 'area' or peripheral studies. As an international relations scholar, Akita is perhaps more at home with a multilateral approach to problems in modern world history in a way that contrasts with most writers in the older tradition of British colonial history. In this, Akita's work most resembles that of Kubicek in this volume, not only because he compares developments in several countries simultaneously, but also in the fact that he hints at a 'world systems', rather than a narrow imperial, approach to the study of capitalism in the modern world.

At the outset, Akita notes that there was a turn to finance capitalism as the main instrument of British influence in East Asia in the late nineteenth century, and that European investment was extremely important, along with inter-Asian trade, in developing a transportation network and basic infrastructure. But he legitimately raises the question whether foreign investment in a host country necessarily constitutes or leads to imperialism by the donor country. He quotes Koala Sugihara to the effect that there was clearly a sense of complementarity between financial interests based in the City of London and inter-Asian economic development.

In the main Akita concurs with the general rendition of events given in *British Imperialism* down to 1911; but he takes strong exception to the Cain/Hopkins account of Anglo-Chinese and, particularly, Anglo-Japanese relations during the period 1919–1939. As one problem area, he highlights the heavy emphasis that Cain and Hopkins place on instruments of financial and monetary control as measures of British power in East Asia to the neglect of the more traditional geopolitical indicators of military and naval strength. He also challenges the role the authors assign to the British government, rather than to the United States of America and to China itself, as the energizing movers in the Chinese monetary reforms of the 1930s. Lastly, Akita asks whether Cain and Hopkins, in attempting to argue that Great Britain and the empire possessed far greater strength in the world than is commonly accepted, and especially in East Asia during the 1920s and 1930s, have allowed their interpretation to outrun the evidence. What about the major problem of appeasement? Here Akita brings to bear a mass of documentation which challenges the Cain and Hopkins revisionist interpretation that Britain somehow took a stronger line against Japanese aggressive expansion in China and Manchuria from 1937 to 1939 than is usually supposed.

A counter model – Britain's military and naval strength in the inter-war period

Student and other readers will want to re-examine here a question noted earlier in the Introduction, that is, whether the Cain and Hopkins approach, for all its ingenuity and sophistication, meets the challenges for a general model of causation for British imperialism. The history of twentieth-century international relations raises questions as to whether any one-track economic assessment of a country's strength – even one as strenuously argued and sophisticated as the Cain/Hopkins finance/service sector model – can suffice as a measure of a country's relative power in the world. Any modern evaluation must also take into account the geopolitical, technological, strategic raw materials and manpower resources at the disposal of a modern nation state. It is not enough for readers to observe that *British Imperialism* does touch briefly at various times on naval and military issues (see especially C&H, I, pp. 86–7, 91, 451, 458, 463–4).[55] The main point, as noted earlier, is that crucial questions concerning war, conquest, territorial acquisition, world balance of power and strategic defence are not among the central problems or major criteria of power analysed systematically or in depth throughout the two-volume study.

Twentieth-century technological breakthroughs in land, sea and air power stood Victorian criteria for maintaining global mastery on their head. In the second half of the nineteenth century the two-power naval standard – possession of large overseas territorial blocks of power together with fortified garrisons and naval bases – had, indeed, been gauges of pre-eminent power. (Some contemporary scholars even questioned whether Britain's nineteenth-century strung-out chain of bases was a source of genuine world hegemony; but she had the advantage of facing no serious challenger for her role.[56]) But with the fleet's conversion to diesel fuel in the early twentieth century many of the older outposts of empire, designed primarily as coaling stations, had already become expendable.[57] And it is possible to argue that the further implications of the revolution in military and naval air power on war-making capacity, though slow to be recognized on both sides of the Atlantic, coupled with the effects of the Statute of Westminster,[58] rendered any conceptualization of

---

55 Cain and Hopkins do deal in depth with these questions in their sub-section on 'The Anglo-German rivalry' and the background to the First World War (C&H, I, pp. 456–65).

56 Gerald S. Graham, *The Politics of Naval Supremacy* (Cambridge, 1965), pp. 118–25.

57 As Paul Kennedy puts it, by the turn of the century sea power as an element in international ascendancy was already on the wane in relation to land-based military power; and Britain's Victorian naval supremacy, bound up with its commercial leadership and a lack of challenge from other nations and empires, was no longer a decisive factor when pitted against the far greater resources, population and industrial bases of the new super powers' (see Paul Kennedy, 'Mahan versus Mackinder: two interpretations of British sea power', in P. Kennedy (ed.), *Strategy and Diplomacy* (London, 1983), p. 48).

58 The Statute of Westminster (1931) is generally regarded as the key statute in the evolution of the self-governing British Commonwealth. It clarified the relationship of the dominion parliaments to the British Parliament. The Dominions could now amend their own constitutions and the British crown lost the right to disallow acts passed by parliaments in the dominions. Most important, the dominions gained control over their own foreign policies, and a declaration of war by Great Britain no longer applied automatically to the self-governing Dominions.

British international power based on the empire and Commonwealth at best problematical, and at worst obsolete. Akita makes this very point about over-stretched British naval power and meagre military capacity and their effects on appeasement foreign policy in the Far East during the 1930s. (See also Nicholas White in this volume, in his brief reference to the fall of Singapore in early 1942.)

Granted that an alert and strong-willed Britain might have stopped Adolf Hitler by calling his bluff while Germany was still militarily weak in the mid-1930s, the fact remains that in 1938–39 Great Britain had to face as potential enemies not only Germany, a nation of more than 80 millions that was under a command economy, was able to raise huge sums for war expenditure, and would soon be amassing an army of an estimated two million, organized into some 106 divisions, but also Japan, a nation of 70 million with a standing army of about one million, which could also mobilize upwards of two million troops if reservists were included.[59] By contrast, England's inability to put more than a handful of divisions into the field in continental Europe was a major consideration both in Hitler's decision to risk general war as a consequence of his invasion of Poland in 1939 and in Stalin's parallel decision to resist overtures for a joint Anglo-Soviet stand against Germany and the resulting Nazi–Soviet Peace Pact of the same year. A restatement of these bare facts is central to any assessment of British power during the inter-war period.[60] The salient point here with reference to the Cain/Hopkins interpretation is that both mainstream historians of the Second World War, supportive of Churchill's position against the appeasers, and modern revisionist apologists for appeasement agree that Britain's inter-war foreign policy was born of a very real geopolitical imbalance of power and military weaknesses as well as a lack of political will.[61] It is one of Cain and Hopkins's contentions (again we are simplifying very lengthy arguments) that Britain's economic initiatives in the fields of international banking and finance between the wars constituted a genuine effort to compensate for such geopolitical and military weaknesses through somehow strengthening the empire and keeping a rearmed Japan and Germany at bay by attempting to maintain friendly relations with them (C&H, II, pp. 90–2, 95–8).

59 The effects of Germany's rapid and potent preparations for war on her overall industrial production in the second half of the 1930s were phenomenal. See R. Berghahn, *Modern Germany* (rev. edn, Cambridge, 1991), p. 146. For army mobilization figures, see T. Taylor, *Sword and Swastika* (rev. edn, New York, 1980), pp. 246–7.

60 A number of historians have contended that this assessment of Britain's relative geopolitical military weakness applied to the 1920s as well as to the period after 1935. Thus, it was recognized that, even under the Locarno treaties of mutual guarantee, Britain had no choice but to entrust the future stability of continental Europe entirely to the army of France (see articles by Arnold Wolfers, S. Borsody and Hajo Holborn in 'The first appeasement era', in Gordon Wright and A. Meija (eds), *An Age of Controversy* (New York, 1968), pp. 178–204.

61 D.C. Watt, 'Appeasement: the rise of a revisionist school', *Political Quarterly*, 36 (1965), pp. 191–213. See also C. Barnett, *The Collapse of British Power* (Atlantic Highlands, NJ, 1973), pp. 113–14, 564; Kennedy, 'The tradition of appeasement in British foreign policy, 1865–1939', *Strategy and Diplomacy*, pp. 23, 27.

Raymond E. Dumett

The movement towards self-government and the transfer of power in India

In volume II as in volume I, some of Cain and Hopkins's most thoughtful and tightly constructed analysis is seen in their sections on British India (I, ch. 10; II, ch. 8). What they have achieved is a deft synthesis of recent revisionist work (by writers such as B.R. Tomlinson) on the economic history of modern India and a redirection of findings in this important sub-field towards a redefinition of London-based imperial interests and the devolution of power in 1947. Questioning older, 'Whiggish', interpretations that the independence of India should be viewed mainly in political and constitutional terms as part of an inevitable and evenly paced process that saw a series of enlightened British responses to Indian nationalist pressures for greater self-government (as embodied in the famous Government of India Acts of 1919 and 1935), Cain and Hopkins maintain that Britain had no clear vision or ordered pathway for Indian independence and that she was quite willing to assert and maintain her overall supremacy by force until at least as late as 1942 and perhaps even later (C&H, II, pp. 194–5, 198). The controlling elements in British long-term policy towards India, they insist (with a nod to their 'gentlemanly capitalist' thesis), were primarily related to fiscal control and currency reserves. Throughout the inter-war period the priority requirement for Britain was to maintain markets for Indian exports abroad so that the latter could 'continue to make remittances to London' (C&H, II, p. 191). Once again, the Cain/Hopkins argument involves the minimizing of British industrial interests and leverage in India. Declining terms of trade and a flare-up of the government's budgetary problems during the late 1920s and early 1930s, they say, fuelled Gandhi's nationalist movement and demands for governmental reform. By 1940 Manchester cotton sales to India were in protracted decline, and thus, Cain and Hopkins insist, British manufacturing interests were much less of a policy determinant than the financial stakes of the City of London. In the Cain/Hopkins interpretation, 1947 marked the crucial turning point, less because of the extreme political pressures and disruption of civil order by Gandhi and Congress and by Jinnah and the Muslim League, which they mention briefly (II, p. 195), than because the British presence in India was no longer economically profitable or fiscally viable (C&H, II, pp. 174–6, 180, 196).

The chapter by Maria Misra on British India in the twentieth century grapples with the issues confronting the imperial government in the 1920s and 1930s from a somewhat different perspective. Like a majority of the other contributors to this volume she is greatly impressed by the depth of the two authors' research and the cohesiveness of their analysis around a central theme; but she is suspicious of economic determinism, and especially of a thesis based primarily on fiscal considerations. Thus, in contrast to Cain and Hopkins, Misra cites a considerable body of evidence to show that there were multiple linkages – social, economic and political – between various British business (including industrial) interests and officials in the government of British India in the twentieth century. In one disarmingly terse sentence, whose potency and implications for the Cain/Hopkins model may easily be overlooked, she writes that the ideological attachment of the Anglo-Indian agency houses 'seems to have been to the principle of extreme business autonomy'. She does not accept the notion that British businessmen involved in India (whether bankers, investors or overseas merchants) necessarily shared the personal values, club affiliations, political ideologies or the policy aims of government officials; rather, they were often at loggerheads with one another.

Misra's paper reinforces another point with reference to the 'industrial minimalist' argument in *British Imperialism*, namely that the power and influence of British manufacturing interests on British Indian policy, seen particularly on questions of free trade and preferences, were far from being a nullity, even though the Government of India did move towards protectionism. In doing this, she mentions the tendency of Cain and Hopkins to trace nearly every important economic fact to their Gladstonian fiscal thesis. By contrast, she argues that the more direct British promotion of Indian industries in 1917 and after had less to do with bolstering India's capacity to make remittances to London and to avoid financial crisis (as Cain and Hopkins suggest) than with the perceived need to develop Indian industrial centres for the production of arms and munitions during the First World War. Misra's chapter ends by calling on Cain and Hopkins for more evidence that it was the conversion of India's longstanding debt to Britain that influenced the timing of the transfer of power and the partition of India and Pakistan in 1947.

To balance Cain and Hopkins's fiscal interpretation, readers should also reconsider the powerful, popular, mass erupting force for freedom that emanated from both the Indian National Congress and Muhammed Ali Jinnah's Muslim League. As in any historical discussion, it is a question of sorting out the primary from the secondary and tertiary considerations. As an alternative to the Cain and Hopkins rendering, students also need to consider the more radical Indian nationalist interpretation which dislikes calling the 1945–47 freedom process a mere 'transfer of power' and lays much greater stress on popular agitation and communal violence as the main cause, not only of the Indian 'independence struggle', but also of the partition (not discussed by Cain and Hopkins) that led to the creation of Pakistan. On this view, it was Muhammed Ali Jinnah's 'direct action' campaign, Hindu/Muslim communal violence and – most decisively – very real British official fears about the continued loyalty of the Indian Army and its ability to maintain order which turned the tide and forced the pace of Britain's abandonment of control under Attlee and the Labour government during 1945–47.[62] This topic for debate may well stand

---

62 For the impact of the 1946 'Direct Action Campaign' on Lord Wavell's decision-making, see Anita Inder Singh, *The Origins of the Partition of India, 1936–1947* (Delhi, 1987), pp. 179–91. See also T.R. Sareen, 'The Indian National Army' and S. Banerjee, 'The R.I.N. Mutiny', in Ravi Dayal, *We Fought Together for Freedom: Chapters from the Indian National Movement* (Delhi and Bombay, 1995), pp. 194–213, 215–37. One need not accept the whole of a radical nationalist interpretation on the potency of rebellions in the army and navy as measurable forces in the

as an example where imperial studies and grass-roots 'area studies' interpretations intersect without remaining totally at odds. Both approaches contain a good part of the truth. At bottom, Cain and Hopkins and the exponents of alternative or opposing nationalist interpretations undoubtedly would agree that it was the Second World War (including, of course, its costs) that was the driving force for radical change.

British Malaya

Nicholas J. White's paper applies the gentlemanly capitalist hypothesis to Great Britain's vital holdings in south-east Asia, an often neglected part of the empire and one that was not included in the Cain/Hopkins two volume work. White takes Cain and Hopkins at their word that 'gentlemanly capitalism' has a specific and measurable meaning and that it should not be interpreted as a vague 'catch-all' phrase that can be taken to explain any or every causal phenomenon about the British Empire. He recognizes that Malaya (or Malaysia as it is today) is one of the least understood parts of the former British Empire; and so, in an approach that is helpful for the new student and the general reader, he provides a brief background history in which he distinguishes between the Federated Malay States, the Unfederated Malay States and the Colony of the Straits Settlements. White was not asked to delve at length into nineteenth-century Malayan history. Had there been space, the story of the slow process by which Britain gradually asserted 'protection' over the indigenous Malay states of Perak, Selangor, Negri Semblan and Pahang between 1873 and 1900 would have afforded an excellent opportunity for examining the possible leverage exercised by City men on the stage by stage incorporation of formerly independent overseas territories into the web of Britain's 'formal empire'. This still remains a profitable area for research and debate by scholars of the decision-making process by which spheres of influence are turned into colonies.[63] What makes White's essay especially stimulating, however, is that he neither accepts nor rejects the gentlemanly capitalist/service sector model in its entirety, but rather that he painstakingly sifts through his evidence on Anglo-Malayan business and governmental elites in order to find the instances where the concept may be applicable and others where it may have little or no validity. He then develops his own subtly textured modification of the Cain and Hopkins argument.

---

independence movement. Most sources agree, however, that a fundamental factor in the *early timing* of British withdrawal was the genuine official fear as to whether the Army of India could be counted on to remain loyal, if British occupation were to be protracted much beyond 1947.

63 See Barbara W. Andaya and L.Y. Andaya, *A History of Malaya* (New York, 1982), pp. 114–204; Chai Hon Chan, *The Development of British Malaya, 1896–1909* (Kuala Lumpur, 1964), pp. 1–83; John Bastin and R. Winks (compilers), *Malaysia: Selected Historical Readings* (London and New York, 1966), pp. 119–257.

A number of interesting new insights emerge from the article on Malaysia. First, White underscores what might be called the 'peripheral theory of gentlemanly capitalism' by pointing out that there were local clones of the London-based service sector elites that sprouted up in Singapore and the Straits Settlements. Yet for White, the businessmen of Singapore and Melaka were no more a unified ideological or lobbying entity than their London counterparts; and the policy agendas of their various sub-units – such as the tin miners and the rubber estate agents – often ran at cross-purposes. Second, just as there was no monolithic unity to the gentlemanly capitalists in London, so too there was little uniformity or unanimity of opinion amongst the various cliques of the British governmental elite, whether in Whitehall or at 'government house' in the Straits Settlements and other colonial possessions. If White's premises on the lack of a close identity of interests between British capitalistic interests and the ruling governmental elite are valid, then the solution may be to retreat to an older and simpler model of highly differentiated and fragmented United Kingdom-wide pressure groups – Liverpool shipping interests, the Manchester cotton textile lobby, various Midland manufacturing interests, plus autonomous banking, mining, tropical commodities and insurance interests (all from London), all trying at various times and with sporadic success to gain support from ministries and departments for their very particularistic policy goals. White's views on the major issues of a 'complementarity of interests' – or the lack of it – should be compared with those of Misra, summarized above.

The chapter on Malaya also has some apposite things to say about the retreat from empire post-1945 and decolonization. With the implication that Cain and Hopkins perhaps missed an opportunity by not delving more deeply into every corner of the British Empire from 1945 to 1990 – particularly in the latter decades of this period – in order to nail home their arguments, White suggests that Malaya could be used to represent the epitome of the Cain/Hopkins fiscal/finance model for decolonization. Underscoring the hypothesis that there is, indeed, a case to be made for the resurgence of British power in a new form in the twentieth century, the White essay urges scholars to take a closer look at post-colonial (1945–80) influences in a wide range of countries, rather than to focus mainly on the 1920s and 1930s, which is what volume II of Cain and Hopkins tends to do. White notes that, for Malaya at least, as early as the 1940s metropolitan planners framed a reinvigorated and progressive 'raj' for the period following the war. This included the evolution of a new political entity, the Federation of Malaya, which, while allowing the states considerable autonomy, embodied British objectives for a strong central government combined with financial stability. In Malaya, White concludes, the British succeeded admirably in maintaining their traditional financial and commercial interests in a drastically altered international environment. In many ways, he suggests – in a most insightful final dictum – this constituted the genuine 'new imperialism'.

CONCLUSION: AREAS FOR FURTHER STUDY AND DEBATE

The contributors hope that the historiographical issues raised in this collection of essays will stimulate further reading, discussion and research among students, scholars and general readers about the causes, nature and structure of imperialism. There is no doubt that *British Imperialism* is an important work which has brought in its wake a renewal of interest in British imperial history. The original and probing thought, the command of source materials, the courage to take risks, not to mention the sheer willpower required to complete the two volumes, are extraordinary by any standard. As noted earlier, many of Cain and Hopkins's separate chapters on British economic penetration in zones such as Latin America, the Ottoman Empire, Egypt, Canada, China and Japan could very easily stand alone as solid introductory syntheses, useful to students in area studies. The writing style is lucid and often entertaining, with frequent clever and epigrammatic asides; though full appreciation of the totality of what the authors have accomplished requires careful rereading and some prior knowledge of and comparison with the larger historiography of imperialism.

The main study against which Cain and Hopkins's work will continue to be matched for some years to come is undoubtedly Robinson and Gallagher's classic *Africa and the Victorians*. Indeed, Cain and Hopkins probably make more critical references to the older partnership's multi-level analyses of nineteenth-century imperialism than to any other work. A major point of contrast lies in the fact that the landmark 1960 study, focusing on one continent, did not cover the entire British Empire, let alone major areas outside it, as the broadly based Cain/Hopkins volumes purport to do. On the other hand, Robinson and Gallagher made extensive use of primary source materials, whereas Cain and Hopkins, given the great scope of their work, were compelled to rely almost entirely on secondary sources. *British Imperialism* is, above all, an economic interpretation (with a unique emphasis on finance and fiscal considerations), whereas Robinson and Gallagher clearly subordinated economic factors in their analysis of causation based mainly on the political calculations of the official mind. Most particularly, Cain and Hopkins disagree fundamentally with Robinson and Gallagher's central emphasis on strategically induced responses by Whitehall to proto-nationalist crises on the periphery – especially Egypt – as the primary explanation for British involvement in the partition of Africa.

This said, it is worth adding that the Cain/Hopkins and Robinson/Gallagher interpretations also have a number of elements in common: (1) both teams (if we include the latter's 1953 article and ancillary publications) devoted nearly as much attention in their scholarship to 'informal imperialism' as they did to the formal empire; (2) both accounts – though especially Cain and Hopkins – tend to gloss over the importance of shifting 'balance of power' alignments in continental Europe (France, Bismarck's Germany, Italy, Russia, Leopold of Belgium) in explaining the motivation (or at the very least influencing the timing) for British imperialistic interventions in other continents; (3) both tend to neglect the motivating importance of irrational factors such as jingo-ism and the search for 'prestige' in the annexation of new protectorates and colonies;[64] and (4) both approaches (in their separate ways) are Anglocentric, with Cain and Hopkins focusing heavily on the financial and service sector of the City of London, coupled with an English socio-cultural history, whereas Robinson and Gallagher concentrated on the calculus of politicians and bureaucrats in Whitehall as the engines of imperialism.

In addition we have suggested a number of thematic topics and possible future regional studies where concepts and principles formulated by Cain and Hopkins might be applied to new or supplementary research. One of the most important of these would be more in-depth studies of pressure group activities by industrial and manufacturers' lobbies as well as by trade associa-tions in the United Kingdom, outside London. By their stringent industrial minimalist line of argument Cain and Hopkins have thrown down the gaunt-let to younger historians who may seek to reassess, through new scholarship, the possible connections between Lancashire and Midland industrial power, Liverpool and Glasgow shipping and trading pressures, and both overseas ex-pansionism and management of the British Empire – the two are not identical phenomena – which may be greater than suggested by Cain and Hopkins.[65] The work of White and Misra in this volume, as well as that of Cain and Hopkins, shows that research by British industrial and commercial pressure groups can also be extended to the study of colonial and overseas municipal chambers of commerce, trade associations, banking houses, mining and railway companies, shipping firms and agency houses, such as those located at Singapore, Cape Town, Bombay, Kingston, Jamaica, Lagos, Hong Kong, Auckland, Sydney, Cairo, Vancouver, Buenos Aires, and many other great metropolitan business centres around the world.

We have also suggested that much more attention could be paid in imperial historical studies generally to micro-analyses of the 'decision-making process', from which we might be able to develop more accurate models about the lines of impact emanating from diverse economic interest groups (not just the gentlemanly capitalists), voluntary associations (some with middle- and working-class affiliations), public and parliamentary opinion, the popular press

---

64 It is interesting in this connection that Cain and Hopkins frequently use the term 'prestige' and give the word high importance in their analysis of English social classes and the rise of the gentlemanly capitalist group on the domestic scene (see, for example, C&H, I, p. 27); but they scarcely use the word at all with reference to the jingoistic land grabs and territorial annexations by the major European powers in raising their flags over new African and Asian colonies and protectorates at the time of the 'new imperialism'.

65 In their conclusions on the limited capacity of manufacturing interests to influence commercial policy in India, Cain and Hopkins tend to focus more on the late nineteenth century, rather than on the first 60 years of the nineteenth or on the twentieth centuries. An indication that the power of the Lancashire cotton lobby was more potent than Cain and Hopkins indicate, particularly in the mid-Victorian period, towards the Indian government, in maintaining a low tariff policy on foreign cotton goods imports can be found in the work of E.C. Moulton, *Lord Northbrook's Indian Administration, 1872–78* (New York, 1968), pp. 174, 191, 212, 213. See also S. Gopal, *British Policy in India, 1858–1905* (Cambridge, 1965), pp. 109–13.

and other 'external factors' on the ultimate control centres in Whitehall and in the colonies. Cain and Hopkins believe that the command hierarchies of both the army and navy, which they did not have time to treat in their two volumes, were closely linked to the gentlemanly capitalist nexus that they claim controlled the economics and politics of the empire. Here is another challenge for others to pursue; and preliminary work in this area is already coming into print.[66] One of the major themes of *British Imperialism* volume II is that the British Empire experienced several upswings in resurgent power during the twentieth century; and to help test this, detailed research on the great support given to the mother country during the two world wars by the empire and the Commonwealth – not only in military manpower, but also in armaments and raw materials – is worthy of more detailed study before we can reach final conclusions on the might of the empire in our own century.[67] Other cyclical dips and revivals occurred during the Cold War and the important period of decolonization.

The list of additional and intriguing research topics is, therefore, potentially endless; and Cain and Hopkins have given impetus to historians to rethink a host of old problems and to ask a myriad of new questions. The subject of race is of obvious importance in imperial studies, not only from the standpoint of oppressed and exploited indigenous peoples, but also for coming to grips with the mentality of European ruling groups and their indigenous collaborators. On the question of further regional topics, not covered by Cain and Hopkins, there is room for new research on the possible intrusion of gentlemanly capitalism into (1) British colonial administration in the Caribbean; (2) Australian and New Zealand 'sub-imperialism' in the south-western Pacific; (3) the separate South Asian territories of Burma and Ceylon; and (4) British and United States oil imperialism in the twentieth-century Middle East, to name but four areas. Andrew Porter has drawn attention to the missionary factor in British imperialism, largely missing from Cain and Hopkins.[68] And the subject of Christian humanitarianism in its broadest dimensions as a social movement (the Anti-Slavery Society, the Aborigines Protection Society) not only for regulating the harsher effects of colonialism, but also as a

66 Such an effort would require a combing of the entrance and commissioning rolls for the Royal Military Academy at Sandhurst and the Royal Naval College at Dartmouth as well as the *Army* and *Navy Lists*. New research by Keith Surridge (University of Notre Dame London branch) on field officers at the time of the Anglo-Boer War suggests that they came largely from lower gentry families. Their attitudes were decidedly anti-urban and anti-City of London, with a strong streak of anti-Semitism. See Keith Surridge, 'British civil–military relations and the South African War, 1899–1902' (unpublished PhD thesis, University of London, 1994). My thanks to Dr Surridge for a personal communication on these points.
67 These are topics worthy of dissertation or book-length research involving careful analysis of statistical data on raw materials, shipping and wartime supplies as well as military manpower. For samples of preliminary or partial contributions, see Raymond E. Dumett, 'Africa's strategic minerals during World War II', in *Journal of African History*, 26 (1984), pp. 381–408; F.W. Perry, *Commonwealth Armies: Manpower and Organization in Two World Wars* (Manchester, 1988), pp. 82–237 and *passim*.
68 Andrew Porter, 'Birmingham, Westminster and the City of London: visions of empire compared', *Journal of Historical Geography*, 21/1 (1995), p. 85.

force for imperial expansion in its own right (South Africa, New Zealand and West Africa) deserves more intensive study in order to determine whether the movement can be connected to, or detached from, gentlemanly capitalism.

One should note finally, in passing, that the impression which *British Imperialism* conveys of a 'gentlemanly capitalist' network of imperialists throughout the greater part of some 788 pages of text is, on the whole, a very respectable (and a strongly masculine) one. One should not forget that 'gentlemanly capitalism' is, after all a 'construct' – an image – but one which now, thanks to Cain and Hopkins, enjoys a life and intellectual force of its own. This could easily lead us into the critical realm of post-colonial discourse theory, a subject that, for reasons of space, we must exclude from the present study.[69] In addition, we hardly need remind readers that the study of women and the empire has blossomed as an important sub-field for imperial and colonial research; and while the constructive overseas work of women who worked as teachers in church schools, as nurses in hospitals or as leaders in colonial and freedom movements deserves increasing attention,[70] there is also a need for critical studies of the role of women as collaborators in imperialism. Though Cain and Hopkins give hints of it, there is much room for further debate on the countless 'ungentlemanly' (to use no stronger term) features of nineteenth-century capitalism and imperialism – in the form of fraud, double-dealing, Social Darwinism, 'land grab', hubris and a nonchalant attitude towards violence, especially against 'subject' indigenous peoples (features obviously shared with American, French and German imperialists) – which have not been sufficiently explored or underscored.[71] Related studies of distinct subdivisions within or on the margins of 'gentlemanly capitalism', such as mining concessionaires, 'filibustering' soldiers of fortune, trading 'ruffians' and sub-circles

69 This touches on a point made by deconstructionists that creative new concepts too easily become axiomatic – seeming to require no further proof. In other words, the new term may develop a force of its own that extends beyond the original historical reality. For a good discussion of the substitution of 'British' for English and other related matters concerning the imperial mentality touched on here, see Robert J.C. Young, *Colonial Desire* (London and New York, 1995), pp. 1–54. For an excellent summary of the literature of post-colonial discourse theory, see Dane Kennedy, 'Imperial history and post-colonial theory', in *Journal of Imperial and Commonwealth Hist.*, 24/3 (Sept. 1986), pp. 345–63.

70 Good recent examples are Margaret MacMillan, *Women of the Raj* (London, 1988); Margaret Strobel, *Gender, Sex and Empire*, American Historical Association Pamphlet (Washington, DC, 1994), pp. 1–24; Antoinette Burton, *Burdens of History: British Feminists, Indian Women, and Imperial Culture, 1865–1915* (Chapel Hill, NC, 1994).

71 We should not lose sight of the fact that the imposition of the ideals and manners of *English* aristocratic gentlemen and 'Englishness' generally on the *British* male citizen was, in fact, part of a very effective piece of image-making during Victorian times and earlier. Cain and Hopkins are aware that the criteria for 'gentlemanliness' and inclusion in the 'elite' classes of London could be very ragged at the edges and shallow at the centre in terms of character and intelligence. They also appreciate the fact that by the end of the century the term had become so diluted that 'gentleman' could include practically anybody. The two authors try to cover themselves on critical questions concerning application of the terminology 'gentleman' to fringe persons by referring to a wider 'order' where 'would-be gentlemen' (or 'proto-gentlemen') could gain admittance (see C&H, I, pp. 21, 41, 358). For a different view of London capitalists and a critique of what was often viewed as the vulgarity and ostentatious display of wealth by parvenus, see Jamie Camplin, *The Rise of the Plutocrats: Wealth and Power in Edwardian England* (London, 1978), pp. 64–5, 95, 97, 108.

of government officials, both at home and abroad, would also make for interesting reading and add to our understanding of the darker side of this strange and multifaceted phenomenon.

★★★

It is in the nature of academic discourse that any seminal work of groundbreaking general theory or radical reinterpretation in history that is worth its salt will be challenged and tested by academic review and debate. Specialists invariably seek, in the interests of truth, to search for errors or omissions, for problems of definition and specification, lapses in logic or oversights in the marshalling of empirical data. We have attempted to take that process a few halting steps forward in the present collection of essays on the Cain and Hopkins model of imperialism, and we hope that the effort is worthwhile. Prior to this publication, only a few of the published reviews have had the space at their disposal to subject *British Imperialism* to systematic analysis; yet we are also aware of the spatial limitations on what could be accomplished in the present volume.

There is no doubt that Cain and Hopkins have produced a most impressive and provocative study. Their book constitutes a milestone in the 100-year-old debate on the economic foundations and development of the British Empire. The approach and method which the two scholars have taken to the study of their topic is radically different from any previous broad survey, incorporating, as it does, a wealth of new material on financial/fiscal imperialism and stretching the scope and framework of 'informal imperialism' beyond all previous bounds. Seeking to reunite the history of the British Empire with the history of the home islands, Cain and Hopkins spend as much time on the domestic economy and society of England as they do on regions overseas; and nearly as much time on British 'informal imperialism' in independent countries as they do on the formal Empire and Commonwealth of the crown colonies, protectorates and self-governing Dominions.

Scholars may not agree with every inference or conclusion that the two scholars have drawn, or on whether their major hypotheses are sufficient to constitute an all-encompassing explanatory paradigm for the British imperial phenomenon. We should keep in mind that Cain and Hopkins have not claimed absolute universality; they have only asked that reviewers consider their belief that the London-oriented financial/fiscal model 'provides the best fit' (C&H, I, p. 48) in comparison with rival theories that also seek to explain a fantastic farrago of myths, facts and interpretations. One of the most thought-provoking legacies of *British Imperialism* lies in the very concept of 'gentlemanly capitalism'. Based in part on the traditions of Marx, Hobson and Schumpeter, coupled with modern interpretations and their own inventiveness, Cain and Hopkins's model is a useful tool for the analysis of both British domestic and external policy formation, pressure group activity, individual and group biographies, plus social and cultural histories about the British Empire, that should survive scholarly exegesis and inspire research and disputation for generations to come.

It is in this spirit of constructive engagement that this volume and this Introduction have been written. The idea has been to probe and debate a bold, revisionist interpretation rather than just to speed its absorption into the historiography. The eight contributions that follow adopt different chronological, thematic and regional perspectives, and each provides a fresh and independent view of the subjects they explore. They vary in the degree to which they concur with the Cain and Hopkins model; and in this Introduction the editor has also put forward his own observations on that interpretation, with the aim of asking new questions and of creating new opportunities for studying the modern age of empires. Cain and Hopkins end the volume with an assessment of the issues raised in those contributions. The larger goal, for everyone involved, is to open the subject to fresh thinking, and to highlight its importance for a generation of readers who now live in a post-imperial age. If the present volume helps to move the study of imperialism and empire forward in these directions, it will have served its purpose.

CHAPTER 1

Gentlemanly capitalism and British economic policy, 1880–1914: the debate over bimetallism and protectionism

E.H.H. GREEN

The period 1880–1914 marked a critical phase in the development of the British economy.[1] In the late nineteenth and early twentieth centuries Britain lost its position as the world's leading industrial nation, being overtaken by the United States and Germany. Furthermore, elements of Britain's manufacturing sector showed signs of fragility in the face of competition both abroad and at home – Britain's share of the world market for manufactured goods fell and import penetration of the British market rose significantly.[2] At the same time British agriculture, especially the arable sector, suffered difficulties, and Britain's rural population steadily declined.[3] However, whilst the visible sector appeared to experience problems, Britain's banking and service sector flourished as never before, and London's position as 'the financial centre of the universe'[4] was both consolidated and extended.

It was, and indeed still is, a matter of debate as to whether the developments outlined above indicated that the British economy was in decline. Recent studies of the period have tended to see change rather than decline as the chief characteristic of the British economy at this time.[5] In particular, Sir John

1 The literature on this period is extensive, but see in particular F. Crouzet, *The Victorian Economy* (London, 1982); S. Pollard, *Britain's Prime and Britain's Decline, 1870–1914* (London, 1988); and the essays on the period 1860–1914 in R. Floud and D.N. McCloskey (eds), *The Economic History of Britain Since 1700* (2nd edn, 3 vols, Cambridge, 1994), II.
2 See D. Aldcroft (ed.), *British Industry and the Growth of Foreign Competition* (London, 1968).
3 See C. O'Grada, 'Agricultural decline, 1860–1914', in Floud and McCloskey (eds), *Economic History*, II, and F.M.L. Thompson, 'An anatomy of British farming', in B. Holderness and M. Turner (eds), *Land, Labour and Agriculture, 1700–1920* (London, 1991).
4 The quotation is from P.J. Grigg, *Prejudice and Judgment* (London, 1953), p. 258.
5 R. Floud, 'Britain 1860–1914: a survey', in Floud and McCloskey (eds), *Economic History*, II.

Clapham's idea of a 'great hinge' in British economic and social life which swung wealth, economic activity and population away from the industrial north and Midlands towards the service sector and the south and south-east has been confirmed. The increasing prominence of the service sector has been seen, in particular by neo-classically minded economic historians, as a 'rational' development, insofar as it represented a transfer of resources, both capital and human, to an area in which Britain enjoyed a clear and growing comparative advantage.[6] However, the work of Peter Cain and Anthony Hopkins offers an alternative explanation. Their studies of 'gentlemanly capitalism' suggest that the growth of the service sector in the late nineteenth and early twentieth centuries, in terms of both its absolute contribution to British GDP and employment and its relative significance vis-à-vis the manufacturing sector, owed more to the British economy's institutional framework and the 'visible hand' of the policy preferences of Britain's governing elite than to the logic of the market. In particular, Cain and Hopkins argue that the adherence of successive governments to the gold standard and free trade strengthened sterling's role as an international currency, reinforced the City's position as a global financial centre, and entrenched Britain as the world's leading shipping, insurance and brokerage market. In Cain and Hopkins's view, Britain's cosmopolitan political economy supported and enhanced the service sector's fortunes, but at the expense of Britain's manufacturers and farmers. Britain's growing invisible earnings demanded that the nation absorb more visible exports in payment for the overseas investment and services provided by its banking and commercial sector.[7] Any effective support for domestic producers would have required Britain to break the circuit of international finance and trade upon which 'the City' relied, for example through tariff protection, but any proposals for such action were rejected. In this respect the 1880–1914 period is central to Cain and Hopkins's analysis, in that for them this apparent cusp in Britain's economic development confirmed and reinforced the existence of a long-term, structural division of interest between manufacturing and finance in the British economy, and illustrated that 'where a choice had to be made, policy invariably favoured finance over manufacturing' (C&H, I, p. 470). For Cain and Hopkins the particular way in which the British economy developed in the late nineteenth and early twentieth centuries, and the policy framework which sustained that development, provide clear examples of 'gentlemanly capitalism' at work.

This essay will examine Cain and Hopkins's thesis through a study of three policy controversies – the debate over empire in the era of the 'new imperialism', and the campaigns for bimetallism in the 1880s and 1890s and for tariff reform in 1903–14. These controversies are of particular significance in the context of 'gentlemanly capitalism'. For Cain and Hopkins the main economic

6 See ibid., and also M. Edelstein, *British Overseas Investment in the Age of High Imperialism* (London, 1979).
7 P.J. Cain and A.G. Hopkins, *British Imperialism*, Vol. I: *Innovation and Expansion, 1688–1914* (London, 1993), *passim*. Referred to hereafter as C&H, I (see references in text).

engine of Britain's imperial growth was not the export interests of Britain's manufacturers but the investment, commercial and carrying interests of the service sector (C&H, I, pp. 1–51). In their schema the political economy of empire was shaped by metropolitan banking, insurance and shipping elites and not by provincial industrialists. The British Empire figures in their work as an institutional mechanism supporting and sustaining the ascendancy of Britain's financial and commercial sector, and hence an examination of British imperial policy in the late nineteenth and early twentieth centuries provides a 'test issue' for the gentlemanly capitalism model. The bimetallic and tariff campaigns are crucial because they challenged, respectively, the gold standard and free trade, the instruments that were defined by Cain and Hopkins as the main ties binding Britain to the international economy. Consequently the alignments of interest and opinion that shaped and informed the bimetallic and tariff debates not only illustrate important aspects of the contemporary response to developments in the British economy, but also offer insights into the influences and constraints on policy-making in the late nineteenth and early twentieth centuries. Given that there must be politics before there is policy, the politics of the bimetallic and tariff debates are crucial to understanding the policy outcomes which saw Britain retain the gold standard and remain almost uniquely loyal to free trade in a protectionist world. The genesis, development and ultimate fate of the bimetallic and tariff reform campaigns can thus shed a great deal of light on whether the structures and requirements of 'gentlemanly capitalism' were the key influence in sustaining Britain's internationalist economic stance.

BRITISH INDUSTRIAL PRODUCTION AND LATE NINETEENTH-CENTURY IMPERIAL EXPANSION

When in 1883 J.R. Seeley famously declared that Britain had 'conquered and peopled half the world in a fit of absence of mind' he was drawing attention to the fact that it was difficult to detect a conscious, guiding imperialist strategy behind the expansion of Great Britain's imperial realm in the nineteenth century. Whatever the merits or demerits of Seeley's argument about the absence of an imperial policy, he was certainly correct insofar as the empire's economic function had rarely been at the centre of public debate. Over the next 30 years, however, the situation changed dramatically. Britain's participation in the 'Scramble for Africa' and other theatres of the 'new imperialism', and the campaigns for empire federation and imperial trade preference, saw the imperial economy become one of the central issues in British politics.

It is not my intention here to explore at length all the factors that led Britain to become a participant in the 'new imperialism'. My primary concern will be to offer a brief discussion of the domestic economic considerations and pressures that helped to shape imperial policy in this period. Of these perhaps the most important was what has been termed the 'fear of the closing door'. The resurgence of protectionism in the late 1870s ensured that territorial expansion carried the threat of the closure by tariffs of areas annexed by protectionist powers. This provoked alarm among British manufacturers, who were concerned at the loss of potential markets and pressed successive governments to avoid this through pre-emptive British annexations.[8] The Royal Commission on the Depression of Trade and Industry, established by Lord Salisbury's short-lived Conservative administration of 1885, expressed a common demand of chambers of commerce when it noted that 'we must display greater activity in the search for new markets';[9] and the Manchester, Glasgow, Birmingham and London chambers were particularly active in the late 1880s in advocating the opening up of 'new countries under the British flag' as a means of relieving the related problems of over-production and the closure of traditional markets and territories colonized by protectionist powers.[10] Given the administrative and military costs attendant upon imperial ventures, and the growing budgetary problems that marked the 1880s and 1890s, governments were in many respects 'reluctant imperialists' in the late nineteenth century: balancing the budgetary (and therefore tax) implications of imperial activity with the potential political cost of appearing 'neglectful' of business opinion was a difficult matter. The possible connections between the perceived needs of British industry and the 'new imperialism' 1890–1914 tend to be minimized by Cain and Hopkins. In fact, it was politically difficult for any government to ignore the demands emanating from Britain's manufacturing centres, and it is not possible to understand late Victorian British imperial expansion without reference to this factor.

That manufacturers demonstrated a clear interest in imperial expansion, and found governments responsive to that interest, seems at first glance to contradict a core element of the gentlemanly capitalist thesis. Moreover, the fact that the London chamber of commerce, which contained many representatives of the service sector, allied itself on the question of empire with Manchester, Liverpool, Glasgow, Birmingham and other chambers in industrial areas, seems to weaken the notion, repeated throughout *British Imperialism*, that there was a gulf between manufacturing and 'City' interests. The domestic forces providing the push for imperial expansion in the late nineteenth century appear to have been drawn from across the spectrum of economic activity.

But although there may have been a consensus on the expediency of preserving and even extending Britain's imperial domain, there were divisions of opinion and interest over the empire's economic function. These differences became very apparent in the difficulties suffered by the Imperial Federation League (IFL). Established in 1884 in order to formulate a means of bringing the empire closer together, the IFL seemed at first to attract cross-party and cross-interest support; but when discussion moved from constitutional, defence and scientific matters to questions of imperial economic organization rifts began to emerge. In particular the notion of establishing an imperial tariff

---

8 See in particular W.G. Hynes, *The Economics of Empire* (London, 1978), *passim*.
9 Royal Commission on the Depression of Trade and Industry, *Final Report*, Cmnd. [4893].
10 See Hynes, *Economics*, and E.H.H. Green, *The Crisis of Conservatism* (London, 1995), pp. 35–41.

regime sundered the IFL and, as its secretary confessed, it became by the early 1890s 'a house divided against itself' and collapsed in 1893.[11] Out of the wreckage of the IFL there emerged two splinter groups, the British Empire League (BEL) and the United Empire Trade League (UETL), the former upholding free trade and the latter raising the banner of imperial preference that Joseph Chamberlain was to wave with such vigour in 1903. It is difficult to establish the precise support bases for the BEL and the UETL, but it is noteworthy that the BEL was chaired by Sir John Lubbock, a scion of a City family, and seems to have had its strongest support in London, whereas the leading figure of the UETL was the tariff enthusiast Sir Howard Vincent, and its strongest sympathizers were in Birmingham and Sheffield.

Many in late Victorian and Edwardian Britain appear to have been for the empire in the same way that many were against sin, that is, they supported a general proposition rather than a particular faith. As a consequence it was possible for imperial expansion to generate support from a wide body of interests and groups. However, as soon as any attempt was made to define the empire's function more rigorously the imperial constituency proved to be highly stratified. It would be reductionist to present the diversity of opinion on the empire as a simple division between provincial manufacturers and metropolitan financiers, but at the same time a key difference of opinion did seem to be between those who regarded the empire as *part* of Britain's broader international economic role and those who regarded it as a distinct, and preferably separate, economic entity. In this respect discussion about the economic function of empire in the late nineteenth century was part of a more general debate about the wisdom of retaining Britain's 'cosmopolitical economy' – a debate which was to be even more sharply focused by the bimetallic and tariff reform campaigns.

ORIGINS OF THE DEBATE OVER A BIMETALLIC CURRENCY STANDARD

The campaign for bimetallism began in earnest in 1881, with the establishment of what was to become the Bimetallic League. The basic premises of bimetallism were simple enough.[12] Bimetallists blamed the cyclical downturns which British industry and agriculture experienced in the mid- to late 1870s, and the recurring recessions of the 1880s and early 1890s, on a worldwide fall in prices which hit the international markets after 1874. The cause of this price fall, according to the bimetallist argument, was the international monetary situation, and more particularly the almost universal adoption of the gold standard by the industrialized nations following Germany's decision to demonetize silver in 1873. This was thought to have had two detrimental effects. First, it

11 Green, *Crisis*, pp. 39–40.
12 For a more detailed introduction to the bimetallic debate see E.H.H. Green, 'Rentiers versus producers? The political economy of the bimetallic controversy, *c*.1880–1898', *English Historical Review*, 103 (1988), pp. 518–612.

had caused an appreciation in the price of gold; second, it had brought about an increase in the amount of work gold had had to do in the international economy as a result of its being the only acceptable standard of exchange for the major powers. These developments, it was argued, had created a severe relative contraction in the world's money supply and, following the quantity theory of money, a concomitant fall in prices.[13]

If the widespread adoption of the gold standard was blamed for the general deflation of the late nineteenth century it was also held responsible for another problem affecting particular trading interests. The corollary of the widespread adoption of the gold standard was an equally widespread demonetization of silver and a divergence in the relative values of the two metals as the price of silver plummeted. While most of the industrialized world had adopted the gold standard, some of the world, most notably South America and the Far East, remained on silver, and trade between the two areas was, according to the bimetallist analysis, gravely dislocated as a result. Silver's depreciation was seen to have substantially diminished the purchasing power of nations on a silver standard for the goods of gold-standard nations. Other harmful effects were also noted. In particular it was argued that whilst the purchasing power of silver had fallen in relation to goods produced in gold regions, its purchasing power with regard to goods produced in silver-using nations had remained constant. This was deemed to have given producers in silver-using countries an enormous competitive advantage over gold-standard producers, with the growth of Indian cotton exports to China at the expense of Lancashire manufacturers being seen as a prime example.[14] At the same time, it was also argued that the relative cheapness of primary products from silver-using states, especially cereals, had been one factor in the increased import of foodstuffs from South America and Asia to Britain.[15] According to bimetallists, the division of the world into gold- and silver-using regions had damaged the trading prospects of British exporters and added to the pressures of import penetration faced by British agriculturalists.

Having defined the problem in monetary terms, bimetallists advocated a monetary solution: they proposed an international agreement for a bimetallic standard in which both gold and silver would be freely convertible and in which their relative value would be fixed at a legal ratio. By abandoning gold and adopting a joint standard, the shortage of money caused by the increased demand for gold would be overcome, as would the problem of falling prices in gold-using nations. At the same time the remonetization of silver, and the action of the fixed ratio, would remove the disjuncture between gold- and silver-using nations, destroy the competitive advantages enjoyed by the latter and thereby reduce competition for British manufacturers in silver markets and stem the flow to Britain of 'artificially' cheap foodstuffs.

13 For a full rehearsal of the bimetallists' arguments on these points see the Royal Commission on Currency (hereafter RCC), *Final Report*, Cmd. [5512], pp. 11–12 (1888).
14 Green, 'Rentiers', pp. 596–8.
15 RCC, *Final Report*, p. 36 for a discussion of this problem.

Support for bimetallism came mainly from those sectors of the economy which felt most hard pressed by falling prices and trade problems with silver-using states. One such sector was British agriculture. When the Royal Commission on Agricultural Depression produced its *First Report* in 1894, bimetallism featured prominently as one of the solutions most favoured by farming witnesses.[16] The leading agricultural members of the commission, Walter Long and Henry Chaplin, produced a special section of the *Report* calling for currency reform,[17] and Chaplin constantly lobbied the Conservative party leadership to take up the cause of bimetallism for the sake of British agriculture.[18] For farmers desperate to see a rise in prices, the explicitly inflationary logic of bimetallism had an obvious attraction. Many farmers, especially arable growers, would undoubtedly have preferred a return to agricultural protection, but, given the prevailing assumptions about the political obstacles to tariffs on foodstuffs, bimetallism seemed to offer a less politically charged alternative. The general inflationary effects of bimetallism meant that it could not be presented as a measure designed to give farming interests any special advantages.

That bimetallism was not simply a vehicle for the agricultural lobby appears to be confirmed by the support it gained from some important sectors of British industry. The cotton industry was particularly interested: Manchester provided the headquarters for the Bimetallic League in its early years, prominent Lancashire cotton bosses were some of the most committed advocates of the bimetallic cause, the United Textile Factory Workers threw their weight behind bimetallism, and in the 1890s Lancashire returned a phalanx of pro-bimetallic MPs to Westminster.[19] Moreover, although Lancashire produced the strongest support for bimetallism, there was also backing for the campaign in Britain's other manufacturing centres, most notably in Glasgow and Birmingham.[20]

With sections of both industry and agriculture blaming the currency situation for falling prices, a form of 'producers' alliance' emerged on the issue of bimetallism. Certainly a conscious attempt was made to foster such an alliance, for when H.H. Gibbs, the longest-serving president of the Bimetallic League, spoke of the damage the currency problem inflicted on the British economy, he was very careful to state that he was 'speaking of productive British industry, and I mean thereby agriculture and the industries that produce goods'.[21] In the bimetallist analysis the fact that Britain's 'productive' sectors were suffering without relief was no accident. Rather, this situation was seen to have developed because, as the cotton boss J.C. Fielden put it,

16 Royal Commission on Agricultural Depression, *First Report* (1894), Cmd. [7400], 'Summary of evidence', (1894), XVI, appendix C.
17 Ibid., p. 33.
18 See for example H. Chaplin to Salisbury, 10 March 1887, Salisbury papers, Hatfield House; Chaplin to Salisbury, 9 Dec. 1892, ibid.; Chaplin to Salisbury, 5 Feb. 1895, ibid.
19 For further details of the cotton industry's involvement see Green, 'Rentiers', pp. 596–7.
20 Ibid., p. 609.
21 H.H. Gibbs, *Address on Bimetallism* (London, 1895), p. 5.

'The capitalist class may be divided into the fixed investment class and the Industrial capitalist', and that whereas 'The former gains by every fall in prices . . . the latter suffers'.[22] That the financial community benefited from a fall in prices whilst the 'productive' sector suffered was inevitable, so bimetallists contended, because 'A fall in prices . . . involves the transference from the active producers of wealth a larger proportion of production in satisfaction of the "fixed charge" due to the passive owners of wealth'.[23] As a result bimetallic campaigners represented their fight as 'a struggle between Lombard Street and the industrial interests of England',[24] identified 'the City' as the common enemy of farmers and industrialists alike, and for much of the 1880s and 1890s poured vitriol on the despised 'money power'.[25]

If opponents of the gold standard were drawn largely from Britain's industrial and agricultural interests, so its greatest supporters were drawn mainly from the City. Giving evidence to the Royal Commission on Currency in 1887 Bertram Currie, chairman of Glyn, Mills and Currie (then Britain's largest private bank) and president of the Gold Standard Defence Association, argued that the fall in prices and appreciation in the value of gold was a good thing because 'England as a country to which large gold debts are due must be drawing advantage from the change, since she must receive from other countries in payment of interest on her gold debts a larger quantity of goods, or money that will buy more goods'.[26] Even more important, Currie saw the reason that Britain enjoyed this advantage as being due to the fact that 'The United Kingdom, and more particularly London is and has been for many years the financial centre of the world', and, further, that 'this supremacy arising . . . in great measure from the knowledge that a debt payable in London will be discharged in a definite quantity of a certain metal . . . could be endangered by the adoption of bimetallism'.[27] Currie, along with most other leading City figures, rallied to defend the gold standard, which they saw as crucial to the preservation and extension of London's dominant international role.[28]

Both the conduct and the outcome of the bimetallic debate proved satisfactory for defenders of the gold standard. From 1881 to 1898, when the campaign effectively came to an end, the bimetallists rarely looked like achieving their goal. In 1886 Lord Randolph Churchill, then Chancellor of the

---

22 J.C. Fielden, in *Proceedings of the Bimetallic League* (London, 1888), p. 82.
23 H.R. Beeton, 'The currency question for laymen', *National Review*, 153 (Nov. 1895), p. 389.
24 G.L. Molesworth, in *Proceedings of the Bimetallic League* (London, 1893), p. 29.
25 See Green, 'Rentiers', p. 600.
26 RCC, *Second Report* (1888), Cmnd. 5248, evidence of B. Currie, examined 8 July 1887, QQ. 6644–6716.
27 Ibid.
28 See Green, 'Rentiers', pp. 604–6. For specific instances of intense City lobbying on the currency question, see Committee of London Clearing Banks to Bank of England, 22 Sept. 1897, discussed at a meeting of the Bank of England Court of Directors, 23 Sept. 1897, Minutes of Court, Bank of England Archives, Ud 8 Apr. 1897–4 Apr. 1898, and also Memorandum from 'The London Bankers' to the Chancellor of the Exchequer, 13 Oct. 1897, Public Record Office, T172/952.

Exchequer, threw a bone in the direction of bimetallic opinion by introducing changes in coinage that led to the Royal Mint purchasing more silver, but otherwise this most unorthodox of politicians proved very orthodox in his economics. In 1887 a Royal Commission on Currency lent an official ear to bimetallic complaints, but signally failed to endorse the bimetallist case. In 1892 bimetallic hopes were dimmed still further when the Liberal Chancellor of the Exchequer, Sir William Harcourt, packed the British delegation to the International Monetary Conference at Brussels with a majority of 'Goldbugs', and thus effectively forestalled any constructive British engagement with the idea of an international currency agreement.[29] Similarly, bimetallic hopes that the Indian currency crisis of the mid-1890s would provide a starting point for an international agreement, through the British government allowing India to adopt a bimetallic standard, were killed off by the decision of Lord Salisbury's third administration to reject overtures from France and the United States on this matter and to place India on the gold standard.[30] In spite of their being well-organized, well-funded and widely supported, the bimetallists were thwarted at every turn.

JOSEPH CHAMBERLAIN AND THE ROOTS OF THE TARIFF REFORM CAMPAIGN

The tariff reform campaign had a larger impact than the bimetallic agitation, but ultimately it suffered a similar fate.[31] Launched by Joseph Chamberlain in May 1903, the tariff campaign was informed by many of the same concerns that had featured in the attack on the gold standard, and indeed drew support from many of the same interests. Britain's farmers, with the arable sector once again taking the lead, were one of the first groups to climb on board the tariff reform bandwagon.[32] The tariff controversy erupted over whether to retain a one shilling per quarter duty on imported corn, imposed in 1901 to help pay for the Boer War. Joseph Chamberlain sought to use this duty to inaugurate a system of imperial tariff preferences, but in farming circles it was also looked upon as perhaps a last chance to obtain tariff protection for British agriculture. As the tariff campaign developed, farming interests were given good cause for optimism. Speaking at Glasgow in October 1903, Chamberlain not only argued for a two shilling per quarter duty on foreign corn but also for duties on imported meat, dairy produce and vegetables.[33] Furthermore, agriculture was the first 'industry' to be investigated and reported on by Chamberlain's

29 Green, 'Rentiers', p. 611; E.H.H. Green, 'The bimetallic controversy: empiricism belimed or the case for the issues', *English Historical Review*, 105 (1990).
30 Green, 'Rentiers', pp. 605–6.
31 For discussions of the tariff campaign see A. Sykes, *Tariff Reform in British Politics* (Oxford, 1978); P. Cain, 'Political economy in Edwardian Britain', in A. O'Day (ed.), *The Edwardian Age: Conflict and Stability* (London, 1979).
32 For a discussion of the agricultural aspect of the tariff campaign see Green, *Crisis*, pp. 207–22.
33 See J. Chamberlain at Glasgow, 6 Oct. 1903, in C. Boyd (ed.), *Speeches of the Right Honourable Joseph Chamberlain* (2 vols, London, 1914), II, p. 167.

Tariff Commission, the body he had called together to construct a 'scientific tariff', and the campaign constantly stressed the general economic, social and, indeed, political importance of a prosperous agricultural sector. Small wonder that there was strong farming support for tariff reform.

The tariff campaign also set out to appeal to British manufacturing industry, and here too it achieved marked success.[34] The 10 per cent all-round tariff on manufactured goods promised by Chamberlain in the autumn of 1903 and confirmed by the Tariff Commission was a tempting prospect for industries concerned about growing import penetration. In particular the iron and steel industry, the metal trades of the Black Country and East Midlands, and significant elements of the engineering and woollen trades showed a keen interest in tariff reform. Hundreds of industrialists assisted the Tariff Commission by providing either written or oral evidence on the condition of their firms or industries,[35] and both the commission and the campaigning organization, the Tariff Reform League, were largely dependent on contributions from industrialists to finance their activities.[36]

Tariff reform, like bimetallism, was presented as a 'producers' policy', on the grounds that domestic agricultural and industrial production were the essence of a genuinely *national* economy. This identification of productive activities with the national interest was underlined by the tariff campaign's carefully drawn contrast between the fortunes of industry and agriculture and those of the service sector under free trade. Britain's position as an international finance and banking sector had, according to the tariff argument, waxed as Britain's industrial and farming interests had waned, with both developments the result of free trade. The reasoning here was straightforward. The interests of the financial sector were deemed to be cosmopolitan: capital flowed to where it would gain returns, insurance flourished no matter whose trade was insured, and bills of exchange could be profitably discounted no matter who presented them. The City's interests were seen to lie in a net expansion of world trade – anyone's trade – and in a continuation of Britain's role as the world's mart. Hence the tariff campaign was infused with a rhetoric openly contemptuous of Britain's financial sector. In September 1903 Joseph Chamberlain was told by one supporter that 'under the present system [free trade] the proportion of placemen, rentiers, agents and distributors is daily increasing and that of producers daily diminishing'.[37] Chamberlain himself stated at

---

34 For the industrial aspect of the tariff campaign see Green, *Crisis*, pp. 223–41, and also A.J. Marrison, 'Businessmen, industries and tariff reform in Great Britain, 1903–31', *Business History*, 25 (1983); idem, *British Businessmen and Protection* (Oxford, 1996).

35 For a detailed analysis of the work of the Tariff Commission see A.J. Marrison, 'British businessmen and the scientific tariff: a study of Joseph Chamberlain's Tariff Commission, 1903–21', unpublished PhD thesis, University of Hull, 1976.

36 See Marrison, 'Scientific tariff'; *idem, British Businessmen*; Green, *Crisis*, pp. 223–41. For the Tariff Reform League's finances see F. Coetzee, 'Pressure groups, Tory businessmen and the age of corruption before the First World War', *Historical Journal*, 29 (1986).

37 E.G. Pretyman to J. Chamberlain, 22 Sept. 1903, Joseph Chamberlain papers, Birmingham University Library, JC 18/18/92.

Birmingham in May 1904 that 'Invisible exports are invisible so far as the working man is concerned. What does he see of them?', whilst a few months earlier Sir Gilbert Parker, the tariff-reforming Conservative MP for Gravesend, had argued that 'For invisible exports there were only invisible commercial travellers'.[38] Nor did the rhetoric cool over time, for in 1908 George Wyndham, a former Conservative Cabinet minister, was telling his father that if Britain continued its drift towards dependence on 'invisibles' it would become 'a nation of bankers and commission agents supporting armies of unemployed loafers'.[39]

The tariff campaign's message was clear. The British economy consisted of productive sectors, industry and agriculture, which would be best served by the national economics of tariff reform, and a non-productive sector, financial services, which was served by the cosmopolitan economics of free trade. This message in part reflected the tariff campaign's experiences in dealing with the service sector. Throughout the campaign, relations between the tariff camp and the City, in particular the banking sector, were always strained and often hostile. Only eight bankers were listed as cooperating with the Tariff Commission, and of these only one was a leading figure in the City.[40] This made life very difficult, with the secretary of the Tariff Commission, W.A.S. Hewins, noting that it was almost impossible to obtain data or detailed descriptions about Britain's role as a financial centre.[41] This lack of cooperation was put down to City hostility. At a meeting of the Tariff Commission in May 1906 Hewins argued that 'The position of the bankers, I gather, is that any change in our fiscal position would be disastrous to London as a banking centre',[42] a view that had been expressed by Sir Felix Schuster in his address to the Institute of Bankers in December 1903.[43] Later assertions at Tariff Commission meetings that 'almost every banker is opposed to tariff reform' were challenged on the basis that 'bankers whose business is largely on the Exchange are against it . . . [whilst] those who are doing general business and who would benefit from the increased prosperity to the country more or less favour it',[44] but this statement turned out to be more an expression of wishful thinking than a statement of fact. Not even the domestic clearing banks provided support for tariff reform.

38 J. Chamberlain at Birmingham, 12 May 1904, G. Parker at Bristol, 20 Feb. 1904, in W.E. Dowding, *The Tariff Reform Mirage* (London, 1912), p. 236.
39 G. Wyndham to C. Wyndham, 4 Nov. 1908, in J. Mackail and G. Wyndham, *Life and Letters of George Wyndham* (2 vols, London, 1924), II, pp. 620–1. Wyndham was the Conservative MP for Dover and had been a Cabinet minister under Salisbury and Balfour.
40 Miscellaneous Lists, n.d., Tariff Commission papers, London School of Economics, TC8/2/17.
41 Tariff Commission, Minutes of Proceedings, 17 May 1906, 31 May 1906 and 23 May 1907 for Hewins's statement of the problem, in ibid., TC2/1/12, 13, 14.
42 Tariff Commission, Minutes of Proceedings, 17 May 1906, in ibid., TC2/1/2.
43 F. Schuster, 'Foreign trade and the money market', address to the Institute of Bankers, 16 Dec. 1903. Schuster was later to become chairman of the Committee of London Clearing Banks.
44 Statement by A. Mosley, Tariff Commission, Minutes of Proceedings, 31 May 1906, in Tariff Commission papers, London School of Economics, TC2/1/13.

THE CAIN/HOPKINS ARGUMENT REGARDING 'GENTLEMANLY CAPITALISM'
AND ITS PERTINENCE TO THE BIMETALLIC AND TARIFF REFORM CAMPAIGNS

Both the nature and the outcome of the bimetallic and tariff campaigns appear at first glance to confirm Cain and Hopkins's arguments. In each case there seems to have been a division of opinion and interest between 'productive enterprise' and services, and in each case it was the policy option favoured by the service sector that won out. However, a more detailed analysis of the interests and issues at play in the bimetallic and tariff debates indicates that neither story is quite as straightforward as it seems.

With regard to bimetallism, it is difficult to attribute the failure of the movement *solely* to City leverage over economic policy-making. To begin with there was some support in the City for bimetallism. H.H. Gibbs, one of the most prominent bimetallic spokesmen, was the chairman of a large merchant bank, a member of the Court of Directors and one-time governor of the Bank of England, and in 1891–2 he was an MP for the City of London. Several other prominent City figures[45] supported bimetallism, and some City firms with strong links to the Far East or South America, like Gibbs's own bank, threw their institutional weight behind the campaign.[46] Bimetallism was certainly a minority taste in the City, but this banking support for currency heresies should not pass unnoticed. The fact that some influential City voices, no matter how few, were prepared to back bimetallism would have been of great help had the 'productive sector' been genuinely united behind the cause. However, a major problem for the bimetallic campaign was that there was no such unanimity. Business opinion on bimetallism was splintered. The Manchester and Liverpool chambers of commerce, two of the most important centres of bimetallic activity, saw support for the campaign fluctuate over time,[47] and whereas the cotton sector appears to have regarded bimetallism as an end in itself, a way of improving trade with India and the Far East, the Birmingham chamber of commerce appears to have seen bimetallism as more of a bargaining tool to induce the United States to reduce tariffs.[48] Furthermore, even though bimetallism enjoyed the backing of these powerful chambers, the Associated Chambers of Commerce voted against bimetallic motions by a substantial majority.[49] In terms of a straightforward breakdown of the interests engaged on either side of the debate, the bimetallic controversy cannot be reduced to a simple clash between rentiers and producers.

The interest group anatomy of the tariff campaign was similarly complex. A comprehensive survey of City opinion carried out on behalf of Joseph

---

45 Notably H.R. Grenfell, another member of the Court of Directors and one-time governor of the Bank of England.
46 See A.C. Howe, 'Bimetallism: a controversy re-opened', *English Historical Review*, 105 (1990).
47 See ibid., and also Green, 'Case for the issues'.
48 Green, 'Rentiers', p. 609.
49 See S.R.B. Smith, 'British nationalism, imperialism and the City of London', unpublished PhD thesis, London University, 1985, p. 76.

Chamberlain by the journalist H.A. Gwynne confirmed that banking opinion was solidly against tariff reform, but at the same time it also indicated that there was substantial support for Chamberlain's proposals in the insurance trade and on the stock exchange.[50] However, the diversity of opinion on tariffs in the City was as nothing when compared to the range of views within British industry. Indeed, the differences of opinion between and within different branches of British manufacturing industry help to explain the creation and work of the Tariff Commission. The chief purpose of the commission, to construct a 'scientific tariff', can be seen – and this was the view of some opponents of tariff reform – simply as an attempt to secure a pseudo-scientific gloss for the tariff project. A more recent and reasoned appraisal is that the Tariff Commission was essential because an economic argument, to be politically credible, must possess at least some degree of internal consistency and hold a plausible claim to scientific validity.[51] However, neither of these explanations grasps the political importance of the Tariff Commission, which was that a 'scientific tariff' was a political necessity if a realistic attempt was to be made to rally the varied and sometimes conflicting interests of a highly stratified industrial sector. British industrialists, in spite of what has been written by those who have seen 'entrepreneurial failure' in the late Victorian economy, were not unimaginative, and they held clear and strong views as to whether a particular tariff regime would help or hinder their businesses. The primary task of the Tariff Commission was to formulate a tariff regime with as broad an appeal as possible, and this proved very difficult.

The personnel assembled in the autumn of 1903 to act as members of the commission gave the project a promising start. A wide range of industries was represented on the commission and, as the most authoritative history of the commission's work has pointed out, this immediately gave and gives the lie to any suggestion that it and the wider tariff debate were simply reflecting the interests of a narrow group of trades unique in experiencing the blast of foreign competition.[52] But hopes of finding an industrial consensus on tariff reform were dashed during the commission's investigations. From December 1903 until the outbreak of the First World War it gathered information from questionnaires circulated to an impressive range of industrial and agricultural concerns, and from witnesses questioned by specialist committees. But there were still huge problems in formulating a tariff policy with *general* appeal. The cotton industry, for example, refused almost en bloc to cooperate with the commission's enquiries. In January 1904 Charles Eckersley, a yarn spinner and a member of the commission, bemoaned the fact that 'When I agreed to become a member, I had no idea that I should be the only representative of the

---

50 H.A. Gwynne, Memorandum on 'Arguments against Mr. Chamberlain's policy', n.d., Dec.(?) 1903, H.A. Gwynne papers, Bodleian Library, Oxford, MS Gwynne, Box 27.
51 See Marrison, 'Scientific tariff'.
52 Ibid., *passim*.

cotton spinning interest'.[53] Some company was eventually found for him, but this did not indicate any weakening of the cotton industry's position. Even the commission's written enquiries were ignored – out of 942 cotton firms which were sent questionnaires on imperial preference, only 44 replied.[54] Nor was it simply imperial preference to which the cotton industry objected. In 1905 the Tariff Commission's Textile Committee noted that the closure of foreign markets by tariffs had affected several branches of the industry, and hence that retaliatory tariffs might have some appeal in cotton districts. In early March 1909 W.A.S. Hewins received a plea from E.A. Bagley, the secretary of the Manchester Tariff Reform League, asking for help to put the tariff reform case to the cotton industry. Later that month Hewins himself lectured 300 Manchester businessmen on the subject of 'Fiscal reform in relation to cotton', emphasizing the damage inflicted by German and US tariffs and indicating the probable benefits of retaliation.[55] Hewins need not have bothered, for the appeal of retaliatory tariffs in Lancashire seems to have been limited to a few manufacturers, while the bulk of producers and more especially the traders and merchants remained loyal to free trade. Moreover, the cotton districts were openly hostile to protective tariffs and imperial preference. The former offered the industry nothing, as there was little or no import penetration; the latter raised 'the greatest fear . . . the cotton industry faced in tariff reform . . . a modification of the Indian tariff'.[56] For the tariff campaign the hostility of the cotton industry seemed insurmountable.

The tariff campaign did not enjoy clear sailing with Britain's other major industries. For example, a leading figure from the woollen industry, W.H. Mitchell, was a founder member of the Tariff Commission. Mitchell was a Bradford mill-owner, a senior vice-president of the Bradford chamber of commerce and a member of the executive council of the UK Chambers of Commerce. In his evidence to the commission he argued that 'the history of the trade of Bradford is a record of a long fight against hostile tariffs for the last 25 years', and he called for protective and retaliatory tariffs in order to check imports and re-open overseas markets.[57] But, as Mitchell told Hewins, his position was not representative. In fact, curiously enough, Mitchell pointed out that his firm, chiefly concerned with spinning yarns, had suffered less from tariffs and foreign competition than those producing finished clothes. This could have implied that finished cloth manufacturers were more likely to support tariffs than Mitchell, and some did, but it also indicated that experiences

53 C. Eckersley to W. Harrison, 1 Jan. 1904, Tariff Commission papers, London School of Economics, TC6/1/6.
54 Marrison, 'Scientific tariff', p. 333.
55 E.A. Bagley to W.A.S. Hewins, 1 Mar. 1909, Tariff Commission papers, London School of Economics, TC8/2/5; W.A.S. Hewins, 'Fiscal reform in relation to cotton', n.d., Mar. 1909, ibid., TC8/2/5.
56 Marrison, 'Scientific tariff', p. 340.
57 T.H. Mitchell, evidence to the Tariff Commission, 8 June 1904, Tariff Commission papers, London School of Economics, TC6/1/24.

in the wool trade were diverse enough to encourage differing viewpoints on the tariff question. This last point was confirmed by A.F. Firth, a Bradford carpet manufacturer, who, in returning a Tariff Commission questionnaire to Mitchell, asked that his views on tariffs be kept confidential because 'my father and brother [partners in the family business] take a different view of the fiscal question from what I do'.[58]

The same problem of divided opinion was evident in a sector generally reckoned to be closely associated with the tariff campaign, the iron and steel industry. Again prominent members of the industry, such as Colonel Allen of Bessemers and the Ebbw Vale Steel Company, and Sir Alfred Hickman, president of the British Iron Trade Association, were active members of the Tariff Commission, while Sheffield had been one of the most important centres of tariff agitation since the 1880s.[59] Yet, in spite of the significant degree of support offered by prominent individuals and firms, the industry was by no means unanimous in its support for tariffs. In 1911, with the Tariff Commission short of funds, an appeal was made to those iron and steel firms employing over 1000 hands who had provided information for the commission's enquiries. However, of the six firms approached, three did not send contributions on the grounds that 'the Board is divided in opinion'.[60]

The lukewarm response of the iron and steel industry may have been due to disillusion at the apparent failure of tariff reform at the 1910 general elections, but this seems unlikely. Divisions of opinion over tariffs not only within sectors of industry but also within individual firms were common before 1910, and were still in evidence in the inter-war years.[61] The divergent and often conflicting views which the Tariff Commission gleaned from British industry made the formulation of a 'scientific tariff' a nightmare. The Tariff Commission's major discovery was that there was no industrial consensus on a specific tariff policy. This lack of agreement ensured that the industrial aspect of the tariff campaign progressed not as the product of 'interest group' politics, that is as a passive receiver and transmitter of the views of pressure groups. Diversity of opinion amongst British industrialists meant that it was impossible for the tariff campaign simply to broadcast *the* industrial interest, for there was no coherent view to broadcast. The tariff campaign was about *constructing*, rather than reflecting, an industrial interest.

Divisions within industry over tariffs were not, however, the only problem the tariff campaign faced. Arguably the greatest obstacle was the hostility of the working class, the largest component of the British electorate. Here two factors were at work. The first was that a system of imperial preference would have required the introduction of taxes on imported foodstuffs. It appears that

58 A.F. Firth to W.H. Mitchell, 11 Feb. 1904, Ibid., TC6/1/24.
59 For Sheffield's pro-tariff outlook in the 1880s see F. Brittain, *Sham Free Trade: What It Has Done for England* (Sheffield, 1885); Green, *Crisis*, pp. 31–5.
60 P.A. Hurd to Sir Vincent Caillard, 19 July 1911, Tariff Commission papers, London School of Economics, TC6/1/1.
61 See Marrison, 'Scientific tariff', *passim*.

Britain's working-class voters, even those engaged in agriculture, put their interests as consumers above their interests as 'producers' – they preferred the bird in the hand of 'cheap food' provided by free trade to the 'work for all' seen lurking in the tariff reform bush. The second obstacle to working-class support was that by 1910 the Liberal and Labour parties had successfully labelled tariffs as a ploy by the rich to foist increased indirect taxation on the poor in order to avoid higher direct taxation.[62] In a political and electoral system increasingly driven by the dynamics of class, the British masses seem to have regarded tariff reform as a policy for 'Them' rather than for 'Us'. The first of these obstacles could have been overcome if the 'food tax' element of the tariff campaign had been abandoned, leaving tariff reform as a policy of industrial protection and/or retaliation. However, such a course of action would have provoked other problems. To have dropped 'food taxes' would have meant abandoning the imperial side of the tariff campaign, which was its initial *raison d'être*. At the same time it could only have been interpreted as a signal that agriculture was not to receive any direct tariff benefits, which was unacceptable to a Conservative party that had for so long identified itself as 'the farmer's friend'.[63] From the outset the tariff campaign had to wrestle with an extremely complex set of interests, and the shifting policy structures of tariff reform in the period 1903–14 reflected the political problems of devising a tariff that could appeal to as many and alienate as few people as possible.

AN HISTORICAL REAPPRAISAL: THE NATURE AND MEANING OF
THE BIMETALLIC AND TARIFF REFORM CAMPAIGNS

The bimetallic and tariff campaigns reveal an alignment of interests that resists reduction to a straightforward 'City versus industry' or 'production versus services' conflict. That there were City opponents of the gold standard and industrial defenders of free trade seems to indicate that there was no clear division between metropolitan finance and provincial industry on these questions.[64] As a consequence it could be argued that neither the nature nor the outcome of these debates provide support for the 'gentlemanly capitalism' thesis. If there was no clear division of interests then there could be no choice for governments to make between them, and hence they could not 'favour' one over the other when it came to policy-making. But, although the bimetallic and tariff debates cannot be reduced to a simple 'City versus industry' or 'producers versus services' divide, this does not mean that a more subtle division between these sectors did not exist and exercised a significant influence over the outcome of the controversies.

62 For the 1910 elections see in particular N. Blewett, *The Peers, The Parties and the People* (London, 1972).
63 See Green, *Crisis*, pp. 189–90, 280–5.
64 See M.J. Daunton, '"Gentlemanly Capitalism" and British industry, 1820–1914', *Past and Present*, 122 (1989).

An important feature of both the bimetallic and the tariff reform debates is that contemporaries had little hesitation in categorizing them as either 'City versus industry' or 'production versus services' issues. In part this can be attributed to the fact that the language of the arguments was informed by a political imperative – for both bimetallists and tariff rerformers the representation of the City as a hostile 'Other' was part of an attempt to construct or 'imagine' a community of producers.[65] But there was more to it than that. At the heart of both the bimetallic and the tariff arguments was a deep concern about the pattern of British economic development. Neither bimetallists nor tariff reformers argued that the British economy was in decline as such: H.H. Gibbs made it clear to W.H. Smith that 'the foundation of the bimetallist contention is *not that the country is not growing richer*', and Joseph Chamberlain was also of the opinion that 'Old England is not going back . . . every year sees a great increase in our acquired wealth'.[66] What bimetallists and tariff reformers contended was that Britain had changed the ways in which it acquired and distributed its wealth, and that this change was fundamentally unhealthy. Thus H.H. Gibbs complained that 'the goods of fortune have been unequally distributed . . . the classes who live upon realised capital have grown richer whilst those who have lessened their capital and income are the industrious producers',[67] and tariff reformers bemoaned the fact that Britain was 'living off its capital' and exporting raw materials and semi-finished goods rather than high value-added finished products.[68] Critics of both bimetallism and tariff reform had no hesitation in accepting that these changes had taken place, but they did not accept that they were necessarily changes for the worse. For example, writing to Joseph Chamberlain to explain his hostility to tariffs, the Duke of Devonshire declared:

> You seem to think that for some reason it must always be necessary for us to export something, whether such exports are required to pay for imports or not. It seems to me that if, to take the extreme case, our imports were balanced by our shipping receipts and by the interest on our foreign investments, the country would be just as much better off than it is now as a man who lived on invested capital is better off than a man who has to work with his hands.[69]

In reply, Chamberlain argued that the aim of the tariff campaign, and the key measure of economic success, was to maintain employment in Britain.[70]

65 See Green, *Crisis*, pp. 233–8. The theoretical perspective developed here is heavily indebted to B. Anderson, *Imagined Communities* (London, 1989).
66 H.H. Gibbs to W.H. Smith, 1 June 1889, H.H. Gibbs papers, Guildhall Library, London, MS 11,021, fos. 671–83; J. Chamberlain to Lord Forrest, 1 April 1903, in J.L. Garvin and J. Amery, *The Life of Joseph Chamberlain* (6 vols, London, 1932–69), IV, p. 169.
67 Gibbs to Smith, Gibbs papers, Guildhall Library, London.
68 See Green, *Crisis*, pp. 235–6.
69 Duke of Devonshire to J. Chamberlain, 13 July 1903, in P. Jackson, *The Last of the Whigs* (London, 1994), pp. 327–8.
70 J. Chamberlain to Devonshire, 29 July 1903, in ibid.

The point Chamberlain was seeking to establish, and which had been made with similar force by many bimetallists,[71] was that productive enterprise carried on within Britain was of greater benefit to more people than income from overseas investment and traded services, which accrued only to a narrow social and geographical section of British society. Implicit in both the bimetallic and the tariff controversies was an ongoing conflict between those who were willing to accept the structural changes taking place in the British economy and those who were not. Hence Winston Churchill argued against tariffs on the grounds that the abandonment of free trade would mean 'exit for ever the banking, broking, warehousing predominance of Great Britain', while Arthur Balfour was told by one Board of Trade official that if Britain did not impose tariffs 'we may become more and more a creditor country – a banking rather than an industrial country'.[72]

An interest group analysis of support for the bimetallic and tariff campaigns shows that it would be reductionist to see either debate as a simple 'City versus industry' or 'production versus services' conflict. However, it is important not to reject one form of reductionism only to replace it with another. That one can find bimetallic bankers and free trading industrialists does not mean that the *issue* of the interests of 'producers' and 'rentiers' was not at stake in both debates: to adopt such a stance is analogous to arguing that class is not an important influence on politics because large sections of the working class have always voted Conservative. For a variety of reasons, some 'rentiers' were of the opinion that their interests were best served by bimetallism and tariffs, whilst some 'producers' felt that the gold standard and free trade were good for them. The bimetallist banker H.H. Gibbs argued that 'a little study of English history might not be an unprofitable occupation for some of our pseudo-monometallic fanatics. They would find that our commercial grandeur was the cause and not the effect of our banking system'.[73] In short, Gibbs took the view that Britain's long-term future as an international financial centre was ultimately dependent upon its productive resources, an argument that was restated during the tariff campaign.[74] Likewise, some manufacturers felt that their interests depended on the maintenance of currency stability and/ or free trade – the cotton industry exemplified the problem here by taking a 'producer' stance on one issue and a 'rentier' position on the other.

Leaving aside any question of 'false consciousness', individuals and groups can define their interests in different ways at different times. Indeed the adoption of different time-frames may in itself lead to a conflict of opinion over the definition of an interest. For example, Gibbs's position was that *in the long run*

---

71 See Green, 'Rentiers', pp. 600–1.
72 W.S. Churchill to J.M. Bayley, 20 May 1903, in R.S. Churchill, *Winston Churchill*, Companion Volume II, part 1, pp. 182–3; P. Ashley to A.J. Balfour, 4 July 1904, Balfour papers, British Library, Add. MS 49870, fols. 38–45.
73 H.H. Gibbs, *The Crisis in Silver* (London, 1893), p. 561.
74 See B. Kidd, 'Colonial preference and free trade', proof copies of a series of articles published in the *Daily Mail*, 5th article, section 1, n.d. [1903], Benjamin Kidd papers, Cambridge University Library, Add. MS 8069.

Britain's banking interest was reliant upon the health of Britain's productive sector. And in similar vein, tariff reformers stressed that they were anticipating future as well as immediate needs and interests, an argument which was given pointed irony by the cotton industry's demand for tariffs after 1945. But although it may be and often is the case that there are considerable differences of opinion on an issue within interests, classes, and other social groups, that does not mean that the issue itself does not exist. Both the bimetallic and the tariff debates posited a choice between accepting or rejecting international 'market' decisions which were swinging the balance of the economy towards the service sector. In the event the path of acceptance was chosen.

In explaining why this choice was made it is difficult to ignore the fact that during both the bimetallic and the tariff debates the policy-making apparatus of the British state revealed a strong bias towards the service sector. During the bimetallic campaign the most powerful permanent officials in the key 'economic departments' of the Civil Service, the Treasury and the Board of Trade expressed marked hostility to bimetallic arguments. Francis Mowatt, Edward Hamilton, Reginald Welby and Robert Chalmers at the Treasury and T.H. Farrer at the Board of Trade were in fact all members of the Gold Standard Defence Association, and Farrer's papers reveal a very close relationship between leading civil servants and City supporters of the gold standard.[75] A similar pattern emerged on the issue of tariff reform, with the Treasury pouring cold water on the tariff campaign.[76] This is hardly surprising, given that in 1898 Robert Chalmers had spoken to T.H. Farrer about 'the unity of the principles which lead you to maintain the two things – free trade and sound currency. One is the obverse of the other, the reverse of the same coin'.[77] Successive British governments were thus offered 'expert' advice from officials committed to the status quo on both the trade and the currency questions.

One possible explanation for the apparent bias of the administrative machine is the close proximity of 'the City' to Whitehall, which gave the world of finance an ease of access to government, and opportunities for close and frequent contact with the senior Civil Service, that was simply not available to voices and interests in the provinces. In short, geography may well be a significant, if often underestimated, factor in the decision-making process. However, there were other factors at work. In January 1888 Edward Hamilton, a Permanent Secretary at the Treasury, noted in his diary that 'it is no use nowadays to attempt to take any financial step without giving the Bankers, which are such a powerful body, an interest and without taking the financial "big wigs" into confidence'.[78] What Hamilton was pointing to here was that there

75 Green, 'Rentiers', pp. 611–12.
76 See in particular 'The fiscal problem', unsigned Treasury memorandum (sent to E.W. Hamilton), 8 Aug. 1903, copy in A.D. Steel-Maitland papers, Scottish Record Office, GD193/88/1/147.
77 R. Chalmers to T.H. Farrer, 19 Nov. 1898, T.H. Farrer papers, London School of Economics, vol. 1, fol. 28.
78 E.W. Hamilton, diary, 7 Jan. 1888, E.W. Hamilton papers, British Library, Add. MS 48647.

was a close *structural* relationship between government and the City. The Bank of England was, after all, the government's banker, and acted as a crucial intermediary in placing government bills on the London market. Furthermore, governments needed the City to take up their various issues, and the question of City confidence was as important in the late nineteenth and early twentieth centuries for the financial security of any government as it is now. The City occupied a key strategic position in the state's financial apparatus, and as a consequence possessed great influence, both direct and indirect. But arguably the most important factor in the 'pro-City' bias of Britain's administrative elite was the fact that, perhaps as a result of the close and frequent contact between them, Whitehall and the 'Square Mile' had by the late nineteenth century come to share a set of assumptions about the 'natural' development of the British economy – they inhabited the same mental world. The leading figures in the key economic departments, especially the Treasury, accepted the structural changes taking place in the British economy as 'rational', even inevitable. Their view of the optimum path of British economic development was informed by a quite conscious emphasis on the overriding importance of the service sector's earnings and the necessity of maintaining Britain's links with the international economy. In 1898 Edward Hamilton estimated Britain's trade deficit at £194 million, but noted that there was no cause for alarm because

> In the first place, we supply foreigners every year with a huge amount of capital . . . the aggregate amount may be put at £2,000,000,000. The interest on this at 4.5% would be £90,000,000, which is being paid in the form of imports without any corresponding exports. In the second place there are also 'invisible' exports to be taken into account in the shape of freights and profits on our vast shipping trade . . . [which] may now be put at £90,000,000. When therefore the excess [of imports over exports] goes on increasing, there is no reason to suppose that it is due to other causes than interest due on the increased capital invested abroad and an augmented carrying trade; and such increases are only compatible with a greatly increasing exporting capacity on the part of other nations.[79]

For Hamilton there was simply no problem – Britain's trade imbalance was the 'natural' outcome of Britain's position as the hub of international finance. As a consequence Hamilton felt there was no need to interfere with the flow of British trade, or to interfere with the 'self-acting' system which had produced the existing patterns of economic activity.

Of course civil servants, although their input should not be underestimated, were not responsible for economic policy. Ultimately elected governments took the key decisions, and for Cain and Hopkins it is in this context that the

---

79 E.W. Hamilton, notes on 'Excess of imports over exports', 28 Nov. 1898, E.W. Hamilton, Private Office papers, Public Record Office, T168/39.

'gentlemanly' aspect of 'gentlemanly capitalism' plays an important role. If the administrative elite shared common ground with the City, Britain's aristocratic *political* elite were, Cain and Hopkins suggest, even more closely entwined with the service sector. The foundation of this link was, it seems, according to the two historians, the 'military–fiscal' state that Britain's aristocratic governments constructed to fight the wars of the eighteenth and early nineteenth centuries, with the alliance between aristocracy and finance being consolidated in the mid-nineteenth century (C&H, I, pp. 12–44). In the period covered by this essay the City–aristocracy nexus was, it appears, extended still further. The British aristocracy, confronted by falling agricultural rents and prices and Radical attacks on landed wealth, sought alternative sources of income to buttress their position. The stock of banking families appears to have risen on the aristocratic marriage market, with banking heiresses proving even more popular than those from across the Atlantic.[80] At the same time many aristocrats traded broad acres for bonds and securities – like Oscar Wilde's Lady Bracknell, it seems they preferred 'the funds' to land.[81] The net result of these trends was that both socially and economically the financial elite and the titled aristocracy were bound together more firmly, thereby strengthening the City's influence over Britain's patrician political elite. Is it surprising that, for example, the Duke of Devonshire should have opposed tariff reform? Here was a man whose income from rentals and bonds had fallen from £170,000 per annum to £15,000 between 1874 and 1896, but who had recovered his position by 1908 as a result of selling 80,000 acres and reinvesting largely in international equities and gilts.[82] Small wonder that Devonshire saw nothing wrong with living off 'invisibles'.

That there was widespread aristocratic interest in City alliances and investments is clear, but it is also evident that many of Britain's 'gentlemen' were not wholly committed to, and indeed displayed some antagonism towards, the supposedly essential mechanisms of 'gentlemanly capitalism'. When the bimetallic campaign was in full swing in 1894–5 the secretary of the London branch of the Bimetallic League, H.R. Beeton, proposed to start a 'guarantee fund' of £100,000. It is significant that, to secure these funds, Beeton looked in the first instance to 'the great territorial Lords', and five months later he was able to note that the guarantee fund was 'assured'.[83] Whether aristocratic support was solely responsible for the deep coffers of the bimetallic campaign is uncertain, but there was clearly aristocratic backing for bimetallism.[84]

80 See Y. Cassis, *City Bankers, 1890–1914* (Cambridge, 1994).

81 See D. Cannadine, *The Decline and Fall of the British Aristocracy* (New Haven, Conn., 1991), pp. 429–43, and F.M.L. Thompson, *English Landed Society in the Nineteenth Century* (London, 1963), pp. 321–4.

82 Jackson, *Last of the Whigs*, pp. 280–8.

83 H.R. Beeton to H.S. Foxwell, 17 July 1894 and 28 Oct. 1894, H.S. Foxwell papers, in the possession of Mr R.D. Freeman.

84 For example, in Jan. 1895 it was noted that the Duke of Portland had given £1000 to the guarantee funds 'in the first place': H. Chaplin to A.J. Balfour, 15 Jan. 1895, Balfour papers, British Library, Add. MS 48772, fol. 104.

Likewise, the tariff campaign attracted strong aristocratic support, with some of the most committed advocates of tariffs being drawn from the patrician elite.[85] That significant elements of the aristocracy were heavily engaged in these campaigns is an indication that some of Britain's titled elite had not bowed to the 'inevitability' of international market decisions, but were prepared to mount a political challenge to them in order to salvage traditional patterns of aristocratic life and wealth. Here the outlook and dispositions of the Earl of Carnarvon offer some intriguing insights into the complex political economy of aristocracy in the late nineteenth and early twentieth centuries. In the early 1880s Carnarvon was so alarmed at the seemingly unstoppable march of anti-landlord radicalism that he sold land, built up a large portfolio of overseas and colonial stocks and drew up advice for his wife to flee overseas in the event of his death. But by the 1890s the apparent success of Lord Salisbury's Conservative administrations in fending off the radical challenge had reassured Carnarvon to the point where he was able to advise the consolidation and even the extension of his English estates.[86]

In short, the political climate helped to shape economic decisions by altering the parameters of economic 'rationality', and large sections of the aristocracy were prepared to support campaigns which offered even a chance of legislation favourable to Britain's agricultural sector and the traditional landed way of life. Likewise, the failure of these movements could encourage them to give up the struggle. In 1910 the Conservatives failed to obtain a popular mandate for tariff reform, and the Liberal government was able to push through the People's Budget with its 'confiscatory' land taxes, and, through the Parliament Act of 1911, bring an end to the aristocracy's veto power over legislation. In the wake of these successive defeats, with their important fiscal and economic as well as political implications, the Earl of Portsmouth, a keen tariff reformer and 'Diehard' peer, informed the Conservative leader that the party's failure had led him to reorder his personal finances. According to Portsmouth the People's Budget represented 'the adoption of a system through which the State . . . could from time to time turn the thumb screw on the capital and savings of the individual', and he pointed out that, as a consequence, 'since that Budget, I have, as indeed have many others, guiltily been transferring our old and making our new investments in securities outside this country, and where the Dividends need not be collected here'.[87] On the basis of evidence like this the specifically 'gentlemanly' aspect of 'gentlemanly capitalism' could be seen as a product of aristocratic weakness and defeat rather than a source of renewed power and authority – an effect more than a cause of Britain's loyalty to the gold standard and to free trade.

85 For aristocratic involvement in the tariff campaign see A. Adonis, *Making Aristocracy Work* (Oxford, 1993); G.D. Phillips, *The Diehards* (Cambridge, Mass., 1979).
86 A. Adonis, 'The survival of the great estates: Henry, 4th Earl Carnarvon and His Dispositions in the 1880s', *Historical Research*, 64 (1991).
87 Earl of Portsmouth to A. Bonar Law, 29 Jan. 1912, A. Bonar Law papers, House of Lords Record Office, 26/1/68.

CONCLUSION

The late nineteenth and early twentieth centuries witnessed the rapid growth of Britain's service sector economy and of significant problems for both the manufacturing and agricultural sectors – this much is clear. The issues at stake are how far this was due to the maintenance of government policies favourable to the former and detrimental to the latter, and in turn how far this was traceable to the influence of Britain's service sector elite in the corridors of power. The bimetallic and tariff reform debates do not provide clear-cut answers to these questions. It is certainly the case that both the gold standard and free trade played a vital role in maintaining London's position at the heart of international finance and commerce, and it is evident that the bulk of City opinion, especially the powerful banking sector, was committed to retaining these policy structures. The currency and tariff debates also indicate that the City was regarded by Britain's administrative elite as the most authoritative voice on economic issues, with the result that City opinion was consulted first and was more likely to be deferred to when any controversy arose. At the same time, however, it is difficult to attribute the failure of either the bimetallic or the tariff campaigns solely to government deference to City opinion and interests. The influence of the City was one factor, but without doubt the most important reason for the failure of bimetallism and tariff reform was that neither campaign succeeded in securing broad enough political or electoral support. Bimetallism, although its importance in certain regions should not be underestimated, was for the most part a secondary issue in late nineteenth-century British politics. Tariff reform became the official policy of one of the major parties, with the Conservatives fighting the 1910 general elections on a tariff reform platform, but a majority of the electorate, for reasons outlined above, remained unconvinced of its merits. Lack of popular support was rather an important obstacle in what was, after all, a mass electoral system.

All this indicates some problematic areas for the 'gentlemanly capitalism' thesis as presently formulated. In Cain and Hopkins's formulation the broad electoral politics of economic policy-making play a less prominent role than the preferences of the decision-making elite in Whitehall and Westminster. One can accept that these decision-makers maintained a policy structure which favoured the service sector, but support for the structures that sustained 'gentlemanly capitalism' extended far beyond the 'gentlemenly capitalists' themselves and their realm of influence. Moreover it is not clear that Britain's aristocratic 'gentlemen', whose role is central in Cain and Hopkins's work, were either united in support of financial/service sector interests or retained the political status and strength to shape policy in the late nineteenth and early twentieth centuries.

Yet it would be wrong simply to discard the 'gentlemanly capitalist' model, for the debates of the period 1880–1914 do indicate that it is of value to an analysis of the development of the British economy and economic policy-making at this time. It is not possible to reduce either the currency or the tariff debates to a simple 'City versus industry'/'production versus services' conflict, for the patterns of support on each issue cut across this divide. However, the basic argument of the 'gentlemanly capitalism' thesis does not require that the pattern of interest be so clear-cut. One does not need to show that the bimetallic and tariff campaigns were a zero-sum game between 'rentiers' and 'producers' to indicate that they were symptomatic of tensions between and controversy about the interests and relative merits of the service and productive sectors.

It is not necessary likewise for the 'gentlemanly capitalism' thesis to demonstrate that the City's interests were the chief determinant of policy. There is an important distinction to be made between the City being in a position to *determine* policy and being able to *influence* policy decisions. An individual, group or interest can influence an event or decision simply by being present, and the influence can be indirect as well as direct. The mere fact of the City's international role, and the growing importance of the City's earnings to Britain's balance of payments, could not but have a profound influence on the way in which people thought about the British economy and its development. This is evident in both the bimetallic and the tariff campaigns, for both debates raised the question of whether the increasing centrality of the service sector to Britain's economic fortunes was a 'good thing', and the economic ideologies that informed these debates were based on clearly annunciated assumptions about whether the trend to 'reliance' on services was the optimum path of development for the British economy. Other issues were at stake too, but this important one was very much to the fore not only in the bimetallic and tariff campaigns but in the more general debate over the 'modernization' of state and society that lay at the heart of late nineteenth- and early twentieth-century British political controversy.

CHAPTER 2

Profit and power: informal empire, the navy and Latin America

BARRY GOUGH

In most general histories of British enterprise and imperialism, the role of the Royal Navy seldom receives the analytical attention it deserves, and it is often marginalized altogether. Cain and Hopkins's bold scheme of analysis, which is based on extensive research, brings scholarship closer to an understanding of the intricacies of imperialism and especially to an appreciation of the inter-relationship between finance and political power both within Great Britain and overseas. By dealing globally with British activities and intentions, with the City of London as the focus of attention, Cain and Hopkins provide an integrative pattern of remarkable force. The importance of sea power does not occupy a large or central place in their study. Yet in two substantial chapters, one in each of their pair of volumes, they oblige historians of Latin America and of the Royal Navy to come to grips with determining techniques of authority and influence in that region, and they force interested students to look more closely at this important question: was the quarterdeck diplomacy of the *Pax Britannica* under the thumb of the City of London?

Early in the imperial progression Sir Josiah Child, seventeenth-century scion of the East India Company, charged all who would read his tract on the future of British trade and dominion to be mindful of his maxim that 'In all things, profit and power ought jointly to be considered'.[1] From about 1651 onwards England enshrined the policy of mercantilism to secure the means of her maritime and naval security, and thereby to create a merchant navy that would be in time of war a nursery of seamen. Statesmen preferred trade to dominion, noted Lord Shelburne at the close of the War of American Independence. Then, as later, Board of Trade decisions favoured commercial pursuits over territorial acquisitions, and the monarchy and its attendant councils customarily

---

1 Sir Josiah Child, *A New Discourse of Trade* (2nd edn, London, 1694), pp. 114–15. See also Charles H. Wilson, *Profit and Power* (London, 1957), p. 1.

regulated policies of trade in such a way as to give assurances to investors and facilitate economic change and expansion.[2]

Commercial pursuits and profits lay at the foundations of England's might, and overseas activities were subservient to that objective. Throughout the greater part of the period 1688–1914 most new accretions of formal empire were seen as encumbrances and little-wanted additions, others were viewed as mere pawns in international diplomacy.

Only in terms of defence and the maintenance of order were some overseas territories held to be valuable: Quebec was still needed to keep the French from threatening the frontiers of the Thirteen Colonies; the Cape of Good Hope to keep the Dutch and then the French from cutting the route to the fabulous Indies; the Falklands/Malvinas to secure sea-lanes westwards to the Pacific; and even New Zealand to exclude the French and deny them access to naval stores. The founding of New South Wales as a convict colony had other motivations attendant on British naval power and security.[3] Only in the early nineteenth century did the motive of providing a vent for Britain's surplus population allow the makers of policy in Whitehall to look on empire as a place for patterned settlement, and by mid-century assisted means of transportation of free settlers, sometimes under corporate control, as in the case of the Christchurch settlement in New Zealand or of Adelaide in South Australia, gave 'empire' a new territorial value. By the end of the century British war planners looked on empire as a means of swelling the ranks of the British Army and providing human additions to an expeditionary force that would come to the assistance of France in a possible war against Imperial Germany.[4]

During the nineteenth century Britain was an aggressive power, not a defensive, weary titan. Even so, British leaders, ever alive to shifting trends in Europe and overseas spheres of rival influence, feared that this mightiest of empires yet would soon falter. They looked on empire for sustenance, assuming that dominion had given them power. Wise men in the City, the successors of Sir Josiah Child, men whom Cain and Hopkins dub the 'gentlemanly capitalists', had no real cause for concern. They were already reordering an empire to suit their purposes. They were expanding the commercial tentacles of authority. This was a new, invisible empire of commerce, one whose progenitor had already been created under the influence of Gladstonian arrangements

---

2 See I.K. Steele, *Politics of Colonial Policy: The Board of Trade in Colonial Administration, 1696–1720* (Oxford, 1968), pp. 4–8. When new colonial populations required representative or self-government, a new discussion evolved around the questions of patronage and local autonomy. Even so, metropolitan interests were still focusing on profits and power, and on security of frontiers. On this and the newer issues of aboriginal trusteeship, see W.P. Morrell, *British Colonial Policy in the Mid-Victorian Age: South Africa, New Zealand, the West Indies* (Oxford, 1969).
3 Alan Frost, *Convicts and Empire: A Naval Question* (Melbourne, 1980).
4 Michael Howard, *The Continental Commitment: The Dilemma of British Defence Policy in the Era of the Two World Wars* (1972; reprint, London, 1989), chs 1 and 2. See also John Gooch, *The Plans of War: The General Staff and British Naval Strategy, c.1900–1916* (London, 1974), and *idem, The Prospect of War: Studies in British Defence Policy, 1847–1942* (London, 1981).

and had laid the firm foundations of a future system that would take Britain well into the twentieth century – despite the financial and human convulsions and damage to the national and imperial fabric experienced by the savage great wars of the century.

THE TOOLS AND TECHNIQUES OF IMPERIALISM

All the more engaging therefore are the arguments put forward by Cain and Hopkins,[5] for they take us back to the problem posed by J.A. Hobson nearly a century ago: where did British capital go, and why? And what were the connections between British investment in a region and British use of force and/or imperialism in that same area? Cain and Hopkins are not deflected by Hobson, nor confounded by the pressing arguments of Lenin, Kautsky and Hilferding (C&H, I, pp. 14–15, 44, 451–6, 465; II, pp. 17, 62, 65). Some students may claim that the two authors are 'hostile to the industrial tradition in British historiography'.[6] However, it may be argued that Cain and Hopkins are essentially structuralist, seeking to examine the economic and social status of the men of the City of London and their interrelationships with leading politicians and government administrators in the higher rungs of the Civil Service. They are also interested in determining the underlying financial causes and motivations for imperial policies; but they take less time to investigate the methods and exact steps by which imperialistic grand designs were forged and implemented.

As early as the Tudor monarchs, and in a way that was certainly well developed by late Stuart times, capitalists were emerging from the aristocratic classes. Persons with money that could be devoted to long-term business ventures on distant seas were investing in the seaborne trades. Such investors – the financial middling classes – demanded stout ships, competent captains and crews and, above all, appropriate means of insurance. Long before the formal empire became fashionable, new empires of trade had been carved out in Hudson Bay, Bombay and Calcutta, West Africa and the Indies. Royal patents, charters and leases allowed economic opportunity for capitalists in distant lands and seas where England would never have dreamed of putting up a fur trade post, a slave factory, a fishing and whaling station or a mart for silks and spices as a state project. The pulsating forces for profit came from the commercial centre, and from a diffuse mix of aristocrats, moneylenders, government 'fixers' and shipowners; and these impulses were re-energized by what was happening on the peripheries of an enlarging maritime world.

---

5 P.J. Cain and A.G. Hopkins, *British Imperialism*, Vol. I: *Innovation and Expansion, 1688–1914*; Vol. II: *Crisis and Deconstruction, 1914–1990* (both London, 1993). Referred to hereafter as C&H, I and II.
6 This was the observation of my student Patrick McElrea, and shared by others in my British Imperial Seminar at Wilfrid Laurier University, 1993–94.

THE ROYAL NAVY AS THE ENABLER OF BRITISH IMPERIALISM

Yet if profit opened the means to power, and ranked first among understood intentions of investors, it was axiomatically true that power afforded the means to profit. Profit and power went hand in hand. Cain and Hopkins acknowledge, in principle, the significance of naval power, and they do not omit the role of the navy.[7] Nonetheless, by focusing so heavily on the profit-generating side of imperialism and on its institutional implications and nuances, they leave aside a considerable amount of material of importance to British and British imperial studies. The 'how to' of empire – or techniques of coercion, control and diplomatic influence abroad – demand greater attention. The security of British capital overseas, as at home, required gunboats and regiments. More-over, in time of war rapid deployment of force, and major battles on land and sea, were undertaken to secure imperial prizes and possibilities.

John Seeley once said that 'the British Empire was acquired in a fit of absence of mind'.[8] Far from any absent-minded approach to the use of force, British policy-makers set about gaining every advantage they could: a sentry box or an anchor of empire here or there, an advantage to imperial strategy in one location or another; and all the while they kept up sufficient troops and warships to be able to master the needs of any crisis or emergency. Both Horatio Nelson and Sir John Fisher advised the statesmen of their respective ages that you could never have too many ships; but, in fact, Parliament, dominated by Smithian political economy, kept the annual Naval Estimates pared to the bone – just large enough that they might pass muster with the naval advocates of the day. The fiscal exigencies of the time mandated re-trenchment in naval expenditures. Britannia might rule the waves, but often she had to do so with the slenderest of means.[9] British statesmen, especially Viscount Castlereagh, one of the architects of the nineteenth-century *Pax Britannica*, thought in terms of bases as being places from which to project power in time of need by rapid deployment. 'Our policy', he remarked at the close of the Napoleonic and American wars, 'has been to secure the Empire against future attack. In order to do this we had acquired what in former days would have been thought romance – the keys of every great military posi-tion.'[10] Small wonder that First Sea Lords such as 'Jackie' Fisher could boast that Britain had the keys to lock up the world. In this sense, imperial acquisi-tion for strategic advantage or leverage gave Britain enhanced means of pro-tecting trade, stamping out illegal trade (including slaving and piracy) and encouraging the legitimate prosecution of commerce, whether it be British or

---

7 Cain and Hopkins take note, for example, that City men favoured a strong navy as a bulwark for their international system. They add that, in general, the City could be counted upon to support Britain's naval building programmes in Parliament – though they 'did not relish paying for' them (C&H, I, pp. 203–4, 239).

8 J.R. Seeley, *The Expansion of England: Two Courses of Lectures* (new edn, London, 1891), p. 8.

9 John F. Beeler, 'A one power standard? Great Britain and the balance of naval power, 1860–1880', *Journal of Strategic Studies*, 15/4 (Dec. 1992), pp. 547–75.

10 Hansard, *Parliamentary Debates*, 1st ser. (1816), v.32, column 1104, pp. 72–81.

non-British. It was in the means of execution of such understood policies that the navy acted out its quiet and unheralded actions in the age of *Pax Britannica*.

The role, or roles, of the Royal Navy in the acquisition and retention of British profit and power have specific links to finance capital and government policy formation. The Lords of the Admiralty, and officers and men generally, did not wish to be classified as tools of the state, and they are not defined as such by Cain and Hopkins or by other historians. But the issue here is this: did the navy act as a leading agent of economic imperialism? And if so, in what ways, if any, did it also respond to the requirements of the gentlemanly capitalists of the City of London and in Whitehall? A selective reading of histories of the navy 'on station' during the nineteenth century yields the undoubted theme that for the greater part of the period 1815–1890 the Admiralty reacted primarily to forces and stimuli on the periphery – in the coastal waters of Australia and New Zealand, the eastern Mediterranean, Sierra Leone and the west coast of Africa, the north-western coast of future British Columbia. Almost without exception, the Lords of the Admiralty reacted to external requirements, the assessment of a local crisis by commanders on the spot. As with the formulation of colonial policy, there was no grand centralized scheme for the exercise of British maritime power. The navy was a reactive force, defensive in nature. To show the flag in support of legitimate trade was perhaps its principal function throughout most of the nineteenth century; and its normal duty assignment lay in 'meeting the needs of each day as they arose'. Secondary themes which run through the naval records on both the North and South Pacific show that the smaller squadrons stationed at Vancouver Island or Valparaiso, or that plied the seas of Polynesia, adhered to the primary need to maintain peace and order, both for the protection of white settlers and for what they and their political masters perceived as the good of 'native peoples', against the disruptive effects of internecine warfare and the corrupting influences of European trading ruffians.[11]

Against the prevailing 'gentlemanly' political economy in Parliament which advocated cutbacks in the Army and Navy Estimates, the First Lords of the Admiralty constantly worried about and lobbied for improvements in the size and strength of the fleet. One of them, Lord Minto, expressed the problem facing the Board of Admiralty in 1841 thus:

11 See Barry M. Gough, *Gunboat Frontier: British Maritime Authority and Northwest Coast Indians, 1846–90* (Vancouver, 1984), pp. 16–23, 204–9, 210–15; Gerald S. Graham, *Great Britain in the Indian Ocean, 1810–1850* (Oxford, 1967); *idem, The China Station: War and Diplomacy, 1830–1860* (Oxford, 1978); Barry M. Gough, *The Royal Navy and the Northwest Coast of North America, 1810–1914: A Study of British Maritime Ascendancy* (Vancouver, 1971); John Bach, *The Australia Station: A History of the Royal Navy in the Southwest Pacific, 1821–1913* (Kensington, NSW, 1986); Jorge Ortiz-Sotelo, 'Peru and the British naval station (1808–1839)', PhD thesis, University of St Andrews, 1993; Barry Gough, 'Sea power and South America: the "Brazils" or South American station of the Royal Navy, 1808–1837', *The American Neptune*, 50/1 (1990), pp. 26–34.

The object to be aimed at is that of maintaining in time of peace a sufficient force for the protection of commerce and in the demonstrations of strength which political events may, from time to time, render necessary, and to keep up such a reserve of ships and stores and men as may, at the shortest possible notice, enable the country to meet every exigency, to exhibit its naval strength unimpaired.[12]

This presented a number of conundrums for the Admiralty, mindful as they always were of balancing Treasury stringencies against the concern about foreign (especially French) naval power and challenges to British maritime primacy.[13] So important is this theme in Admiralty papers – of maintaining the superiority of the fleet against that of rivals, and pressing this argument in discussions over the annual Navy Estimates – that it is surprising that historians of the empire hardly ever take their scholarly investigations beyond these shores, as blue-water maritime historians do. The role of the navy as an instrument of empire, as Peter Cain has suggested, has hitherto been conceived as primarily a problem for naval historians. But can modern imperialism mean anything without analysis of the tools and methods used to enforce the law and executive authority? The term *Pax Britannica*, though it also has broad cultural connotations, certainly encompasses the maintenance of order and stability in various regions of the world; and yet this concept hardly ever appears in *British Imperialism*. How can we explain the formidable phenomenon of the Victorian empire without describing the leading agency for overseas coercion and the enforcement of 'the British peace' – the navy? One might just as well try to explain the structure and power of the Roman Empire at its height without analysing the vaunted legion.

In general terms there is no doubt but that the exercise of British naval influence was viewed as an adjunct to British foreign policy, a policy which had its roots in maintaining security and ascendancy against all rivals. Thus, there is great room in this area for a more detailed application of, and also challenges to, the Cain/Hopkins theories. Provided that the European equipoise was not disturbed,[14] fleet movements in the main could be controlled by consular activities and local financial considerations in overseas places of influence. After 1815 the Royal Navy undertook some largely unheralded and still little studied humanitarian duties, including the suppression of the slave trade, opening the seas for legitimate commerce, surveying far-off waters and coasts, and putting down indigenous 'coastal tribes' that contested the imperium and especially interfered with legitimate commerce and European lives. In some

12 'Lord Minto on the administration of the navy, 1841', National Maritime Museum, Greenwich, ELL 239.
13 France remained the principal naval rival to Britain for most of the nineteenth century, and the technological rivalry between the two powers helped shape the exclusivity of that rivalry. C.I. Hamilton, *Anglo-French Naval Rivalry, 1840–1870* (Oxford, 1993), p. 13.
14 As it was during the Crimean War, when Britain and France came to the perceived aid of the Ottoman Empire in order to keep Russia from making strategic gains towards the Mediterranean. The same mentality of pre-emptive, or reactionary, response lay beneath British defence doctrine for the nineteenth century in regards to the security of India and trade in eastern seas.

locations, such as the Falkland Islands, British naval power was used to secure places regarded as fundamental to British maritime pre-eminence. 'It is a growing opinion among naval and mercantile men', remarked Lord John Russell in 1841, in assessing the advantages of having a governor on the Falklands/ Malvinas, 'that a settlement on the Falkland Islands would be of essential service to our merchant vessels in the voyages from our more distant possessions. It may be that a mere guard, to occupy a post in the vicinity of the best harbour, is all that can be effected with advantage.'[15] Naturally, such imperialistic naval operations were always conducted according to the principle of the least possible expenditure, but they were intended to achieve the maximum mercantile advantage, especially to British shipping. Elsewhere, the navy's main assignment – and this was particularly true in Latin America – was to maintain the flow of legitimate commerce and to provide a political climate for the encouragement of British business. Working in close conjunction with British consuls, who were enjoined by the Foreign Office to report regularly on the state and prospects of British exports and imports, naval officers had strict orders to facilitate improved commercial relations, provided that Britain was not engaged in domestic quarrels ashore or war with any legitimate governments.

But in general, historians of these interventions are content to treat the role of the navy in cursory fashion. As in the general literature of British imperial and Commonwealth history, so it is with Cain and Hopkins. 'The Navy was not only the key to the defence of Britain,' they write, '. . . but also the crucial safeguard for the enormously complex chain of economic interests which Britain had built up over the centuries without which she would be an offshore island of Europe rather than a great world power' (C&H, I, p. 458). Doubtless investor confidence varied according to risk. More volatile locations required the security afforded by the white ensign flapping in the breeze on a sloop-of-war at anchor or in the offing. Undoubtedly, too, British naval units were sent to secure the assets of British banks ashore. In the Cain/Hopkins analysis, finance seems all-powerful in influencing policy. The navy appears as the tool of the metropole, and seldom do strategic, humanitarian or strict legal concerns intrude on the discussion; in fact, they are relegated to insignificance.

If the country's power rested on credit and the navy, as Cain and Hopkins contend, then more discussion of what one would call today 'security issues' ought to be part of their argument. Investor confidence demanded gunboats. Besieged consuls pressed upon by British bankers and investors called for men-of-war. And the pulls of the oceanic frontiers and peripheries continually engaged the Royal Navy in unpleasant police duties that were far different from the great campaigns of Trafalgar and the major encounters of the wars of empire ending in 1815. Admittedly, Cain and Hopkins do mention fears of a French blockade, and they do discuss Anglo-German naval rivalry and occasionally the vital role of coaling stations. But when they generalize that

---

15 Russell to Lieutenant-Governor R.C. Moody, 23 August 1841, *Correspondence Relative to the Falkland Islands*, printed 22 June 1843, *Parliamentary Papers*.

'the relationship between naval predominance, the security of Britain and her empire and confidence in the British as the world's banker and commercial intermediary was very well understood before 1914' (C&H, I, pp. 86, 461), a cry goes out for detailed examples and further explanation.

In each of the major geographical areas considered in the vast Cain and Hopkins study the Royal Navy kept units; it also kept ships-of-war at several smaller 'foreign' stations. The number of ships, their guns and complements were all known to parliamentarians, and the Naval Estimates annually clocked the imperial obligation on distant seas and counted every pound, shilling and pence.[16] Cabinets determined the allocation of resources by station. Each station had a zone to patrol, a squadron of ships, a base of operations. Each commander-in-chief answered to the Lords of the Admiralty, who in turn took their cue from the Cabinet and invariably the Secretary of State for Foreign Affairs. In China seas, West African and East Indian waters, the Mediterranean and Pacific oceans British fleets were maintained, linking the metropole to its peripheries. Of all the stations, China commanded the largest armament, with next-ranking North America and West Indies on the one hand and the Mediterranean on the other requiring equal numbers of ships and men, followed in descending order of size by the west coast of Africa, the Pacific and the south-east coast of America (the last two monitoring Latin America).[17]

THE CASE OF SOUTH AMERICA

The South America station in the nineteenth century

On the South America, or 'Brazils', station, the Royal Navy assumed a particularly important role, and a study of it reveals the closeness of the links. Here a vast informal empire had to be maintained, by consular activities, diplomatic pressure and naval influence.

The Spanish and Portuguese empires in Latin America had been built on grand scales. However, they were prone to administrative difficulties, illicit trade and contraband and, not least, the perils of revolution and the predatory encroachments of the other great powers. Napoleon's invasion of the Iberian Peninsula precipitated the revolutions in Spanish America, and ended with a war of independence against Spain. At the local level unstable political conditions and upheavals led to a variety of overlapping and sometimes competing political and administrative responses from local authorities or pretenders. In such circumstances, British naval officers were puzzled and even amused by the difficulties ashore. During the period of insurgency in Latin America and

16 See Appendix C, 'Distribution of the Royal Navy, 1861–1874, showing Naval Estimates, number of ships and men by area and date', as obtained from *Parliamentary Papers*, in Gough, *Royal Navy and the Northwest Coast*, p. 248; see also C.J. Bartlett, 'The mid-Victorian reappraisal of naval policy', in K. Bourne and D.C. Watt (eds), *Studies in International History: Essays Presented to W. Norton Medlicott* (London, 1967), p. 248.

17 This analysis is based on naval statistics referred to in note 16.

the heroic struggles of Bolivar and San Martin, the British officers on the South America station had to concern themselves with radical political upheavals on shore. At the same time they witnessed the radical transformation of the map of the western hemisphere.

South America in the age of revolutions

During that protracted period of insurgency, when revolution and civil war were common, and repression was feared from the European continental powers who had dominated the affairs of South America before the independence achievements of the 1820s, the Royal Navy's ships on station provided a constant reminder of British policies and interests. British priorities were to foster the cause of peace and order for the purpose of profit, and to promote the health and trade of states in South America. To a considerable extent, the pursuit of those objectives meant preventing the former imperial powers, Spain and Portugal, from reasserting their old dominance. Equally, the Royal Navy watched the threatened rivalry of the two other nations that had extensive, indeed growing, commercial and diplomatic interests in South America, namely France and the United States. In the words of the liberator Bolivar, 'Only England, mistress of the seas, can protect us against the united force of European reaction'. And the eminent diplomatic historian, Sir Charles Webster, summed it up aptly in noting that 'by her two main agencies – her trade and her fleet', Britain was able to establish a very strong presence in Latin American affairs.[18]

A second duty of the Royal Navy on the coasts of South America was to check the South Atlantic slave trade. Directed primarily against Brazil (a number of whose states had plantation economies still based heavily on slave labour), this policy, administered from the Foreign Office with close cooperation from the Admiralty, represented the enlargement and continuation of efforts by British anti-slavery organizations, begun in 1807, to eradicate totally the Atlantic slave trade. The Royal Navy had an onerous task, for the places of disembarkation on the Brazilian coast were numerous and invariably out of the way. Despite the signing of a strengthened anti-slave trade treaty between Britain and Brazil in 1826, which made Brazilian involvement after 1830 the equivalent of piracy, the trade had continued unabated for another twenty years. Intervention against the slave trade, which had been a British demand as one price of the international recognition of Brazil's independence and stature among nations, was unpopular and ineffective until more consistent coercive naval action was employed after 1845, under the leadership of Lord Palmerston.[19] Final abolition in the 1850s also depended on the Brazilian

18 Bolivar, quoted in Dexter Perkins, *The Monroe Doctrine, 1823–26* (Cambridge, Mass., 1968), pp. 322–3; Sir Charles K. Webster, *Britain and the Independence of Latin America* (2 vols, London, 1938), I, p. 11.
19 Leslie Bethel, *The Abolition of the Brazilian Slave Trade: Britain, Brazil and the Slave Trade Question, 1807–1869* (Cambridge, 1970), pp. 242–387.

government being willing to enforce the treaties. But the Foreign Office's action and the anti-slave trade squadron's hard work constituted together 'the main factor leading to the effective ending of the trade almost immediately'.[20] The considerable expenditure in men, money and ships required for this achievement suggests a strong humanitarian component in Royal Navy actions and in British imperialism in the South Atlantic.

The Royal Navy's South America station: stabilization and restrained intervention

Meanwhile the critical state of affairs ashore also demanded steady protection by units of the navy. In 1808 the Admiralty established the South America station, and the admiral commanding was given specific instructions to give 'permanent protection' to 'the coasts of the Portuguese dominions'. Brazilian political stability answered to Foreign Office initiatives, for in that same year, 1808, Lord Strangford was sent as envoy-extraordinary to the Portuguese court in Rio de Janeiro, and under successive diplomats consuls and ambassadors pursued the policy of peace for the purpose of profit. They sought to maintain strict neutrality. At the same time the Admiralty reminded British naval commanders in Latin American waters that 'to give countenance and protection to this extensive commerce, and to support the influence of British interests in these countries is the first and indispensable duty of the squadron placed under your command'.[21]

Financial matters never lay far beneath the surface of amphibious foreign policy-making. Quarterdeck diplomacy kept a keen eye on Britain's overseas investment portfolio. In what may have been one of the closest tie-ins between City of London interests and the South Atlantic *Pax Britannica*, naval officers were reminded that the British had some £10 million invested in South American states, and that the civil state of none of these states was tranquil.[22] Moreover, France, the United States and Portugal also competed strongly for commercial pre-eminence in various South American market areas, more especially in the Rio de la Plata. In this region the Portuguese had a settlement. Montevideo and Buenos Aires were rivals in the hide and beef export trades and also kept ambitiously watchful eyes on the interior provinces to the north, which were drained by the Parana River. Consular reports flowed into London proclaiming to the Foreign Office the rich possibilities of trade in Central and South America, the high risks of doing business, the instability of governments, and the necessity for naval protection.[23]

20 Bethell, article in *The Cambridge History of Latin America*, Vol. III: *From Independence to c.1870* (Cambridge, 1985), p. 224.
21 See Instructions, William Wellesley-Pole to Rear-Admiral Sir William Sidney Smith, 25 Jan. 1808, Adm. 2/1365; Canning to Admiralty, 25 Dec. 1807, secret, Adm. 1/4206; and Rear-Admiral Baker to Captain Waldegrave, [?] April 1831, Adm. 1/35, in Public Record Office, Kew, England.
22 Baker to Waldegrave, n.d., April 1831, Adm. 1/35.
23 R.A. Humphreys (ed.), *British Consular Reports on the Trade and Politics of Latin America, 1824–1826* (London, 1940).

In these circumstances, commanding officers of British warships had to be exceedingly careful not to be construed as agents for British commercial bullying. Moreover, they certainly could not side with insurgents and revolutionaries against legitimate local governments. This was the case even though the Foreign Office might have come to the conclusion that the maintenance of the independence of the South American states constituted the preferable course of action if British commercial and political interests were to be sustained and enhanced. To send an armed party from a warship to secure a limited objective on shore afforded a tempting response for any frustrated commanding officer who saw British property and lives at risk. In 1831, for instance, British and French naval commanders combined forces and landed seamen and marines to protect nationals at Rio de Janeiro. The Admiralty was bound to denounce such practices as 'inexpedient and unsafe', and stated in the clearest language possible: 'Remonstrance with the civil authorities on shore is the duty of the British resident.'[24]

Armed naval interventions

'It took adroit diplomacy', wrote one admiral in praise of a commodore, Bowles, who was leaving station at the conclusion of a difficult tour of duty in the Rio de la Plata, 'for the maintenance of friendly relations with the heads of the contending parties on each bank of the river; a relationship not very easy to maintain without having had a due observance to that system of neutrality, which has been so strongly recommended [by the government] and so successfully adhered to.' Bowles himself, seeking the award of a Companion of the Order of the Bath, pointed out that his services in protecting British commerce ashore and afloat under circumstances of particular duty were carried out without any loss of life or even molestation.[25] Naval power was exceedingly pervasive and often took the form of a blockade against recalcitrants ashore. It was rare, and indicated desperate circumstances, for a British naval captain to send a landing party ashore – to secure a bank's assets, to dissuade the patriots from making a forced levy on British merchants, or to protect a customs house against interference. In those extraordinary instances when 'gunboat diplomacy' appeared justified, the Foreign Office was sensitive to the dangers of forceful intervention. Every time the British attempted armed coercion of local governments they tended to get their hands burned. Lord Aberdeen, the Foreign Secretary, learned this lesson in the Rio de la Plata affair of 1845 when seeking to assist Montevideo's independence and to safeguard British trade in the face of 'senseless and barbarous' interference from the Argentine leader, General Juan Manuel de Rosas. Customarily, the navy's duties were confined to the small-scale operations it could perform

24 Rear-Admiral Sir Thomas Baker to Secretary of the Admiralty, 14 June 1831, and Admiralty Minute of 16 August 1831, Adm. 1/36.
25 Bowles to C. Wood, 27 July 1838, Adm. 1/1568, Cap. B174.

most effectively: 'check piracy, protect trade, prevent the abuse of the right of blockade and keep any acquisitive European power from intervening'.[26]

For all this, most specialists in the history of British foreign policy agree that Latin America in the first half of the nineteenth century stands as a classic case where British intervention – particularly through the use of the fleet – helped to determine the course of history outside Europe in a decisive way.

The Falkland Islands, 1832–33

As long as Britain held predominance at sea, Spain had no good chance of reasserting her former authority in South America; meanwhile, provided local governments were in agreement, the whole continent lay open to commercial penetration by British and other European traders. For this reason the British kept a high priority on securing the sea-lanes, and this is the fundamental reason why they re-established their authority in the Falkland Islands in 1832–33. The Falkland Islands provide us with one of the best examples in the nineteenth century of where the navy, in conjunction with commercial and settler interests, took the lead in expanding imperial territorial control through the annexation of a new colony. Here the British sought to oust the Argentine occupants, and to control local fishing and sealing waters. They claimed that their rights there were incontestable, and they brushed aside what they regarded as Argentine pretensions.[27] Only in the Falklands did the British send landing parties ashore with the determination to stay. In other locations they did so only for short periods, and always exercised 'minimum intervention'. When they stood aside to watch others contend for empire or to observe local states quarrel over ancient questions, as in the War of the Pacific, nicely assessed by Cain and Hopkins, they did so with a keen eye to a potential wrap on the knuckles from the Lords of the Admiralty or the Foreign Office. Amphibious diplomacy required a deft hand.

The transmission of bullion

From all major South American ports – Rio de Janeiro, Montevideo, Callao in Peru, San Blas in Mexico, and others – ships of the Royal Navy acted in direct association with the Bank of England and British investors in yet another way. They kept up an extremely important function as freighters of bullion, specie, bank notes and bills of exchange. This little-known function of the navy is another contribution it made to the peaceful benefits of the *Pax*

26 G.S. Graham and R.A. Humphreys (eds), *The Navy and South America* (London, 1962), p. xxxiv. For further particulars on British policy for promoting trade see D.C.M. Platt, *Finance, Trade and Politics in British Foreign Policy, 1815–1914* (Oxford, 1968), pp. 322–3; John F. Cady, *Foreign Interventions in the Rio de la Plata, 1838–50: A Study of French, British and American Policy in Relation to the Dictator Juan Manuel Rosas* (Philadelphia, 1929); Henry S. Ferns, *Britain and Argentina in the Nineteenth Century* (Oxford, 1960).
27 Barry Gough, *The Falkland Islands/Malvinas: Contest for Empire in the South Atlantic* (London, 1992) may be consulted for an examination of British motivations and actions.

Britannica, and it demonstrates a clear association with the aims and interests of the City of London. The conveyance of specie or 'freight' was authorized by government and controlled by regulation. At a time of periodic anarchy, HM's ships were symbols of security to nervous merchants, besieged governments and anxious creditors. The navy was the Securicor or seagoing 'Wells Fargo' of that age, and it suffered no ambushes or hold-ups. On one occasion a British man-of-war, the *Gorgon*, was lost while carrying freight, but it was later salvaged. Fraudulent practices sometimes occurred (one shipper fooled a captain by shipping lead instead of silver); and naval officers were not immune from corruption. Ships took on 'freights' from the west coast of Mexico all the way round to Rio, and conveyed the highly valued cargoes to Portsmouth and thence by heavily guarded coach to the Bank of England. Almost every man-of-war returning from Rio upon completion of a three- or four-year commission took home a handsome 'freight'. The scheme made capitalists of admirals, commanding officers and ships' crews, and aided the humanitarian relief of aged sailors at Greenwich Hospital.[28]

Epilogue: Early Twentieth-Century Developments

Thus the imperial fabric was held together by an almost invisible web of connecting forces and influences, of which the Royal Navy was one of the most important. In Latin America a British realm of influence – what some, including Robinson and Gallagher, D.C.M. Platt and Cain and Hopkins, would call an 'informal empire' – had been erected in place of the old dominions of Portugal and Spain. The financial gains were high, and the investments well worth while, for Latin America then was the equivalent of the ASEAN states of our own times. Once the United States had supplanted British naval power in the western hemisphere, as it did clearly after 1914, American interventions replaced British and French; and because the strategic aspects were of greater importance to Washington, and military traditions different, a heavier-handed procedure was put in place. The more benign symbol of the white ensign supporting consuls and bankers ashore gave way to a new system of Yankee imperialism, as at Panama in 1903. Such changes fall outside our immediate concern here, but it can be observed that in the Caribbean and in the Isthmus of Panama United States investors and strategists took on an energized mode of expansion, one that the British neither wished to pursue nor had the force to compete with. Indeed, actions by United States Secretaries of State Blaine and Olney gave credence to the argument that there was now an 'American empire' that linked the Atlantic to the Pacific not only across the continent but through Caribbean seas, Panama and Nicaragua and thence to Hawaii and Alaska by sea. Even the greatest naval power, Britain, could not forestall such ambitions, especially since state-of-the-art

---

28 See Barry Gough, 'Specie conveyance from the west coast of Mexico in British warships, 1820–1870: an aspect of the *Pax Britannica*', *The Mariner's Mirror*, 69/4 (Nov. 1983), pp. 419–33.

naval units were direly needed in home waters. Thus the South America station, along with others such as the Pacific, the North American and the West Indies, was closed down, and the old techniques of the *Pax Britannica* under the aegis of the Royal Navy came to an end. But the usual outlets of investment for the gentlemanly capitalists in support of informal imperialism remained intact. The City continued to issue bonds for loans to Latin American governments. The internal transportation infrastructures of Central and South America were built up with the aid of British capital. Whole indigenous economies continued to be tied to the heartland of Threadneedle Street. And a new empire had replaced an old. As Cain and Hopkins show, capital went to places of opportunity, and the service sector helped shape official British preferences for formal and informal empire. In the navy the state provided an agency of support for official policy, which under the aegis of the *Pax Britannica* was to pursue peace for the purpose of profit.

In 1901 the First Lord of the Admiralty, Lord Selborne, minuted that it was on its credit and its navy that the strength of Britain rested, and he noted that these were twin pillars of power.[29] Nothing had really changed from Sir Josiah Child's maxim of three centuries before. Throughout the intervening years the one had reinforced the other, and made its companion possible. Naval history has not yet done all that it can to examine such issues in the breadth and depth they deserve. Moreover, the disparate, chaotic nature of imperial–Commonwealth history reflects the 'cutting to the chase' of popular concerns. Renewed focus on finance by Cain and Hopkins adds mightily to the discussion, and brings us closer to understanding the totality of both the imperial achievement and British economic success in the nineteenth and twentieth centuries. In particular, the two-volume study demonstrates how new empires replace old, how the movement of British wealth left the formal empire behind, and how formal colonial structures and informal political links were often mere conveniences, designed to serve greater financial ends.

29 Quoted in Brian McKercher (ed.), *Anglo-American Relations in the 1920s: The Struggle for Supremacy* (Edmonton, 1990).

CHAPTER 3

The late nineteenth-century British imperialist: specification, quantification and controlled conjectures

LANCE DAVIS

Despite the title of volume I, *British Imperialism, Innovation and Expansion, 1688–1914*, Cain and Hopkins, though they have certainly analysed innovation and expansion, have not really written about British imperialism. What they have constructed is an excellent book about the power of the 'City', the landed gentry and 'the higher ranks of the new urban middle classes'; they have, in a way that I would not have believed possible, underscored the importance of innovations in finance and in services; and they have posed, although they have not solved, a fascinating political conundrum.

In this paper I want to touch briefly on five separate but related issues that are raised by their work: the nature of the British Empire; the structure of British foreign investment in the years 1865–1914; the importance of 'gentlemen capitalists'; the motives that underlay the behaviour of those 'gentlemen capitalists'; and, finally, the nature of the political conundrum.

THE DEFINITION OF EMPIRE

If, as Cain and Hopkins argue, it was the landed gentry, the 'moneyed men of the City' and the upper reaches of the urban middle classes who were most heavily involved in imperial finance and trade, then how, anyone trained as a 'blue-water' imperial historian may well ask, is it possible to assert that Cain and Hopkins have not written about imperialism? The answer, of course, lies in the definition of the empire – for without an empire it is difficult to talk about imperialism. There was a time when all historians thought they understood the term 'the British Empire'; but, since Robinson and Gallagher published 'The imperialism of free trade', the boundaries of that empire have become very murky indeed.[1]

The usefulness of any definition, however, depends on the questions to be addressed. If, for example, the question involves only the gains or losses from trade, the choice of the definition of empire would be relatively trivial, although one would want to explore the basis for any economic or political barriers to that trade – transport costs, tariffs, VERS (voluntary export restrictions), VIERS (voluntary import and export restrictions), imperial preference, quotas, direct restrictions on investment, or 'most favoured nation' treaties. In the case of the British Empire, however, most of the literature, to say nothing of almost all the rhetoric, has focused not on trade but on 'exploitation', a term that, although often used, is also not well defined. To the extent that 'exploitation' involves taking something from someone without providing an adequate quid pro quo, no person or country can exploit another unless they are able to exercise some form of legal (or illegal) coercive power. Thus, an empire without coercion is hardly an empire at all; and it certainly is not an exploitative empire. As Joseph Schumpeter wrote more than half a century ago:

> where free trade prevails no class has an interest in forcible expansion. . . . Where the cultural backwardness of a region makes normal intercourse dependent on colonization, it does not matter, assuming free trade, which of the civilized nations undertakes the task of colonization. Dominion of the seas, in such a case, means little more than a maritime traffic police. Similarly, it is a matter of indifference to a nation whether a railway concession in a foreign country is acquired by one of its own citizens or not – just as long as it is built.[2]

Cain and Hopkins have not unhesitantly accepted the Gallagher and Robinson position about the nature of the informal empire, but neither have they entirely rejected it. In their own words:

> The coverage offered by the present study examines the central issue of the exercise of power in international relations by considering both regions which were brought into the formal empire and those which remained outside it. . . . Accordingly, we have examined the leading constituents of the constitutional empire, Canada, Australia, New Zealand, India, and Africa, in some detail. . . . Outside the formal empire, we have chosen as case studies South America, China, and the Ottoman Empire, regions where

---

1 Cain and Hopkins correctly point out that Gallagher and Robinson did not invent the term, but they certainly made it famous. P.J. Cain and A.G. Hopkins, *British Imperialism: Innovation and Expansion, 1688–1914* (London, 1993) (cited hereafter as C&H, I), pp. 7–8; J. Gallagher and R.E. Robinson, 'The imperialism of free trade', *Economic History Review*, 2nd ser., 6 (1953).
2 Joseph A. Schumpeter, *Imperialism, Social Classes, Two Essays* (New York, 1955), pp. 75–6.

Britain's presence was both prominent and subject to keen rivalry from other powers.

(C&H, I, p. 8)

Clearly, the ability to exercise power is at the centre of any question about Britain's (or any other country's) ability to exploit its less developed neighbours, but Cain and Hopkins offer no measure of that power.

DID BRITISH INFORMAL IMPERIALISM EXIST IN SOUTH AMERICA?

It is the South American case that represents Cain and Hopkins's most serious attempt to exposit the nature of 'informal empire', but their argument raises at least as many questions as it puts to rest.[3] Unlike Robinson and Gallagher, who concluded that British policy was designed to promote 'indirect political hegemony' in South America in support of her commercial interests, Cain and Hopkins tend to agree with D.C.M. Platt, who has argued that British governments intervened in South America's internal affairs only when international law had been broken or when British lives and property were at risk.[4] While Cain and Hopkins believe that Platt may have somewhat overstated his case, they conclude: 'nevertheless, on the evidence presently available, Platt's case would seem to hold for most of the continent and for the greater part of the period under review' (C&H, I, p. 277). Despite the absence of evidence of direct political involvement, Cain and Hopkins appear to include large parts of South America in Britain's informal empire, at least for the years after 1875. Their evidence is, however, subject to more than one interpretation – or at least to a quite different interpretation. Consider their argument:

There was, of course, no formal partition of South America. Considerations of cost, logistics and diplomacy were always on hand to restrain the major powers at moments of crisis. Far more important, however, was the fact that official political intervention was rarely demanded by economic interests, nor was it seen by the Foreign Office as appropriate. . . . Consequently, as we have seen, British strategy relied on self-policing and self-regulating mechanisms, and especially on the disciplines imposed on South American governments by their need to remain credit-worthy. . . . When the rules were broken the penalties were severe: Peru was ostracized by the City following its bad default of 1876; and its subsequent economic development

---

3 The authors do make an excellent case that the British were in a position to 'exercise power' in Egypt (C&H, I, pp. 362–9); but, constitutional issues aside, most historians would have placed that country in the 'formal' rather than the 'informal' empire, at least after 1882. As an aside, even though they are speaking only of Africa, the authors write: 'In retrospect, we can see that the problem was not that Britain's informal empire had broken down, but that it had never come into being except, for an illusionary moment, in Egypt' (p. 395). In many ways that conclusion could be generalized to include the entire 'informal' empire.

4 D.C.M. Platt, 'The imperialism of free trade: some reservations', *Economic History Review*, 2nd ser., 21 (1968), pp. 21–41. Platt concludes: 'In practice, Government assistance was insignificant.'

was seriously hampered by its inability to borrow abroad; elsewhere, financial crises were met by the standard penalties of retrenchment and deflation which were imposed, directly or indirectly, by external creditors.

Successive debt crises gave Britain more, not less, influence in the three major republics [Argentina, Brazil and Chile]. Private investors moved further into the economy through purchases of public utilities and banks, and by investing directly in manufacturing and processing activities, while the public sector fiscal and monetary priorities were set by borrowing requirements which were linked to the needs of open, export economies. Consequently, public expenditure, tariffs and the exchange rate were all profoundly influenced by foreign influences. . . .

The degree of penetration, direct and indirect, must surely be seen as infringing the sovereignty of the recipients, even as it boosted their incomes.

(C&H, I, pp. 312–13)

Although one could interpret this set of events as evidence of informal empire, it might also be seen as a normal scenario in a world characterized by free trade and by the free international movement of private capital. In any but a world marked by governments that make economic decisions – or that put pressure on private institutions to make economic decisions (the recent South American debt crisis, for example) – for solely political reasons, one would seldom use the pejorative term 'ostracized' to characterize the behaviour of a lender who declines to extend further credit to a defaulting debtor: in fact, over the past few years American newspapers have been full of stories of commercial bank and savings and loan executives who had been faced by substantial civil or criminal penalties for failing to deny further credits to borrowers who had become bad credit risks.

Moreover, it does not seem either unreasonable or counter-intuitive to assume that a businessman who wants to continue to borrow might, quite rationally, decide that it is more profitable to put his financial house in order, even if that strategy is costly, than to accept the protection of the bankruptcy laws. Nor does the fact that the Japanese have recently invested heavily in a wide range of American businesses – in banks, in public utilities, in manufacturing and processing activities, in the American movie industry and, God help us, even more unthinkably, in an American baseball team – lead any but a few 'Japan bashers' to conclude that America has become a part of Japan's informal empire.

In fact, the United States provides an interesting counter-example to the Cain and Hopkins conclusion. The authors deny informal empire status to the United States. They write:

In the case of the largest newly settled country, the United States, there was no question of her economic relationship with Great Britain involving any form of economic subordination. In the late nineteenth century the United States already had a population equivalent to that of the great European powers and a large and growing industrial sector based on the home market.

The capital which she borrowed from Britain provided her with only a small portion of her investment needs.

(C&H, I, p. 231)

Some readers may find it difficult to reject that conclusion.

BRITISH INVESTMENT IN THE USA IN THE NINETEENTH AND TWENTIETH CENTURIES

Consider, however, the United States in terms of the Cain/Hopkins definition of informal empire. Did the United States borrow heavily from Great Britain? The answer is definitely yes. Overall, between 1865 and 1914 about one-quarter of all overseas finance channelled through the London Stock Exchange was directed toward that country. Moreover, although foreign capital accounted for only about 5 per cent of the $60 billion increase in the nation's capital stock that occurred between 1799 and 1900, for some periods the infusions represented a much larger share of total investment; and during those crucial decades, they almost certainly played a critical role in shaping American development. In the years 1815–40, foreign investment accounted for about 20 per cent of new capital formation, in the Civil War decade perhaps three-quarters of that amount, and even in the 1880s for more than 8 per cent. As late as 1903–14, years when long-term American capital *exports* totalled more than three-quarters of a billion dollars, long-term foreign investment in the United States exceeded $1.2 billion.[5] Were Americans 'ostracized' by European bankers when they defaulted on their debts? Again the answer is yes. In 1841 and 1842 nine American states stopped payment of interest on their debts; of the nine, two repudiated them outright; and Florida pleaded minority. Jeffrey Williamson concludes that of the total of $174 million of American debt held in England in 1838, 'almost the whole was in default or repudiated by 1842'.[6]

The European reaction was one of horror and outrage. *The Times* denounced all Americans and 'prophesied that the American name would not recover for a half a century [from] the slur which has been cast upon it by the temporary or complete failure of some states to pay their debts'. American agents seeking new infusions of British capital were not only faced by the anger of the editors of *The Times* – 'that there is a class of securities to which no abundance of money, however great, can give value; and in this class their own securities stand preeminent' – but also by the refusal of British bankers even to discuss new loans. As Paris Rothschild told Duff Green, 'You may tell your government

5 Lance E. Davis and Robert J. Cull, *International Capital Markets and American Economic Growth, 1820–1914* (New York, 1994), pp. 2–3.
6 Jeffrey G. Williamson, *American Growth and the Balance of Payments, 1820–1913: A Study of the Long Swing* (Chapel Hill, NC, 1964), p. 106. For the $174 million estimate Williamson cites Leland Jenks, *The Migration of British Capital to 1875* (London, 1963), p. 106.

that you have seen the man who is at the head of finances for Europe, and that he has told you that they can not borrow a dollar, not a dollar.'[7] Moreover, some four decades later, when eight states again defaulted, the British reaction was hardly less intense; and the issue was still being debated in Parliament in the 1930s.[8]

Did British 'private investors move further into the economy through purchases of public utilities and banks, and by investing directly in manufacturing and processing activities'? Again the answer is yes. Not only did the British invest in American rails – Robert Fleming, the entrepreneurial force behind three Scottish-American trusts, for example, argued that 'Scottish capital made possible the building of the American railroad network many years earlier than would otherwise have been possible' – and in a myriad of mines, cattle ranches, farms, citrus groves and timberland in the south and west; but they invested in public utilities, banks, manufacturing firms and processing enterprises as well.[9]

Between 1865 and 1914 American public utilities – firms producing gas and electricity, telephone and telegraph services, and purified water for public consumption – sold $207.4 million in securities on the London Stock Exchange. At the same time, nine commercial banks – five in the west – also turned to that market for financial support. These figures do not include the investments made by British insurance companies; and, although there are still no precise estimates of the level of their investment in the years before the First World War, it was almost certainly substantial. Mira Wilkins, for example, concludes that 'foreign insurance firms, especially those in the fire and marine field, taking advantage of profitable opportunities, did substantial business in the United States. . . . they were also large investors in American securities, government and railroad bonds, . . . some also owned real estate and some did real estate financing in the United States'; and Cleona Lewis places the level of foreign insurance companies' investments in the USA at $313 million in 1934.[10]

In the case of manufacturing, as early as the 1870s no fewer than eight iron and coal companies – firms that ranged alphabetically from the Alton Coal, Coke, & Iron Company to the Southern States Coal, Iron, and Land Company Ltd – received infusions of British capital. Those transfers ranged from $24,000 to $8.8 million. By the end of the period (1914), British, Dutch,

7 Jenks, *The Migration of British Capital*, pp. 103, 106. The editorial is from *The Times*, 5 May 1842. The Rothschild quote is from a letter from Duff Green to John C. Calhoun, 24 Jan. 1842, in *The Correspondence of John C. Calhoun* (Washington, DC, 1900), pp. 841–2. Reginald C. McGrane, *Foreign Bondholders and American State Debts* (New York, 1935), pp. 265–6.

8 Cleona Lewis (assisted by Karl T. Schottenbeck), *America's Stake in International Investment* (Washington, DC, 1938), p. 62. See also McGrane, *Foreign Bondholders*, pp. 384–5.

9 Fleming is cited in W. Turrentine Jackson, *The Enterprising Scot: Investors in the American West after 1873* (Edinburgh, 1968), p. 71.

10 Mira Wilkins, *The History of Foreign Investment in the United States to 1914*, Harvard Studies in Business History, 34 (Cambridge, Mass., 1989), p. 535; Lewis, *America's Stake*, p. 140.

German, French, Swiss and Canadian investors held $122.4 million of the common and $27.5 million of the preferred shares of the United States Steel Company; and those figures do not include substantial holdings in both Bethlehem and Otis Steel.[11] Again, beginning with the manufacturing subsidiaries opened by the Scottish firms of J. & J. Clark in Newark, New Jersey, and by J. & P. Coats in Pawtucket, Rhode Island, British investment in the sewing thread industry increased rapidly; and by 1900 almost every American manufacturing plant was British owned.[12]

In the case of processing, between 1888 and 1891 24 British 'syndicates' purchased and reorganized more than 80 American breweries, including the St Louis Breweries (capitalization £2.85 million) and the Chicago Breweries Ltd (£2.271 million). Although those investments had declined from their early 1890s peak, Cleona Lewis estimated the level of investment at $75 million in 1899 and $58 million in 1914.[13] In 1889 the British purchased Pillsbury Mills, the nation's principle flour producer, and launched Pillsbury-Washburn with a capital stock of £1 million and debenture debt of £635,000. At the time the conglomerate was organized, it included three Pillsbury mills, two Washburn mills, two water power companies and a number of grain elevators; and the newly integrated firm was recognized as the largest milling company in the world.[14]

Finally, were the 'public sector fiscal and monetary priorities set by borrowing requirements which were linked to the needs of an open, export economy'? Again the answer is yes. During the 1870s the federal government was twice forced to turn to the British capital market to refund $1.5 billion in Civil War debt. Again, in 1895, the federal government found its gold reserves so depleted that, to remain on the gold standard, it was forced to turn to a syndicate led by J.P. Morgan to buy '$3\frac{1}{2}$ million ounces of gold amounting to $65.1 million. At least half was to be obtained in Europe in amounts not to exceed 300,000 ounces per month'. In the words of one of Morgan's fans, 'he saved the gold standard'.[15] Be that as it may, the costs of the débâcle were not insignificant. In exchange for the gold, the bankers received $62.3 million of 30-year – 4 per cent bonds, a yield of 3.75 per cent at a time when governments were yielding only 3.0 per cent. Moreover, although the 3.75 per cent yield translated into a price of $104\frac{1}{2}$ per cent of par value, the bankers sold those bonds at $112\frac{1}{4}$; and those bonds were soon selling for 123 per cent of par value.

11 Wilkins, *Foreign Investment*, p. 263; Lewis, *America's Stake*, p. 101.
12 Wilkins, *Foreign Investment*, pp. 361–8; Lewis, *America's Stake*, pp. 100–1.
13 Wilkins, *Foreign Investment*, p. 325; Lewis, *America's Stake*, p. 89.
14 Wilkins, *Foreign Investment*, p. 320; Lewis, *America's Stake*, p. 101. See also Charles B. Kuhlman, *Development of Flour Milling in the United States* (Boston, 1929), p. 134.
15 Paul Studenski and Hermann E. Kroos, *Financial History of the United States: Fiscal, Monetary, Banking, and Tariff, including Financial Administration and State and Local Finance* (New York, 1952), pp. 226–31. The fan was Ron Chernow: see his *The House of Morgan: An American Banking Dynasty and the Rise of Modern Finance* (New York, 1990), pp. 71–7.

The historian's choice, then, appears to lie between either selecting a definition that includes the United States in Britain's informal empire or abandoning the term 'informal empire' altogether. Perhaps it is merely my suppressed nationalistic chauvinism coming through, but I tend toward the latter option. But what of the formal empire – how exploitable were the parts of the world that were actually painted red? Take, for example, Canada – it appears to have been a favourite of Cain and Hopkins, and it seems representative of the colonies with responsible government – in the years after those colonies had been granted responsible government and Dominion status. The authors write: 'Given the extent to which Canada's determination to avoid the American embrace put her in the hands of the London money market, it is clear that the Canadians, when they had to choose, preferred informal economic dominance from London to political control by the United States' (C&H, I, p. 270). No one denies that, from the point of view of the self-governing colonies, there were benefits to be had from membership in the empire as long as the costs were not too high; but two questions remain: first, was it economics or politics that kept Canada 'in the hands of the London money market'?; and second, did empire membership make it possible for Britain in some sense to exploit the colonials? Let us examine these issues in turn.

There may, of course, be any number of reasons why Canadians looked to London rather than to New York; and, certainly, politics could have been one. Most economists, however, would prefer to explore the implications of economic rationality (i.e. lower interest rates and, thus, higher profits) before accepting a conclusion that is unsupported by direct evidence. Moreover, that preference becomes particularly marked when the evidence shows that American firms were also borrowing heavily in the London market at the same time. The data in Table 3.1 indicate that, between 1901 and 1930 – years for which we have very good data – the ratio of British to American investment in Canada was closely and negatively related to the ratio of interest rates in Britain to interest rates in the US. That is, as interest rates in the US declined relative to interest rates in Britain, so the level of British investment in Canada declined relative to American investment in that country.[16] Given that evidence, it seems reasonable to conclude that it was economic efficiency – to say nothing of profitability – rather than politics or fear of the Americans that accounted for the observed pattern of international investment.

---

16 The investment figures are from Frank A. Knox, '*Excursus*: Canadian capital movements and the Canadian balance of international payments, 1900–1934', in Herbert Marshall, Frank A. Southard, Jr., and Kenneth W. Taylor, *Canadian–American Industry: A Study in International Investment* (New Haven, Conn., 1936), p. 299. The American interest rates are the yields on bond buyer, high-grade municipal bonds reported in Sidney Homer and Richard Sylla, *A History of Interest Rates*, 3rd edn (New Brunswick, NJ, and London, 1991), pp. 342, 351. The British interest rates are the yields of consols reported in Brian R. Mitchell (in collaboration with Phyllis Deane), *Abstract of British Historical Statistics* (Cambridge, 1962), p. 455.

TABLE 3.1

BRITISH AND AMERICAN CAPITAL INVESTED IN CANADA, AND COMPARATIVE INTEREST RATES, 1900-1933

| Year | British and American capital invested in Canada | | | | Interest rates | | Ratio of UK/US |
	by Great Britain ($ millions)	by the United States ($ millions)	by Great Britain (%)	by the United States (%)	in Great Britain (%)	in the United States (%)	interest rates
1900	1050	168	86.2	13.8	2.80	3.25	.86
1901	1065	186	85.1	14.9	2.90	3.10	.94
1902	1077	210	83.7	16.3	2.90	3.18	.91
1903	1106	232	82.7	17.3	2.80	3.30	.85
1904	1135	258	81.5	18.5	2.80	3.40	.82
1905	1212	290	80.7	19.3	2.80	3.48	.80
1906	1280	319	80.1	19.9	2.80	3.43	.82
1907	1346	345	79.6	20.4	3.00	3.67	.82
1908	1526	378	80.1	19.9	2.90	3.87	.75
1909	1740	414	80.8	19.2	3.00	3.76	.80
1910	1958	487	80.1	19.9	3.10	3.91	.79
1911	2203	563	79.6	20.4	3.20	3.98	.80
1912	2417	645	78.9	21.1	3.30	4.01	.82
1913	2793	780	78.2	21.8	3.40	4.45	.76
1914	2779	881	75.9	24.1	3.30	4.16	.79
1915	2772	1070	72.1	27.9	3.80	4.24	.90
1916	2840	1307	68.5	31.5	4.30	4.05	1.06

1917	2739	1577	63.5	36.5	4.60	4.23	1.09
1918	2729	1630	62.6	37.4	4.40	4.57	.96
1919	2645	1818	59.3	40.7	4.60	4.50	1.02
1920	2577	2128	54.8	45.2	5.30	4.97	1.07
1921	2494	2260	52.5	47.5	5.20	5.02	1.04
1922	2464	2593	48.7	51.3	4.40	4.19	1.05
1923	2471	2794	46.9	53.1	4.30	4.23	1.02
1924	2373	3094	43.4	56.6	4.40	4.19	1.05
1925	2346	3219	42.2	57.8	4.40	4.09	1.08
1926	2592	3109	45.5	54.5	4.60	4.08	1.13
1927	2638	3339	44.1	55.9	4.60	3.97	1.16
1928	2699	3552	43.2	56.8	4.50	3.98	1.13
1929	2774	3794	42.2	57.8	4.60	4.29	1.07
1930	2792	4099	40.5	59.5	4.50	4.08	1.10
1931	2729	4056	40.2	59.8	4.40	3.88	1.13
1932	2687	4045	39.9	60.1	3.70	4.33	.85
1933	2732	3967	40.8	59.2	3.40	4.30	.79

Sources: Frank A. Knox, 'Excursus: Canadian Capital Movements and the Balance of International Payments, 1900–1934' in Herbert Marshall, Frank A. Southard Jr, and Kenneth W. Taylor, *Canadian-American Industry: A Study in International Investment* (New Haven, Cn.: Yale University Press, 1936), pp. 299–300. Sidney Homer, *A History of Interest Rates*, Second Edition (New Brunswick, N.J.: Rutgers University Press, 1977), Table 51, p. 372 and Table 59, p. 426.

What can be said about the potential for exploitation – did fear of the Americans lead Canada into Britain's exploitable web? Once again, the evidence suggests otherwise. Obviously, in the more recent past we have witnessed a rising crescendo of anti-American rhetoric north of the border; but there was little evidence of such feelings before 1911.[17] In the nineteenth century, the Canadians do not appear to have been excessively worried about the economic and political intentions of their American neighbours.

In 1863, with an American army poised on the Canadian border, the only response the British received to their request for local financial or military support was the curt reply, 'the best defence for Canada is no defence at all'.[18] Again, it was only after the US Congress made it abundantly clear that there was to be no NAFTA (North American Free Trade Area) in the 1870s that the Canadians were forced to abandon any hope for successful implementation of their Continental Policy – a policy based on free north–south trade. Even then, it was only with great reluctance that Sir John A. Macdonald turned instead to his now famous National Policy – 'a program of railroad building, industrialization, tariff protection, and western settlement inaugurated in the years after 1879'.[19] Finally, in the years after 1880, when residents of the western United States railed against foreign investment and successfully enacted legislation that prohibited or greatly circumscribed a foreigner's ability to own land, there was no parallel response against American financial invasions north of the border.[20] For example, despite the fact that, by 1909, American citizens or corporations controlled 90 per cent of the available timber in British Columbia, there was no significant Canadian response.[21]

If Yankeephobia was neither widespread nor intense – and certainly not sufficient to lever the Canadians into unprofitable economic arrangements – what were the legal institutions that might have permitted the British to exploit their Canadian subjects? With three notable exceptions – control of crown lands, the ability to erect tariff barriers, and foreign affairs – responsible government carried with it the right of Canadian citizens to control the Dominion's own affairs. The Canadians saw to it that the first two restrictions went by the board almost immediately, and they unilaterally repealed the third

17 For a balanced discussion of the impact of American investment on the Canadian economy, see Hugh G.J. Aitken, *American Capital and Canadian Resources* (Cambridge, Mass., 1961). For a less balanced presentation, see Kari Levitt, *Silent Surrender: The American Economic Empire in Canada* (New York, 1970).

18 Newcastle papers, Newcastle to Sir George Monk, governor-general of Canada, 30 June 1863.

19 Aitken, *American Capital*, p. 132.

20 The legislative response occurred at both the federal and state levels. The US Congress passed a bill controlling ownership in the territories in 1887; and by 1900, 30 of the 45 states had passed laws that in some way restricted alien ownership of land: *Statutes at Large of the U.S.*, 24 (1887), pp. 476–7. See also Roger V. Clements, 'British investment and American legislative restrictions in the trans-Mississippi West, 1880–1900', *Mississippi Valley Historical Review*, 42 (1955), pp. 216–17; Edward P. Crapol, *America for Americans: Economic Nationalism and Anglophobia in the Late Nineteenth Century* (Westport, Conn., 1973), p. 117.

21 Mira Wilkins, *The Emergence of Multinational Enterprise: American Business Abroad from the Colonial Era to 1914*, Harvard Studies in Business History, 34 (Cambridge, Mass., 1970), p. 138.

as soon as the citizens of the ex-colony recognized the costs imposed by the constitutional limits.[22]

Control of crown lands might have given the British a little leverage, but the ability to prohibit tariffs on British imports would certainly have produced positive benefits to British incomes. About tariffs, Cane and Hopkins write: 'On the other hand, a united Canada was not possible without protection, it was the effects of this protection, and of declining manufacturing competitiveness, which were rapidly undermining Britain's commodity exports by 1914, while finance, commerce, and services sustained her informal economic empire in Canada' (C&H, I, p. 273). It was, however, an 'empire' without coercive power; and it is not clear how much the world would have changed if Canada had severed her formal political connections with the mother country. The nation's federal and provincial governments and its businessmen were already beginning to shift the country's financial ties from London to cities south of the 49th parallel, and the choice of tariffs as the appropriate institution to 'unite Canada' speeded up that shift. Because institutions designed to overcome informational asymmetries in colonial securities issues had long existed, the British were well placed to evaluate portfolio investments in the Dominion; but they were much more poorly placed than their American competitors to evaluate direct investment alternatives.[23] Thus between 1897 and 1914 British direct investment increased slightly less than twice – from $142.7 to $281.3 million – while American direct investment almost quadrupled – from $159.7 to $618.4 million.[24] Moreover, in 1897 the American share of total Anglo-American investment in Canada was less than 15 per cent; and, in the absence of any informational asymmetry, one would expect that the ratio of American to Anglo-American direct investment would approximate to that figure. In fact, by 1897 US direct investments in Canada were already larger than Britain's – a state of events that leads one to conclude that the tariff-induced bias was having a significant effect on relative investment flows well before the turn of the century.

Finally, it is not clear that, the merchant marine aside, British 'finance, commerce, and services' would have been adversely impacted had Macdonald's

22 In the case of Canada that final break did not occur until the Chanak incident forced the Canadians to recognize the implications of decisions made at the Imperial Conference of 1921. Until then, Canada's position in the empire meant that, in 1914, when Britain went to war, Canada was legally at war. In 1939, despite the absence of any legal requirements, Canada voluntarily entered the war on the side of Britain. In neither case, however, was either empire membership or cultural inheritance sufficient to induce the government to draft soldiers for overseas combat. Richard A Preston, *Canada and 'Imperial Defense': A Study of the Origins of the British Commonwealth's Defense Organization, 1867–1919*, Duke University Commonwealth-Studies Center, Publication No. 29 (Durham, NC, 1967), ch. 15.

23 For an analysis of informational asymmetries in Canadian portfolio investments, see Ann Carlos and Frank Lewis, 'International financing of Canadian railway development', paper presented at the New York University Salomon Center, Conference on Anglo-American Finance: Financial Markets and Institutions in 20th-Century North America and the UK, New York, 10 Dec. 1993.

24 Lewis, *America's Stake*, p. 606; Donald G. Patterson, *British Direct Investment in Canada, 1890–1914: Estimates and Determinants* (Toronto and Buffalo, 1976), p. 49.

Continental Policy been implemented in 1870 and Canada become a part of America's 'informal empire'. British finance, commerce and services were freely exported to the US; unlike current French policies about movies and television, there were, then as now, no American tariffs on the flows of finance and services. Thus, in the case of Canada – and almost certainly Australia, New Zealand and South Africa as well – it does not appear that empire membership gave British investors, bankers and businessmen an exploitative edge over potential competitors from Canada, from the United States, or from Timbuctoo.

THE STRUCTURE OF BRITISH PORTFOLIO INVESTMENT, 1865–1914

If we exclude the alleged 'informal empire' and the colonies with representative government, we are left with only the dependent colonies and India as political units whose citizens might have been exploited by the 'gentlemen capitalists' operating through the good offices of Downing Street and Whitehall. How important were those financial links, and how do they compare with the links to the informal empire, to those colonies with responsible government, and to the United States and the rest of the world? Tables 3.2 and 3.3 provide a summary of the overseas capital passing through the London Stock Exchange in the years between 1865 and 1914.

During that time the London market channelled about $32.2 billion to governments and firms located in almost 175 countries, colonies and princely states. Of that total, the domestic economy received something more than a quarter, other countries and their colonies about half – the US alone drew $5.2 billion, or about three-fifths of the UK domestic total – and the empire just less than a quarter. Of that last fraction, however, the colonies with responsible government received seven out of every ten dollars. If the focus is narrowed to the overseas sector, the total was $23.3 billion; and that figure was divided in a ratio of 7:3 between 'foreign' countries and their colonies and the British overseas empire. Again, however, the colonies with responsible government received $2.30 for every $1 directed toward the dependent colonies and India.

Thus, if we deny the relevance of the informal empire, and if we conclude that there were no exploitative profits to be earned in the colonies with responsible government, the exploitable empire received less than 7 per cent of all – and less than 10 per cent of all overseas – capital passing through the London Stock Exchange. Moreover, even if the analysis is narrowed to private sector finance – both Marx and Lenin would have argued that it was the capitalists in the private sector who were the chief beneficiaries of empire – those fractions rise to only 7 and 11 per cent respectively. In either case, unless those investments in the dependent empire were extremely profitable – and there is no evidence that they were – they hardly provided enough tail to wag the dog.

TABLE 3.2

LONDON STOCK EXCHANGE: ALL CAPITAL, BY TYPE OF GOVERNMENT, 1865-1914

PANEL A: IN US $ MILLIONS

Years	All capital			UK			Foreign			Responsible government			Dependent colonies and India		
	Total	Private	Gov't	Total	Private	Gov't	Total	Private	Gov't	Total	Private	Gov't	Total	Private	Gov't
1865–69	1808.6	1141.2	667.4	630.4	623.4	7.0	918.1	315.5	602.6	79.5	29.5	50.0	180.5	172.7	7.9
1870–74	3193.2	1266.9	1926.3	553.7	518.9	34.8	2410.5	633.3	1777.2	154.5	67.6	86.9	74.4	47.1	27.4
1875–79	2440.2	672.0	1768.2	517.8	426.0	91.8	1477.7	170.3	1307.4	307.0	48.7	258.3	137.7	27.0	110.7
1880–84	2534.3	1377.1	1157.2	660.1	520.5	139.6	1277.4	655.6	621.8	444.3	129.3	315.0	152.6	71.7	80.8
1885–89	3055.4	1966.8	1088.6	836.1	740.1	96.0	1495.7	965.6	530.1	536.7	185.1	351.6	186.9	76.1	110.9
1890–94	2424.8	1562.6	862.2	735.8	620.6	115.2	1137.8	724.7	413.1	402.1	177.4	224.7	149.1	39.9	109.3
1895–99	2703.0	1850.7	852.3	1128.7	988.3	140.4	1021.4	505.8	515.6	309.4	183.1	126.4	243.5	173.6	69.9
1900–04	3870.5	2124.4	1746.1	1932.2	972.8	959.4	1065.8	767.5	298.2	628.8	211.1	417.7	243.7	173.0	70.7
1905–09	4622.1	3041.9	1580.2	846.9	618.9	228.0	2403.7	1595.0	808.7	958.5	601.7	356.8	412.9	226.3	186.6
1910–14	5526.1	3452.6	2073.5	1064.7	701.3	363.4	2731.8	1846.3	885.5	1282.9	623.0	659.9	446.6	282.0	164.6
Total	32178.2	18456.3	13721.9	8906.5	6730.9	2175.7	15939.9	8179.7	7760.2	5103.7	2256.5	2847.3	2228.0	1289.2	938.8

TABLE 3.2
(CONT'D)
PANEL B: % OF ALL CAPITAL

Years	All capital			UK			Foreign			Responsible government			Dependent colonies and India		
	Total	Private	Gov't	Total	Private	Gov't	Total	Private	Gov't	Total	Private	Gov't	Total	Private	Gov't
1865–69	100.00	63.10	36.90	34.86	34.47	0.39	50.76	17.45	33.32	4.40	1.63	2.76	9.98	9.55	0.43
1870–74	100.00	39.67	60.33	17.34	16.25	1.09	75.49	19.83	55.66	4.84	2.12	2.72	2.33	1.47	0.86
1875–79	100.00	27.54	72.46	21.22	17.46	3.76	60.56	6.98	53.58	12.58	2.00	10.59	5.64	1.11	4.54
1880–84	100.00	54.34	45.66	26.05	20.54	5.51	50.40	25.87	24.53	17.53	5.10	12.43	6.02	2.83	3.19
1885–89	100.00	64.37	35.63	27.37	24.22	3.14	48.95	31.60	17.35	17.56	6.06	11.51	6.12	2.49	3.63
1890–94	100.00	64.44	35.56	30.34	25.59	4.75	46.92	29.89	17.04	16.58	7.32	9.26	6.15	1.65	4.51
1895–99	100.00	68.47	31.53	41.76	36.56	5.19	37.79	18.71	19.07	11.45	6.77	4.68	9.01	6.42	2.59
1900–04	100.00	54.89	45.11	49.92	25.13	24.79	27.54	19.83	7.71	16.25	5.45	10.79	6.30	4.47	1.83
1905–09	100.00	65.81	34.19	18.32	13.39	4.93	52.00	34.51	17.50	20.74	13.02	7.72	8.93	4.90	4.04
1910–14	100.00	62.48	37.52	19.27	12.69	6.58	49.44	33.41	16.02	23.22	11.27	11.94	8.08	5.10	2.98
Total	100.00	57.36	42.64	27.68	20.92	6.76	49.54	25.42	24.12	15.86	7.01	8.85	6.92	4.01	2.92

Source: L.E. Davis and R.A. Huttenback, *Mammon and the Pursuit of Empire* (Cambridge: CUP, 1986), pp. 40–1.

TABLE 3.3

LONDON STOCK EXCHANGE: ALL OVERSEAS CAPITAL, BY TYPE OF GOVERNMENT, 1865–1914

PANEL A: US $ MILLIONS

Years	All overseas capital			Foreign			Responsible government			Dependent colonies			India		
	Total	Private	Gov't	Total	Private	Gov't	Total	Private	Gov't	Total	Private	Gov't	Total	Private	Gov't
1865–69	1178.2	517.7	660.4	918.1	315.5	602.6	79.5	29.5	50.0	29.8	21.9	7.9	150.8	150.8	0.0
1870–74	2639.5	748.0	1891.5	2410.5	633.3	1777.2	154.5	67.6	86.9	12.6	9.9	2.7	61.9	37.1	24.7
1875–79	1922.4	246.0	1676.4	1477.7	170.3	1307.4	307.0	48.7	258.3	5.9	2.5	3.4	131.8	24.5	107.3
1880–84	1874.3	856.7	1017.6	1277.4	655.6	621.8	444.3	129.3	315.0	35.9	19.4	16.5	116.7	52.4	64.3
1885–89	2219.3	1226.7	992.6	1495.7	965.6	530.1	536.7	185.1	351.6	40.2	31.3	8.9	146.7	44.8	102.0
1890–94	1689.0	942.0	747.0	1137.8	724.7	413.1	402.1	177.4	224.7	33.9	18.4	15.5	115.2	21.5	93.7
1895–99	1574.3	862.4	711.9	1021.4	505.8	515.6	309.4	183.1	126.4	110.9	94.3	16.6	132.6	79.3	53.3
1900–04	1938.3	1151.6	786.7	1065.8	767.5	298.2	628.8	211.1	417.7	122.1	97.7	24.5	121.6	75.3	46.3
1905–09	3775.1	2423.0	1352.2	2403.7	1595.0	808.7	958.5	601.7	356.8	185.7	125.5	60.3	227.2	100.8	126.4
1910–14	4461.4	2751.3	1710.0	2731.8	1846.3	885.5	1282.9	623.0	659.9	243.5	181.2	62.4	203.0	100.8	102.2
Total	23271.7	11725.4	11546.3	15939.9	8179.7	7760.2	5103.7	2256.5	2847.3	820.6	602.0	218.6	1407.5	687.3	720.2

TABLE 3.3
(CONT'D)
PANEL B: % OF ALL OVERSEAS CAPITAL

Years	All overseas capital			Foreign			Responsible government			Dependent colonies			India		
	Total	Private	Gov't	Total	Private	Gov't	Total	Private	Gov't	Total	Private	Gov't	Total	Private	Gov't
1865–69	100.00	43.94	56.06	77.93	26.78	51.15	6.75	2.51	4.24	2.53	1.86	0.67	12.80	12.80	0.00
1870–74	100.00	28.34	71.66	91.33	23.99	67.33	5.85	2.56	3.29	0.48	0.38	0.10	2.34	1.41	0.94
1875–79	100.00	12.80	87.20	76.87	8.86	68.01	15.97	2.53	13.44	0.31	0.13	0.18	6.85	1.27	5.58
1880–84	100.00	45.71	54.29	68.16	34.98	33.17	23.70	6.90	16.81	1.91	1.03	0.88	6.23	2.80	3.43
1885–89	100.00	55.27	44.73	67.40	43.51	23.89	24.18	8.34	15.84	1.81	1.41	0.40	6.61	2.02	4.59
1890–94	100.00	55.77	44.23	67.36	42.91	24.46	23.81	10.50	13.30	2.01	1.09	0.92	6.82	1.28	5.55
1895–99	100.00	54.78	45.22	64.88	32.13	32.75	19.65	11.63	8.03	7.04	5.99	1.05	8.42	5.04	3.39
1900–04	100.00	59.41	40.59	54.99	39.60	15.39	32.44	10.89	21.55	6.30	5.04	1.26	6.27	3.89	2.39
1905–09	100.00	64.18	35.82	63.67	42.25	21.42	25.39	15.94	9.45	4.92	3.32	1.60	6.02	2.67	3.35
1910–14	100.00	61.67	38.33	61.23	41.38	19.85	28.76	13.97	14.79	5.46	4.06	1.40	4.55	2.26	2.29
Total	100.00	50.38	49.62	68.49	35.15	33.35	21.93	9.70	12.23	3.53	2.59	0.94	6.05	2.95	3.09

Source: L.E. Davis and R.A. Huttenback, Mammon and the Pursuit of Empire (Cambridge: CUP, 1986), pp. 40–1.

While British portfolio investment underwrote domestic capital formation in nearly 175 countries and colonies between 1865 and 1914, four frontier countries – Argentina, Australia, Canada and the United States – were the recipients of just less than one-half the overseas total.[25] In many respects the four countries were similar; but they differed in some important aspects, and, as a result, they offer a rich opportunity for comparative study. Over the half-century under study, all four were rapidly developing frontier economies; all were largely populated by European immigrants or their descendants; and all drew heavily, or at least importantly, on European, particularly British, capital. Thus a more detailed examination of the transfers to those countries should provide some clues about the nature of 'finance capitalism' in Great Britain.

All four countries sold substantial blocks of securities on the London capital market during the years between 1865 and 1914; and those funds flowed into a wide variety of public and private enterprises. Governments in each country borrowed; but so did railroads, private manufacturing and commercial firms, financial enterprises (banks and insurance companies, for example), public utilities, and a myriad of land-related endeavours.[26] Table 3.4 provides an estimate of the industrial distribution and timing of those flows. Although there was substantial year-to-year and country-to-country variation, overall, transportation (almost entirely railroads) received about 60 per cent of the total and governments an additional quarter. At the same time, the agriculture and extractive sector was the beneficiary of about 7 per cent, manufacturing and commerce $3\frac{1}{2}$ per cent, public utilities about 3 per cent, and finance about 2 per cent. If, on the one hand, imperial policy or some hidden agenda of the 'gentlemen capitalists' was influencing those flows, we might expect to see a substantial level of temporal association among the transfers to the four countries – or, if one concludes that the United States was not a part of the informal empire, between the other three, or, if there was no informal empire, at least between the two representatives of the formal one. If, on the other hand, the flows were demand driven, we would expect little temporal association between the flows. Each would have been primarily influenced by economic opportunities in the recipient country; and, a few extraordinary events like the world wheat boom aside, there is no reason to expect that, in any particular year, investment opportunities in Argentina would have been the same as those in Australia, Canada or the United States.

The calculations reported in Table 3.5 are designed to shed some light on the question of causality – were the flows demand or supply driven? The figures reported are the coefficients of determination (r_{xy}^2's) between the capital flows to pairs of countries. Overall (Table 3.5a) there is little evidence of

25 The four countries received $10.9 billion of the $23.3 billion in British portfolio investment that flowed overseas between 1 Jan. 1865 and 31 Dec. 1914. The data in this section of the paper all come from the Davis–Gallman, 'Capital created and called' tape created from the London Stock Exchange transactions reported monthly in *Investors' Monthly Manual*.
26 In this analysis, the land-related industries have been combined in the Agriculture & Extractive sector. That sector is a combination of firms in agriculture, mining, petroleum and chemicals, and the financial land and development industry.

TABLE 3.4

CAPITAL CREATED AND CALLED: LONDON STOCK EXCHANGE, FOUR FRONTIER COUNTRIES, 1865–1914, BY INDUSTRY

PANEL A: US $000

Years	Manufacturing & Commercial	Financial	Government	Agricultural & Extractive	Transport	Public utilities	Total
1865–69	447	6,428	26,393	9,096	106,191	9,016	157,572
1870–74	18,708	5,843	608,231	34,547	363,605	11,651	1,042,585
1875–79	329	6,967	1,057,074	8,219	286,923	12,296	1,371,808
1880–84	7,423	24,451	127,148	73,868	516,836	3,261	752,986
1885–89	57,461	28,467	261,277	89,869	669,256	30,969	1,137,299
1890–94	56,523	43,669	80,663	66,509	508,235	2,490	758,089
1895–99	47,863	11,627	106,316	125,019	168,861	8,673	468,359
1900–04	8,611	7,896	68,947	57,562	929,185	6,463	1,078,664
1905–09	41,047	16,391	134,459	85,903	1,544,442	90,354	1,912,597
1910–14	140,396	55,964	314,562	211,262	1,378,826	142,641	2,231,652
All years	378,806	207,704	2,785,070	761,854	6,472,359	317,814	10,911,610

PANEL B: % OF FOUR-COUNTRY TOTAL

Years	Manufacturing & Commercial	Financial	Government	Agricultural & Extractive	Transport	Public utilities	Total
1865–69	0.28	4.08	16.75	5.77	67.39	5.72	100.00
1870–74	1.79	0.56	58.34	3.31	34.88	1.12	100.00
1875–79	0.02	0.51	77.06	0.60	20.92	0.90	100.00
1880–84	0.99	3.25	16.89	9.81	68.64	0.43	100.00
1885–89	5.05	2.50	22.97	7.90	58.85	2.72	100.00
1890–94	7.46	5.76	10.64	8.77	67.04	0.33	100.00
1895–99	10.22	2.48	22.70	26.69	36.05	1.85	100.00
1900–04	0.80	0.73	6.39	5.34	86.14	0.60	100.00
1905–09	2.15	0.86	7.03	4.49	80.75	4.72	100.00
1910–14	6.29	2.51	14.10	9.47	61.78	6.39	100.00
All years	3.47	1.90	25.52	6.98	59.32	2.91	100.00

Notes: In Canada and Argentina government loans in support of railroads have been assigned to transport. In Australia, since the rail network was almost all government financed, some fraction of government loans were assigned to transport.
Source: Davis–Gallman tape of capital created and called up on the London Stock Exchange, 1865–1914.

TABLE 3.5

R2 MATRICES: CAPITAL CREATED AND CALLED ON THE LONDON STOCK EXCHANGE,
FOUR FRONTIER COUNTRIES, 1865–1914

TABLE 3.5A

TOTAL CAPITAL CALLED, FOUR FRONTIER COUNTRIES

	Argentina	Australia	Canada	United States
Argentina	1.000	–	–	–
Australia	0.027	1.000	–	–
Canada	0.104	0.049	1.000	–
United States	0.001	0.004	0.026	1.000

TABLE 3.5B

TOTAL MANUFACTURING & COMMERCIAL CAPITAL CALLED, FOUR FRONTIER COUNTRIES

	Argentina	Australia	Canada	United States
Argentina	1.000	–	–	–
Australia	0.001	1.000	–	–
Canada	0.447	0.068	1.000	–
United States	0.247	0.016	0.084	1.000

TABLE 3.5C

TOTAL FINANCIAL CAPITAL CALLED, FOUR FRONTIER COUNTRIES

	Argentina	Australia	Canada	United States
Argentina	1.000	–	–	–
Australia	0.047	1.000	–	–
Canada	0.000	0.023	1.000	–
United States	0.004	0.009	0.052	1.000

any significant degree of association between the gross flows. The coefficients
– that is, the fraction of the variation in the flow to one country that can be
'explained' by the flow to the other – range from a high of 10 per cent in the
case of the Canada–Argentina pair to a low of 0.4 per cent for the US–
Australia regression. Nor does disaggregation do much to improve the apparent level of temporal association (see Tables 3.5b–3.5g). For the six industries
in the four countries there are 36 pairs of series of annual capital flows. For ten
of those comparisons, the coefficients are less than 0.01 (that is, less than 1 per
cent of the variation of the flow to country A can be 'explained' by the flow
to country B); for eight, the coefficients are less than .05, for another six,
less than .1, and for seven, less than .2. In only five of the 36 pairs does the
'explanatory power' of the capital flowing to one country account for more than

TABLE 3.5D

TOTAL GOVERNMENT CAPITAL CALLED, FOUR FRONTIER COUNTRIES

	Argentina	Australia	Canada	United States
Argentina	1.000	–	–	–
Australia	0.150	1.000	–	–
Canada	0.052	0.253	1.000	–
United States	0.005	0.010	0.024	1.000

TABLE 3.5E

TOTAL AGRICULTURAL & EXTRACTIVE CAPITAL CALLED, FOUR FRONTIER COUNTRIES

	Argentina	Australia	Canada	United States
Argentina	1.000	–	–	–
Australia	0.000	1.000	–	–
Canada	0.494	0.001	1.000	–
United States	0.162	0.004	0.192	1.000

TABLE 3.5F

TOTAL TRANSPORT CAPITAL CALLED, FOUR FRONTIER COUNTRIES

	Argentina	Australia	Canada	United States
Argentina	1.000	–	–	–
Australia	0.000	1.000	–	–
Canada	0.064	0.019	1.000	–
United States	0.082	0.041	0.176	1.000

TABLE 3.5G

TOTAL PUBLIC UTILITY CAPITAL CALLED, FOUR FRONTIER COUNTRIES

	Argentina	Australia	Canada	United States
Argentina	1.000	–	–	–
Australia	0.002	1.000	–	–
Canada	0.104	0.117	1.000	–
United States	0.111	0.016	0.270	1.000

Source: Davis–Gallman tape of capital created and called on the London Stock Exchange, 1865–1914.

one-fifth of the variation of the flow to the other. Of the five that are marked by coefficients greater than .2, the largest are for Canada–Argentina Manufacturing & Commerce and Agriculture & Extractive comparisons – in those two cases, the 'explanatory' power reaches almost one-half. The coefficients for the other three suggest that about one-quarter of the variance can be 'explained'; and even for those three, it is difficult to argue that a major determinant of the size of the flow has been uncovered.

Taken together, the evidence from both the gross and the disaggregated flows strongly suggests that for the four countries, at least, the size and composition of the capital flows reflected conditions of domestic demand rather than British policies that might have affected supply. It would be an interesting exercise to apply the same technique to the flows to the dependent colonies and India. That exercise might help us to decide whether those transfers were demand or supply driven; and if, unlike the case of the 'big four', the transfers were found to be supply induced, that fact might be taken as evidence of possible politically rooted exploitation. If not, it would appear that market forces were at work in the dependent empire as well as in the four largest recipients.

GENTLEMEN CAPITALISTS

Cain and Hopkins argue that, by the late nineteenth century, both British 'national policy and Britain's unofficial presence abroad' were the product of an original coalition of the 'eighteenth-century landed gentry' and the new 'moneyed men of the city' – a coalition that had been somewhat altered in the second half of the next century 'to give greater prominence to financial interests, the leading beneficiaries of economic reform', and to reach out and encompass 'the higher ranks of the new urban middle class, who were co-opted into defence of property and order' (C&H, I, p. 467).

One can hardly argue with that conclusion; and, at the same time, it appears that those groups played an equally important role in overseas investment. Tables 3.6 and 3.7 report the results of a survey of 79,944 stockholders of 260 British, foreign and empire firms chartered between 1883 and 1903.[27] Table 3.6 suggests that businessmen turned first to the domestic economy, then, with somewhat less enthusiasm, to those parts of the world *not* painted red, and only then, and with a marked lack of enthusiasm, to the formal empire. In fact, they were less than half as likely to invest in an empire enterprise than they were to put their savings to work at home. The elites, on the other hand, while having a slight preference for foreign as opposed to domestic opportunities, were half as likely again to channel their accumulations to the formal empire as they were to place those resources in domestic enterprise. Nor, as Cain and Hopkins argue, and as Table 3.7 confirms, were all members of the middle class identical. Although the elites in London were less likely to invest in the domestic economy than their downstate (rural) counterparts, they displayed about the same taste for foreign and empire investment. Not so the London business community. Although London merchants displayed only a

27 See L.E. Davis and R.A. Huttenback, *Mammon and the Pursuit of Empire: The Political Economy of British Imperialism, 1860–1912* (Cambridge, 1986), ch. 7.

TABLE 3.6

INDEX OF RELATIVE EQUITY HOLDINGS, BY OCCUPATION (UNITED KINGDOM = 100)

	Location of investments		
Occupation	United Kingdom	Foreign	Empire
Businessmen			
Merchants	100	173	76
Manufacturers	100	24	13
Professional & management	100	66	64
Miscellaneous businessmen	100	100	41
All businessmen	100	86	45
Elites			
Financiers	100	228	97
Military officers	100	63	76
Peers & gentlemen	100	97	166
Miscellaneous elites	100	200	260
All elites	100	115	153

Source: L.E. Davis and R.A. Huttenback, *Mammon and the Pursuit of Empire* (Cambridge: CUP, 1986), p. 212.

TABLE 3.7

RELATIVE ATTRACTIVENESS OF HOME, FOREIGN AND EMPIRE INVESTMENTS: EQUITY HOLDINGS OF PRIVATE FIRMS BY OCCUPATION AND LOCATION OF STOCK (RATIO IS LONDON TO NON-LONDON)

	Location of investments		
Occupation	United Kingdom	Foreign	Empire
Businessmen			
Merchants	19	135	110
Manufacturers	44	140	162
Professional & management	22	114	126
Miscellaneous businessmen	2	40	635
All Businessmen	17	122	142
Elites			
Financiers	61	105	103
Military officers	132	108	94
Peers & gentlemen	49	102	205
Miscellaneous elites	152	129	90
All elites	62	106	102

Source: L.E. Davis and R.A. Huttenback, *Mammon and the Pursuit of Empire* (Cambridge: CUP, 1986), p. 216.

slightly greater preference for empire investments than did their counterparts in the rest of the country, overall, the businessmen in the metropolis were about 40 per cent more likely to invest in formal empire and about a quarter more likely to place their resources in the foreign sector than were businessmen in rural areas or in provincial cities like Manchester, Leeds or Glasgow.

AN ALTERNATIVE HYPOTHESIS

If the political manipulations associated with empire do not provide an adequate explanation of the observed capital flows, is there a viable alternative explanation? Let us initially assume, as the evidence presented in this paper strongly suggests, that the international capital flows emanating from Great Britain between 1865 and 1914 were demand, rather than supply, driven; and that the 'gentlemen capitalists' displayed a greater affinity for empire investment than their less socially acceptable peers. Moreover, let us further assume, as the external evidence indicates, that, in the recipient countries: (1) domestic savings rates were either relatively low or – as in the case of the United States (and, after the turn of the century, in Australia and Canada as well) – although relatively high, not high enough to have underwritten the short-term surges in investment demand that characterized those nations' development; (2) the average level of investor sophistication was much lower and the geographic concentration of knowledgeable investors much higher than in the United Kingdom; and (3) there were important institutional differences between the domestic capital markets and the London Stock Exchange.[28] Taken together, these assumptions provide the basis for an economic model that appears to explain investor behaviour better – both the behaviour of the 'gentlemen capitalists' and the middle class in Britain and of the 'plebs' overseas. Both groups – island residents and 'colonists' – received information about alternative investments; but there was an asymmetric bias in the way that they processed that information. As a result, overseas investors required a stronger signal about the safety of certain investment choices than did their British counterparts. Although not everyone in Britain received precisely the same information, the culmination of a long process of investor education coupled with the financial innovations that underwrote the development of the British capital market meant that the average British investor was better informed

28 For a more complete discussion of the implication of these assumptions for the American case, see L. Davis, R. Cull and R. Gallman, 'Sophisticates, rubes, financiers, and the evolution of American capital markets: U.S.–U.K. finance, 1865–1914', paper presented at the NBER's Franco-American Economic Seminar, Boston, Mass., July 1993, and at the South American Econometric Conference, Tucuman, Argentina, Aug. 1993; Davis and Cull, *International Capital Markets*; and L. Davis and R. Cull, 'International capital movements, domestic capital markets, and American growth, 1820–1914', in S. Engerman and R. Gallman (eds), *The Cambridge Economic History of the United States*, Vol. II (Cambridge, forthcoming 1998). For the Canadian experience, see L. Davis and R. Gallman, 'Domestic savings, international capital flows, and the evolution of domestic capital markets: the Canadian experience', paper presented at the All-UC Group in Economic History, Fall Conference, University of California, Los Angeles, Nov. 1993, and at the Southern Economic Association, New Orleans, Nov. 1993.

and better able to take advantage of that information than the typical colonist or citizen of the less developed world. In Britain, savers (that is, potential investors) were relatively sophisticated; and they were experienced in investing in pieces of paper – that is, in the stocks and bonds – that were alleged to represent debt and equity claims on enterprises far removed, both geographically and industrially, from the savers' immediate experience. Even in Britain, however, not everyone received the same information; savers were more confident about the information they received about investments in places and industries with which they were most familiar; and not everyone was equally familiar with the entire range of investment alternatives. As a result, *ceterus paribus*, when the British saver calculated the potential gains from each of a set of alternative investment choices, he or she applied a lower uncertainty discount to information about the better-known alternatives.

For example, although he would have been willing to invest abroad if the discounted relative returns made that investment the alternative of choice, a Liverpool bicycle manufacturer might have tended to rely more heavily on (that is, he discounted less) information about Midlands textiles and Leeds city bonds than he would have on the information he received about American breweries and the bonds of the province of Quebec. Conversely, a British country gentleman might have thought that he was better informed about investments in Delhi, where his cousin worked, than about those same Midland textile firms; and a London merchant may have felt more confident about commercial investments in Buenos Aires, where his firm had an office, or about the bonds of the Grand Trunk Railway – his City-based broker, partner in Baring Brothers and fellow club member, had told him that those bonds had some (explicit or implicit) government guarantee – than about coal mines in Scotland. Again, while neither the gentleman nor the merchant was unwilling to invest in the domestic British economy, they applied a higher uncertainty discount to those alternatives when they calculated the relative values of domestic and overseas alternatives, and, because of that discount, the distant alternatives appeared more rewarding.

In the receiving countries, however, the problem was quite different. Savings may have been scarce or they may have been plentiful, but, unlike their British counterparts, savers had not been educated in the value of 'pieces of paper'; and they were unwilling to risk their accumulations in activities that they could neither see nor touch. Farmers saved, but they invested in their farms. Merchants saved, but they invested in commercial buildings and inventories. Manufacturers saved, but they invested in new factories and machines. In short, before they were willing to risk their accumulations in regions and industries far removed from their own experience, these potential investors had to be educated about the safety and potential profitability of 'depersonalized' capital.[29] These were lessons their British counterparts had learned

29 In the American case, it has been the subject of a wide range of studies. See, for example, L. Davis, 'The capital markets and industrial concentration: the U.S. and the U.K., a comparative study', *Economic History Review*, 19/2 (1966); B. DeLong, 'Did Morgan's men add value?', in

from their experience with government bonds during the Napoleonic Wars and from railroad securities in the Hudson era.

Moreover, education also often involves institutional innovation. For example, an American merchant in Chicago may have learned that a stock or bond offered by J.P. Morgan was a safe investment, and, as a result, he would have been willing to invest in the equity shares of US Steel when they were offered. At the same time, although the firm was located in the same city, he may have viewed the bond issues of McCormick Reaper – a firm as yet without the Morgan imprimatur – as too uncertain (that is, subject to a very large discount in his profitability calculation). That discount, however, would have been revised substantially downward when Morgan folded McCormick into his new International Harvestor conglomerate. With Morgan's blessing, those shares suddenly looked profitable, although, in fact, nothing 'real' had changed. Similarly, the imprimatur granted by an official listing on the New York Stock Exchange might have convinced a St Louis brewer that an Argentine government bond was 'safe', while a Kansas City bond was still subject to his high uncertainty discount.

In neither case, however, was the imprimatur a free good. In the former case, Morgan earned monopoly rents – his commission charges were not low; in the latter case, a listing on the New York Stock Exchange was expensive for the firm (the requirements were draconian and, therefore, the signal was costly) and expensive for the investor (the Exchange set monopoly-level minimum commissions). Those profits, of course, did not last forever. Once the majority of investors had reached the educational levels that had been attained by the typical British investor by the middle of the nineteenth century, the monopoly profits were largely competed away; but that level of sophistication was not achieved, even in the United States, before the First World War, and it may well have been much later.

There were, of course, some sophisticated investors in the receiving countries. In the United States, for example, there were investors in Boston who were able to process efficiently information on western railroads and copper mines; and there were investors in Philadelphia who were as informed as anyone in the world about economic activity in the upper Mid-west. Such informed investors, however, were neither typical nor numerous; and they did not control a sufficient volume of savings to meet the demand of all the firms and governments that were unwilling or unable to meet the signalling costs imposed by the institutions that had emerged to grant a generally accepted 'safety imprimatur'. In short, there was room in the local developing economy for foreign investment; and, given the relative level of sophistication and the financial innovations that had been introduced over the previous century and a half, the British investor stood ready to reap the profits.

P. Temin (ed.), *Inside the Business Enterprise: Historical Perspectives on the Use of Information* (Chicago, 1991); and N. Lamoreaux, 'Banks, kinship, and economic development: the New England case', *The Journal of Economic History* (Sept. 1986).

In Britain, however, there were still some informational asymmetries. Because of the relative uncertainty discounts, domestic investment appealed to the typical member of the burgeoning middle class; foreign investment lured the nation's merchants and financiers; and the empire beckoned peers and gentlemen as well as London businessmen.

The story is simple. The driving force behind investment was profits, not political manipulation. Those profits were, in turn, supported by a high level of investor sophistication and by efficiently operating domestic and foreign capital markets. Some informational asymmetries, however, still remained, and those asymmetries supported what has been termed Britain's 'dual capital market' – a domestic market that served the needs of middle-class investors, particularly those living in the provinces, and an international market that served the interests of the 'gentlemen capitalists'. The domestic British capital market has frequently been the subject of severe criticism; but the relatively slow innovation of the corporate form of organization, the variety of domestic firms that did successfully raise resources on the London Stock Exchange, and recent work on the role of the commercial banks in industrial finance, all suggest that the market was, in fact, very well served.[30]

CONCLUSION AND CONUNDRUM

As Cain and Hopkins have argued, the innovations in finance and services, and in ocean transport that made it possible to trade British manufactures for American cotton and Canadian wheat, had paid off handsomely; and the 'gentlemen capitalists' could reap the rewards. But did the typical British investor need the empire to harvest those returns?

Certainly from the empire investors' point of view, the empire was good business. If risk-adjusted earnings in the empire were above domestic, the empire relationship produced a significant positive return for those investors. If they were lower than those available at home or in the foreign sector, as far as the owners of those empire investments were concerned, returns were still higher than they would have been had the political links been dissolved and the private sector been forced to shoulder directly the costs that had been socialized. Loss of the dependent empire would certainly have cost those investors their subsidy, perhaps the basis for some of their allegedly exploitative profits,

30 For a discussion of the slow rate of corporate formation, see Sir John Clapham, *An Economic History of Great Britain* (Cambridge, 1952), vol. II, p. 1. For a comparison with the American experience, see George Heberton Evans, Jr., *Business Incorporations in the United States, 1800–1943*, National Bureau of Economic Research, Publication No. 49 (New York, 1948). In terms of the relative availability of capital in London, note that among other enterprises that were able to float equity issues in the late nineteenth century was the Wembley Park Construction Company, a firm chartered to build the Eiffel Tower in Wembley park. Finally, on the role of British commercial banks, see Forest Capie, 'Prudent and stable (but inefficient?): commercial banks in Britain, 1890–1940', paper delivered at the New York University Saloman Center, Leonard N. Stern School of Business, Conference on Anglo-American Finance: Financial Markets and Institutions in 20th-Century North America and the UK, Dec. 1993; Forrest Capie, 'Structure and performance in British banking, 1870–1939', in P. Cotterell and D. Moggridge (eds), *Money and Power* (London, 1988), and Forrest Capie and Michael Collins, *Have Banks Failed British Industry?* (London, 1992).

and perhaps (although this is unlikely) their entire investment (any attempt at nationalization might have brought forth the wrath of the international community).[31] In the case of the self-governing colonies, the increases in taxes that would have followed the shift in costs from the mother country to the four Dominions would have somewhat reduced the profits on their investments. Thus, it must have paid at least some fraction of the empire component of the 'gentlemen capitalists' to lobby to keep the formal ties with the empire in place. However, even if we assume that they were responsible for all overseas investments, the empire's share of those flows was only about 30 per cent. At the same time, a fairly substantial portion of the middle classes had few, if any, investments in the dependent empire; and, although many gained from trade with the Dominions, it is not obvious that those gains can be traced to their empire connection – they may have gained a little from the shipping and cable subsidies, but for the most part they traded on the same basis as their competitors in Germany and the United States. They did, however, have a substantial financial interest in the empire – they paid for a large fraction of the subsidy. Despite the overall regressiveness of the British tax system, the middle and upper classes shouldered about two-thirds of the total tax burden. Moreover, it appears that, of that two-thirds, the middle class paid about 70 per cent in 1880; and their share had risen to almost 85 per cent by 1906. The 'gentlemen capitalists'' contribution was some 30 per cent in 1880, 15 per cent in 1906.[32]

Finally, the political power of the 'gentlemen capitalists' must have been at least somewhat on the wane. The three electoral reform acts (1832, 1867–68 and 1885) had gradually increased the fraction of enfranchised adult males in England and Wales from an estimated one in seven and a half in 1831 to one in five in 1833, to one in three in 1869, and to two in three in 1886. Although the franchise remained somewhat more restricted in Scotland and Ireland, the percentage gains were even more spectacular; and by 1886, three in five adult males could vote in Scotland and one in two in Ireland.[33] Of course, as Hopkins points out, 'the political parties, run by gents, reorganized to mobilize and incorporate the new voters'; but reorganization probably involved some power sharing and it certainly involved some accommodation.[34]

The conundrum then, a puzzle that Cain and Hopkins note but do not resolve: how did the 'gentlemen capitalists' pull off this political–economic version of the Great Train Robbery? Cain and Hopkins write:

31 It is interesting to speculate why the Chinese attempt, despite that country's location thousands of miles away from Europe, engendered an international military response, while Mexico, located on the American border, was able to nationalize foreign investment successfully. See Peter Fleming, *The Siege at Peking: The Boxer Rebellion* (New York, 1959); Clark W. Reynolds, *The Mexican Economy: Twentieth-Century Structure and Growth* (New Haven, Conn., 1970); and James D. Cockcroft, *Mexico: Class Formation, Capital Accumulation, and the State* (New York, 1983).
32 Davis and Huttenback, *Mammon and the Pursuit of Empire*, pp. 250–1, 316.
33 These figures were compiled by David Butler and James Cornford. They are cited in Chris Cook and Brendan Keith, *British Historical Facts, 1830–1900* (New York, 1975), pp. 116–17.
34 Anthony Hopkins, private communication, 31 Jan. 1994.

The international order that was erected on the basis of free trade and the gold standard served the purposes of finance and services rather better than it did those of manufacturing: the increasing scale and complexity of multilateral trade relations gave the City opportunities and commitments that extended far beyond the distribution of British manufactures. Moreover, when a choice had to be made, policy invariably favoured finance over manufacturing. The empirical evidence is compelling: the manufacturing lobby always put its case, but it rarely got its way, whereas the City's needs were very much to the fore in all the examples we have examined . . .

. . . . When this [a disaggregation of what has been termed the 'business' lobby] is done, the contrast commonly drawn between officialdom and business loses much of its validity because it is apparent that an important segment of the non-industrial business elite consisted of gentlemen who moved in the same circles and shared the same values with those who had their hands on the levers of power – and often managed their investments too. Imperial and imperialist policies did not issue from a conspiracy by a covert minority but from the open exercise of authority by a respected elite who enjoyed the deference of those they governed. Like-mindedness was certainly extended abroad, but it began at home.

(C&H, I, pp. 470–1)

Those observations are certainly correct, but they do not explain why, given the answer provided by the economic calculus, the 'respected elite' continued to enjoy 'the deference of those they governed'. Obviously, the established policy of recruiting the bureaucracy from the public schools and from Oxbridge meant that the men with 'their hands on the levers of power' did share the views of the 'gentlemen capitalists'. Moreover, it is clear that the House of Commons was 'a quintessentially patrician legislative body dominated by the elite classes, business, and the professions. The members had attended ancient universities and the major public schools and they were "club men" with a vengeance'.[35] But none of these factors was immutable. In a democracy, rules can be changed and politicians defeated; and even in California, lobbyists have discovered that, in the face of widespread public concern, their efforts are not always successful.

Cain and Hopkins have written a superb book; I don't remember when I have learned so much from a single work. They have also, perhaps unintentionally, set a future research agenda – an agenda, not for economic, but for social and political, historians, and not for imperial, but for British, historians. The problem has been sketched out, but it will be the next generation of historians who will have to solve the mystery of the 'Great Train Robbery'. Let me close, on the basis of no evidence at all, by suggesting three possible solutions to that mystery:

---

35 Davis and Huttenback, *Mammon and the Pursuit of Empire*, ch. 9 and p. 317.

1. Political change comes, but it does not come quickly. Political institutions are only gradually modified, and, in the case of the British Empire, those innovations were delayed until the middle of this century.
2. The newly enfranchised working classes derived real psychological benefits from living in a country that 'ruled' an overseas empire that spanned the globe, was populated by almost 450 million people, and included almost 13 million square miles of territory.[36] That is, the social revenues exceeded the social costs.
3. The traditional middle class was doing so well within the existing domestic economic institutional structure that they were happy to pay a bit of money to let the 'gentlemen capitalists' be diverted into playing the empire game instead of turning to issues of Bismarckian domestic institutional reform.

Almost certainly, none of these three top-of-the-head alternatives will stand up under any even semi-serious academic scrutiny, but, if we are ever to understand the evolution of the British economy, it is necessary to solve the mystery. Cain and Hopkins are to be commended both for what they have and for what they have not done. They have explained the role of overseas finance and services in Britain's prosperity and they have implicitly posed a question that is fundamental to our understanding of the evolution of British society.

---

36 As an aside, at the time of the Falklands War, those islands represented three-quarters of the land mass of the British overseas empire.

CHAPTER 4

Economic power at the periphery: Canada, Australia and South Africa, 1850–1914

ROBERT KUBICEK

In minimizing colonial autonomy, Cain and Hopkins register their 'dissatisfaction with the peripheral thesis' and the 'claim that the fundamental cause of imperialism is to be found on the periphery itself'. They also stress that the machinations of financial capital have more explanatory power than the needs of industrial capital in identifying the source of the actions of the imperial state.[1] In reaching these conclusions they devote considerable space to the temperate zone colonies of the empire established by substantial European migrant populations (see esp. C&H, I, pp. 202–75, 369–81; II, pp. 107–45). Here we examine the options open to imperial policy-makers to impose their priorities in Britain's relations with the expansive settlement colonies of Canada, Australia and South Africa. This approach has been suggested by Donald Denoon's work, which compares six polities in the southern hemisphere, including Australia and South Africa, and which probes their relationship with the metropole and emphasizes that 'settler capitalists' pursued export-led development to considerable material advantage.[2] While Denoon does not concern himself with Canada, he does make reference to how his settler societies fared in relation to the USA. Since Cain and Hopkins's first volume concentrates on the period 1850–1914, this chapter will do the same. In each colonial case we begin with 1911. This year has been selected for two reasons: by then all three colonies had a central government; and at that particular juncture political and economic developments in each illuminate particularly well both

1 P.J. Cain and A.G. Hopkins, *British Imperialism*, Vol. I: *Innovation and Expansion, 1688–1914* (London, 1993), pp. 10–11 (hereafter cited as C&H, I). Volume II of their two-volume study, *British Imperialism: Crisis and Deconstruction, 1914–1990* (London, 1993) is hereafter referred to as C&H, II.
2 D. Denoon, *Settler Capitalism: The Dynamics of Dependent Development in the Southern Hemisphere* (New York, 1983).

the differences and the similarities in their internal dynamics and in their relations with the metropole.

CANADIAN DEVELOPMENT

In 1911 Wilfrid Laurier, Canada's long-serving Liberal prime minister, was turfed out of office over his trade policy, a reciprocity package with the United States designed to obtain better access for Canadian agricultural production that reduced modestly protective tariffs against American manufacture. His opponents argued that this initiative undermined the imperial connection and set Canada 'on the road toward commercial and eventually political union with the United States'.[3] His defeat may be viewed less as a function of Canada's relations with its neighbour or its 'mother country' and more as the result of local regional rivalries; seen, that is, as a victory for central Canadian manufacturers who claimed it was in the nation's interest to continue to protect their enterprises with high tariffs, a policy followed since 1879. On the other hand, it could be judged to be a defeat of western Canadian agrarian aspirations. Whatever the differences among Canadians that the election accentuated, a smooth transition to a new government followed.

Regional interests and factions of capital could destabilize political practice while contending for advantage. Old ethnic tensions and new peoples also offered the potential for serious political disruptions. But Laurier could claim that ethnic cleavages had been harnessed to a greater national enterprise.[4] The northern half of North America had absorbed technologies, capital and people at an enormous rate. To employ Immanuel Wallerstein's construct, 'a semi-peripheral state' of considerable stability and substance had emerged.[5]

In their approach, Cain and Hopkins view Canada's viability as the result, in no small measure, of 'a collaborating economic elite who clung to, and depended upon, British power and British capital' (C&H, I, p. 265). But does this view give sufficient weight to the leverage and options that Canadians had acquired on their own?

White colonists have been dubbed by Ronald Robinson 'the ideal prefabricated collaborators'.[6] They profited from doing business with Britain, which in

3 R. Craig Brown and R. Cook, *Canada, 1896–1921: A Nation Transformed* (Toronto, 1974), p. 180.
4 'I am', complained Laurier, 'branded in Quebec as a traitor to the French, and in Ontario as a traitor to the English. In Quebec I am branded as a Jingo, and in Ontario as a Separatist. . . . I am neither, I am a Canadian. . . . I have before me as a pillar . . . a policy of true Canadianism, of moderation, of conciliation.' Quoted in K. McNaught, *The Pelican History of Canada* (Baltimore, 1969, 1976), p. 211.
5 I. Wallerstein, 'The rise and future demise of the world capitalist system: concepts for comparative analysis', *Comparative Studies in Society and History*, 16 (Sept. 1974), pp. 387–415.
6 R. Robinson, 'Non-European foundations of European imperialism: sketch for a theory of collaboration', in R. Owen and B. Sutcliffe (eds), *Studies in the Theory of Imperialism* (London, 1972), p. 124. For Robinson's comment that 'Australasian, Canadian and South African colonies . . . by 1919 . . . had taken off into virtual economic and political independence', see his 'Imperial theory and the question of imperialism after empire', *Journal of Imperial and Commonwealth History*, 12 (Jan. 1984), pp. 45–6. Cf. R.W. Winks, 'On decolonization and informal empire', *American Historical Review*, 81 (1976), pp. 540–56.

turn saw its interests maintained. Identified as such at an early date by the British official mind, the white settlers of British North America, as in the case of the reciprocity negotiations with the United States at mid-century, 'possessed considerable influence', inducing 'Britain to negotiate for the terms they desired by exploiting British fears of annexation'.[7]

Collaborators had options; they also had objectives. These can be illuminated by adopting Warwick Armstrong's terminology – he defines them as a 'national ruling coalition'.[8] Whatever their nationalist characteristics, their roots were overseas. Massive immigration from Britain (especially from Ireland and Scotland) after 1815 produced a dominant cultural group which spoke English and had a sense of being British but which did not 'replicate exactly the political and social values of the Mother Country, particularly its class structure. . . . They were British but British in their own way.'[9] With a mix of loyalties – British, ethnic (i.e. Irish, Scottish), local and even national – these migrants and their offspring adapted the political institutions they understood. In these the leadership of French-speaking Canadians found a subordinate yet proactive place. This migrant group also adapted financial institutions, so that by an early date a viable banking structure had emerged. It used political means to secure capital to transfer technology with which its members were familiar, to nurture a revolution in transportation: 'By the mid-1850s, the Canadian government, Canadian railways, Canadian banks and London financiers were bound together in a web of interrelated investment activity.' Since the financial system in which British merchant banks like Glyn and Baring operated was locally developed, they could not dictate to it; rather, their options were to avoid it or cooperate with it. By the mid-1860s local politicians and administrators had fashioned a sufficient fiscal autonomy to give substance to the political devolution provided by the grant of responsible government.[10] In 1867 'the constitution of Canada, as it appears on the statute books of the British Parliament, had been designed to secure capital for the improvement of navigation and transport'. That design, as Harold Innis documented, was very much locally inspired and driven.[11]

7 J.B. Ingham, 'Power to the powerless: British North America and the pursuit of reciprocity, 1846–1854', *Bulletin of Canadian Studies*, 8 (Spring 1984), pp. 132–3. See also P. Baskerville, 'The pet bank, the local state and the imperial centre, 1850–1864', *Journal of Canadian Studies*, 20 (Fall 1985), pp. 22–46, and M.J. Piva, 'Financing the union: the Upper Canadian debt and financial administration in the Canadas, 1837–1845', ibid., 25 (Winter 1990–91), pp. 82–98, whose financial studies confirm the existence of considerable local initiative in shaping events.

8 W. Armstrong, 'The social origins of industrial growth: Canada, Argentina and Australia, 1870–1930', in D.C.M. Platt and G. di Tella (eds), *Argentina, Australia and Canada* (London, 1985), p. 81.

9 P. Buckner, 'Whatever happened to the British Empire?', *Journal of the Canadian Historical Association*, new ser., 4 (1993), p. 18.

10 W.L. Marr and D.G. Paterson, *Canada: An Economic History* (Toronto, 1980), pp. 243–5; P. Baskerville, 'Imperial agendas and "disloyal" collaborators: decolonization and the John Sandfield Macdonald ministries, 1862–1864', in D. Keane and C. Read (eds), *Old Ontario: Essays in Honour of J. M. S. Careless* (Toronto, 1990), pp. 236, 248.

11 H.A. Innis, *Essays in Canadian Economic History* (Toronto, 1956), quoted in C&H, I, p. 264; Buckner complains that the authors' work, 'a sophisticated form of economic reductionism, . . .

Coincidental with, and to some extent underpinning, the state's deliberate effort to integrate Canada into the world economy through a transport system geared to staple production, dynamic domestic development was under way. As early as the 1860s 'partial industrialization' – dairy processing and milling, farm equipment manufacture and small urban consumer industries – threw up 'a modern, wage-earning working class'. There evolved, as well, a social class made up of 'small businessmen, professionals and administrators' which minimized the need for external expertise.[12] Elements of this group invented or adapted technologies for extraction and processing or acquired the knowledge to run the latest sophisticated equipment imported from the US or Britain.[13] Put another way, Canada had substantial numbers of its own modernizers who proactively selected and used both the financial and the technical tools of empire.

High on the national ruling coalition's agenda was the establishment of its own dependent hinterland. Whether this initiative was 'a defensive reaction to the threat of the United States'[14] or reflected aggressive sub-imperialist ambitions or both, the objective was realized. A dependent hinterland also served the regional and class interests of central Canada, with which the state was closely identified.

Much is made by Cain and Hopkins of the financing of the Canadian-Pacific Railway (CPR) (C&H, I, pp. 268–9). That British, but not exclusively British, interests financed the ambitious undertaking and received lavish state subsidies is not disputed. But it was 'built ahead of demand for its services'. 'Since private interests expected the railway to yield relatively low internal rates of return over its early life, government aid was required to build the line.'[15] Meanwhile, Canadian investors were not overburdened by their government's debt load. They used their surplus capital to meet domestic demand triggered by partial industrialization for other important elements of infrastructure such as housing.

Once constructed, the railway provided the means to divert British capital on very advantageous terms and integrate the western hinterland into the central Canadian orbit. Development of the lead, silver and zinc lodes of the rugged Kootenay and Boundary area of British Columbia depended upon transportation. The geography of the remote region made it easy for branch

---

exaggerates the British role in bringing about Confederation' and provides evidence which contradicts their claim 'that Canada was dominated by British capitalists after 1867': Buckner, 'Whatever happened?', p. 14.

12 Armstrong, 'Social origins', pp. 82–3.

13 These developments can be traced in works of historical industrial archaeology. Cf. R. Pomfret, 'Mechanization of reaping in nineteenth-century Ontario: a case study of the pace and cause of the diffusion of embodied technical change', *Journal of Economic History*, 36 (1976), pp. 399–415; D. Newell, *Technology on the Frontier: Mining in Old Ontario* (Vancouver, 1986); J. Lutz, 'Losing steam: the boiler and engine industry as an index of British Columbia's deindustrialization, 1880–1915', *Canadian Historical Association Papers* (1988), pp. 168–208.

14 R. Pomfret, *The Economic Development of Canada* (Toronto and New York, 1984), p. 120.

15 Marr and Paterson, *Canada*, p. 324.

lines to enter the area from the US and the early phases of mining were carried out with American capital and expertise. Its full incorporation into an 'inland empire' based on Spokane was a distinct possibility. However, the CPR reached British Columbia in time to deflect this trend, and its branch lines brought other sources to influence the mining field's development. Though US capital was not entirely displaced, it came to play a less important role in the mines of the region.

Meanwhile, British capital came in. In the 1890s a substantial number of British investors had assets in British Columbia, obtained through trust companies which held shares in locally founded enterprises. Such mining trusts obtained properties at inflated prices from Canadian or US interests. They were given bad advice by their engineers, who were often ignorant of the characteristics of local ore bodies or engaged in speculation to advance their own income. For such reasons, British investors 'in Canadian mining . . . lost over $150 million between 1890 and 1914'.[16] Meanwhile, in the case of British Columbia, Canadian investment became pronounced and eastern Canadian control significant with the emergence of the Consolidated Mining and Smelting Company of Canada, a subsidiary of the CPR.[17] These shifts in transportation links, capital flows and corporate control secured the Kootenay region for the Montreal–Toronto metropole. They also ensured the viability of British Columbia, which in 1907 styled itself, appropriately enough, the 'Mineral Province of Canada'. The CPR, with its western terminus at tide water, also fuelled the ambitions of the Canadian metropole to fashion a presence in the Pacific. Canadian entrepreneurs, along with Australasian interests, pressured the British government to provide a substantial loan and subsidies to build and run the Pacific Cable, which opened in 1903.[18]

Canada emerged as a state that, through facilitating the transfer of capital and technology, assisted its own capitalist classes and thereby gained advantage from the impact of British and American imperialism, economic and political. Rising living standards were testimony to this reality and to the fact that the terms of capital borrowing and the uses to which that capital was put did not significantly accentuate elite advantages at the expense of marginalizing significant groups (with the exception of native Indians and Chinese migrants). At the same time a dynamic middle class, which had its origins in British migrants and their descendants adapting European values, skills and technology for the exploitation of local resources, fashioned a domestic economy.

---

16 D.G. Paterson, *British Direct Investment in Canada, 1890–1914: Estimates and Determinants* (Toronto, 1976), p. 102.
17 J. Mouat, 'Creating a new staple: capital, technology and monopoly in British Columbia's resource sector', *Journal of the Canadian Historial Association*, new ser., 1 (1990), pp. 215–37; *idem, Roaring Days: Rossland's Mines and the History of British Columbia* (Vancouver, 1995), pp. 130–50.
18 L.E. Davis and R.A. Huttenback, *Mammon and the Pursuit of Empire: The Political Economy of British Imperialism, 1860–1912* (Cambridge, 1986), p. 181; Treasury to Colonial Office, 28 April 1899, Public Record Office, T7/31, in which the Treasury reluctantly agrees to an imperial subsidy for an undertaking of 'much greater importance to Australia and Canada than to the United Kingdom'.

A synergy evolved between this domestic economy and the staple-led export economy, fostering diversification. The extraordinary wheat boom of the early twentieth century was balanced by other staples and a local demand for domestically produced goods which had been in place for decades.[19] Over the period 1850–1914, dependence on capital and technology sought out by collaborators transferred and created wealth as well as empowered the state. Choosing advantageous integration in the world economy, the Dominions minimized their dependence on the mother country. Significantly enough, Denoon's findings for settler societies in the southern hemisphere are replicated in the Canadian experience, that is in the northern hemisphere, and despite a hegemonically disposed neighbour.

THE AUSTRALIAN EXPERIENCE

Alfred Deakin, Laurier's counterpart in Australia and a heavyweight in British–Dominion relations, was out of office in 1911. In his place was Andrew Fisher, a former coalminer and union leader from Queensland who had emigrated from Scotland in 1885. Absolute majorities in both the House and the Senate made it 'the first time in the history of the world that a social-democratic party had achieved such a position'.[20] But as the creation of the Commonwealth a decade previously had shown, class priorities had not displaced regional and national objectives. Australia too had forged 'national coalitions' and variants of a liberal polity within a capitalist economy. But the Australian continent did not, of course, have a central state, either embryonic or in the making, when it became integrated into the world economy by wool and gold at mid-century. In the 1870s and 1880s Australia received significant additional inputs of capital, immigrants and technology.[21] Then there existed six colonies, some with tiny populations and all with small ones, most of whom lived in port cities, the rest in mining camps or on pastoral farms. All but Western Australia had obtained responsible government some time before. So here, as in Canada, the transfer of power had been substantial,[22] with the result that land policy, banking arrangements, railway developments, tariff arrangements and immigration policy were in the hands of local politicians elected on a broad-base franchise. These small, self-governing colonies, remote and insular, managed to dictate to a surprising degree the terms on which they received capital, immigrants and technology. For almost 20 years from 1873 the economies of these various states, and certainly those of the most populous, New South Wales and Victoria, featured remarkable growth. This growth was fuelled by a large infusion of British capital: some £150

19 C.B. Schedvin, 'Staples and regions of Pax Britannica', *Economic History Review*, 2nd ser., 43 (1990), p. 552.
20 R. Ward, *The History of Australia: The Twentieth Century, 1901–1975* (London, 1976), p. 76.
21 Schedvin, 'Staples and regions', pp. 536–45.
22 Cf. J.W. Cell, *British Colonial Administration in the Mid-Nineteenth Century: The Policy-Making Process* (New Haven, Conn., 1970), p. 212.

million in the 1880s. Two-thirds of this flowed into government loans and £50 million went to individuals and companies, particularly in mining and in land. State and private indebtedness grew accordingly in an orgy of speculation and overcapitalization. Public debt rose from £39 million to £194 million, or from £20 to £50 per head of population. Railways, telegraphs, gang ploughs, mechanical reapers, steam vessels, refrigeration were some of the tools transferred which allowed for increasing sheep and grain production and profitable access to core-state markets. Also, in the mining sector railways, telegraphs and chemical and metallurgical developments fostered 'the rush that never ended'.[23]

'Almost until 1890 there seemed to many to be no limit to Australia's progress though in fact it was a case of sowing the wind to reap the whirl-wind.'[24] The ensuing depression bottomed out in 1893–94, but recovery was slow. Eight years of drought and falls in commodity prices in world markets plagued the continent. While booms and busts were a function of a world economy in which Australians were increasingly involved, they were also a function of local decision-making[25] and climatic conditions. By taking advantage of core-state surpluses and needs, collaborators had transformed a group of weak and remote peripheral polities into dynamic, semi-peripheral entities. Colonial states and their capitalists and pastoralists also used core-state resources obtained on favourable terms to exploit hinterlands and outbacks.

Cain and Hopkins's exposition is sensitive to these developments. It sees, for example, the bust of the 1890s as 'internally generated rather than wilfully imposed from without'. But its aftermath witnessed, it is argued, 'the tightening of London's grip on colonial economic life' (C&H, I, p. 256). Thereafter Australians, apparently cowed by adversity, would heed conditions 'imposed from without'.

This assertion ignores what occurred in the mining sector of London's venture capital market. The Western Australian gold-mining boom saw speculators conducting gambling operations 'on a huge scale'. Though the Coolgardie–Kalgoorlie fields yielded much gold, the mines were used 'as speculative counters rather than business units. . . . As a result of such conditions of the c. 500 mines in which British investors were interested only 14 paid dividends in 1898 and 23 in 1899'.[26]

But if London promoters made the market, it was Australian-based claim or mine owners who often benefited. A Melbourne syndicate made a 'fantastic profit'[27] selling out its control of gold-bearing property on the Coolgardie

23 Cf. G. Blainey, *The Rush That Never Ended: A History of Australian Mining*, 3rd edn (Melbourne, 1978).
24 A.G.L. Shaw, *The Story of Australia*, 4th edn (London, 1972), p. 151.
25 '. . . the critical decisions in capital formation and in the orientation of the economy were taken in Australia, by Australians and in the light of Australian experience': N.G. Butlin, *Investment in Australian Economic Development, 1861–1900* (Cambridge, 1964), p. 5; cf. L. Trainor, *British Imperialism and Australian Nationalism: Manipulation, Conflict and Compromise in the Late Nineteenth Century* (Cambridge, 1994), pp. 3, 120–9, 179–80.
26 A.R. Hall, *The London Capital Market and Australia, 1870–1914* (Canberra, 1963), p. 177.
27 Blainey, *The Rush*, p. 176.

field. Other reefs or lodes pegged by local prospectors yielded no gold, but they gave them ample opportunity to exploit the Westralian boom at the expense of overseas investors. In London, the financial press complained,

> the ordinary investor is rapidly coming to the conclusion that the mines, rich as some of them undoubtedly are, are not being worked in the interests of their rightful owners, the shareholders, but that the latter are being made the cat'a-paws of sharpers, not only in the markets, but among the very officials who are paid to serve the shareholders' interests.[28]

Melbourne's streets were not lined with gold, but its suburbs were adorned with palatial houses belonging to Victoria's equivalent of the US robber barons.

If, as Cain and Hopkins suggest, Whitehall favoured the needs of financiers at the expense of industrialists, the latter's opportunities were limited by the needs of Australia's economy. Armstrong notes the phenomenon of partial industrialization occurring here, though at a later date than in Canada.[29] Opportunities for the import of British manufactures were limited not only by pro-tectionist measures but also by the modest requirements of pastoral production specifically and the relatively primitive stage of development generally outside urban centres. Here, where comparative advantage operated, demand was met by local 'small-scale enterprises employing simple technologies'.[30]

Meanwhile, the federation movement gained momentum, enabling Aus-tralians to save themselves from their own excesses, mediate class antagonisms and defuse colonial rivalries. They also sought to be better positioned to obtain credit ratings in London's money market through the solidities of a central government. But the local constitution-makers were so little concerned with placating Britain's gentlemanly capitalists that they chose to adapt ele-ments of US federalism. Joseph Chamberlain, the British colonial secretary, tried without success to provide special protection in the Commonwealth constitution for British investors in the Western Australian goldfields.[31] The remarks of Richard Gardiner Casey, a self-made Australian entrepreneur who was in London at the turn of the century seeking finance to restructure a pastoral enterprise, are instructive of what had come to pass. He deliberately stopped negotiating with the representatives of bondholders, concluding: 'I think this did good, as it showed I did not mean to be unduly squeezed.' Subsequently the bondholders' representatives were 'very civil and conciliat-ory'. The reconstructed company with Casey as its chair paid dividends of up to 20 per cent on the eve of the First World War.[32]

28 *Investors' Monthly Manual, 1900*, p. 503, quoted in Hall, *London Capital*, p. 178.
29 Armstrong, 'Social origins', p. 91.
30 S. Macintyre, *The Oxford History of Australia*, Vol. IV, *1901–1942: The Succeeding Age* (Mel-bourne and Oxford, 1986); Denoon, *Settler Capitalism*, pp. 213, 223, notes that the settler colonies failed to follow the US example of diversification in their preoccupation with staple exports; perhaps they were pursuing the rewards of comparative advantage.
31 J. La Nauze, *The Making of the Australian Constitution* (Melbourne, 1972), pp. 259–60.
32 Macintyre, *Oxford History*, IV, p. 5.

No 'national coalition' or left-leaning party governed South Africa in 1911. Rather, a Transvaal-based political party led by the former Afrikaner generals, Louis Botha and Jan Smuts, formed the government, having won the unitary state's first election the previous year. A party identified with mining capital, which had profoundly shaped the country's industrial development, formed the offical opposition. Meanwhile, the gold-mining companies had struggled. As a senior partner in the most important mining house observed, 'the fact is, South African mines are a dead letter and nobody wants to touch them'. A pleasant, though wishful thought, he added, was that the South African government would nationalize them.[33] Britain had won the South African War, but from the view of imperialists such as Alfred, Lord Milner, it had lost the peace.[34] In the process finance capital had not been advantaged. To explore the reasons for these developments we turn to Sir Edward Hamilton, 'the Gladstonian Under-Secretary at the Treasury'.[35]

This well-placed Whitehall official with access to the City, having dined with Alfred Rothschild in late August 1899 as the South African crisis was about to erupt into war, observed: 'He and Natty [Rothschild] are most strong about keeping the peace. They had telegraphed this latest news from Pretoria to [Joseph] Chamberlain and also to Arthur Balfour.' Chamberlain, in a note to the Rothschilds which Hamilton saw and considered 'a distinct snub', made it clear 'that he would prefer not having their unofficial communications from Pretoria'.[36] Is this a case of the Birmingham-based Colonial Secretary representing industrial capital overriding the dictates of finance capital as represented by the Rothschilds? If so, it would challenge Cain and Hopkins's argument. But Chamberlain and his brother had invested in South African gold mines. They were therefore not disinterested parties when it came to mining profits and were likely to be sensitive to the effect that political crises had on stock market behaviour. Moreover, they must have understood that much of the capital which went into mines paid for much expensive British-made equipment.

In setting out the historiographical debate, Cain and Hopkins observe:

> At one extreme [is] . . . the interpretation, formulated by Hobson, that events in southern Africa were driven by a conspiracy of financiers who hijacked the apparatus of state power in the interests of private profit; at the other extreme is the view that agents of the state on the periphery of empire

---

33 F. Eckstein, 3 Oct. 1913, Barlow Rand Archives, Johannesburg.
34 L. Thompson, *The Unification of South Africa, 1902–1910* (Oxford, 1960), pp. 16–17.
35 Cf. C&H, I, p. 152. Hamilton, who fits their discussion of gentlemanly capitalism and the links which existed between Whitehall and the City, disliked the policies of Chamberlain, the Birmingham-based Colonial Secretary, but also his social position and temperament. 'He', concluded Hamilton, 'was not born, bred or educated in the ways which alone secure the necessary tact and behaviour of a real gentleman' (diary entry, 3 Dec. 1899, British Library, Add. MS 48675).
36 Diary entries, 24 and 25 Aug. 1899, British Library, Add. MS 48675.

harnessed both Whitehall and the mine-owners for their own (greater or lesser) ends.

(C&H, I, p. 370)

Having made this distinction they follow the work of radical or neo-Marxist analysis without making it clear that such analysis assumes that the changing needs of Eurocentric capitalism drove imperial activity. That part of the so-called liberal school of South African historiography advocating central push factors is also emphasized, rather than those elements stressing peripheral pulls.[37]

The analysis also does not sufficiently differentiate between the sources of mining capital or establish fully the motives of those who assembled it. The authors minimize the importance of French and German capital in the forma-tion of De Beers Consolidated and Rand undertakings. The architect of the Corner House, the dominant gold-mining house, which had raised most of its capital in France and Germany and whose major subsidiary was realizing huge profits, neither demanded nor required intervention in the Transvaal state.[38] Representatives of this foreign capital wanted less but got more imperial state intervention.

A third limitation of the authors' approach is to give insufficient emphasis to the transformation wrought by South Africa's mining revolution. Before the mining boom began in the 1870s, South Africa was integrated into the world economy through the staple wool. A banking structure with attending credit facilities evolved – 23 banks by 1860, mostly in the Cape, with total assets of £1.3 million. But the region's population of European descent was very small, and parts of it were only marginally integrated into the world economy and were little supplemented by the immigrants who were. Its sub-stantial native peoples were even more isolated. Thus on the eve of the mining boom South Africa was partly in the peripheral stage and partly outside the orbit of the world economy. As such it was much less developed than either the Australian or Canadian colonies.

Transformation through mining featured three significant developments. Exploitation of gold and diamonds after the mid-1880s used sophisticated,

37 See, for example, the radical work of R.V. Turrell, *Capital and Labour on the Kimberley Diamond Fields, 1871–1890* (Cambridge, 1987); and J.J. Van-Helten, 'The Rothschilds, the Exploration Company, and mining finance', *Business History*, 28 (1986), pp. 181–205; the liberal, metropolitan-centred analysis of A. Porter, *The Origins of the South African War: Joseph Chamberlain and the Diplomacy of Imperialism, 1895–1899* (Manchester, 1980); and the liberal approach with a peripheral emphasis of A.J. Jeeves, 'The Rand capitalists and the coming of the South African War, 1896–1899', *Canadian Historical Association Papers* (1973), pp. 61–83, as well as D.M. Schreuder, *The Scramble for Southern Africa, 1877–1895* (Cambridge, 1980), and R.I. Rotberg, *The Founder: Cecil Rhodes and the Pursuit of Power* (New York, 1988); see also note 39 below.
38 War, observed Julius Wernher, would be a 'great misfortune' and a guarantee of independence for the Transvaal a necessity. Quoted in R. Kubicek, *Economic Imperialism in Theory and Practice: The Case of South Africa Gold Mining Finance, 1886–1914* (Durham, NC, 1979), p. 72. Also see R. Kubicek, 'Mining: patterns of dependence and development, 1870–1930', in Z.A. Konczacki, J.L. Parpart and T.M. Shaw (eds), *Studies in the Economic History of Southern Africa* (London, 1991), II, p. 81.

extensive technology and was, therefore, capital-intensive. Secondly, mining capital was highly speculative, volatile and crooked. Despite the potential of the gold reefs to be exploited as long-lived industrial concerns based on a stable price for the product, much financing and profit-taking was speculative. Insider traders made enormous fortunes but many investors in Europe lost heavily. Thirdly, the industry had access to cheap labour which was mobilized through precedents already established in subsistence and commercial agriculture. Moreover, Africans denied the peasant option by white agricultural and pastoral activity were bundled into migratory labour systems. In South Africa, then, a staple-led development with unique characteristics unleashed major social and economic discontinuities which had fostered political instability.

After starting on the process of decolonization with a grant of responsible government to the Cape in 1872, and despite backing off after the first South African War, the imperial state did not relinquish, and, indeed, for a time intensified, its interventionist strategy. By 1907, however, it resumed what it had started in 1872 with grants of responsible government to the Transvaal and the Orange Free State. In the interim, intervention intensified because of the gold-mining industry, though the links of cause and effect are not to be found in the conspiracy theories of the Hobsonites, as Cain and Hopkins make clear. But neither are they to be found in proactive, metropolitan-based impulses. The authors go some distance towards recognizing peripheral discontinuities when they observe: 'The discovery of gold gave the [Transvaal] Republic the resources to underwrite its political independence, and the Boer leaders, headed by Kruger, took the opportunity to embark on a programme of modernisation and expansion' (C&H, I, p. 374). But they underestimate the extent of the peripheral disequilibriums unleashed. One of these featured the local nexus of economic and political power shifting from the Cape Town–Kimberley to the Pretoria–Johannesburg axis. In Canada and Australia after 1870, economic development within the world system did not redistribute power locally. Rather, in the case of Canada, the Montreal–Toronto axis of central Canadian dominance was strengthened, while in Australia, the dominance Melbourne and Sydney exerted on their hinterlands was also reinforced.

In South Africa, the Transvaal, once a bankrupt polity, fed on the revenues derived from gold-mining to pursue a policy of economic nationalism. It granted local concessions to provide the mines with materials like explosives, obtained loans to finance building its outlet to the sea at Delegoa Bay so that the Cape and Natal could be bypassed, pursued territorial expansion (i.e. Swaziland) and built up a formidable armoury. The mining houses' financiers found the Transvaal state's policies and administrative practices bothersome but tolerable. To some extent they fell in with the imperial factor's initiatives, though Milner never thought that what he called 'money bags' could be trusted.[39]

The Cape, increasingly denied its sub-imperialist ambitions, enlisted core-state support for its designs. Cecil Rhodes was a Rand mine controller but he

39 C. Headlam (ed.), The Milner Papers, 1931–33, I, pp. 324–5.

was also a Cape politician and capitalist.[40] In supporting its client, Britain hoped to curtail the ambitions of other core-states in southern Africa, notably Germany, which was challenging its hegemonic position, and with whom relations were increasingly antagonistic. Gold-mining upset the local distribution of political power and thwarted the ambitions of the Cape, the imperial state's client.

CONCLUSION

If the world capitalist system could integrate the staple-led economies of Canada and Australia into its orbit with considerable material advantage to the 'semi-peripheral' states and without major discontinuities and decreasing imperial state interventions, why did it not duplicate the feat in South Africa? Here there were massive discontinuities, major interventions and disappointing material development. If metropolitan money markets, stock markets and financial institutions had the clout and vision Cain and Hopkins claim for them, then one should be struck by the similarities in peripheral developments evolving in the settlement colonies. The migrants, capital and technology and political forms that were available to them in the last half of the century were quite similar. However, their physical characteristics, demographic patterns and political cultures were different, with the result that different mixes of factors of production were imported and with different results.

Edward Hamilton's preferences rather than Joseph Chamberlain's policies may have been a more accurate reflection of those most influential in setting imperial priorities. After all, Hamilton and his Treasury colleagues got away with very uncivil servant-like interventions in the political process of blocking Chamberlain's attempt to introduce imperial preference.[41] Ironically, Chamberlain's efforts to elicit substantial imperial funding to provide infrastructure in the dependent tropical empire so as to entice private financial capital were thwarted by the Treasury.[42] But it is also problematic that Britain pursued effectively either the strategy of the civil servant, representing gentlemanly capitalists, or of the Colonial Secretary, the embodiment of industrial interests, in relations with settler societies. The settlement empire had opted for protection against British as well as foreign imports.[43]

40 Cf. C. Newbury, 'Out of the pit: the capital accumulation of Cecil Rhodes', *Journal of Imperial and Commonwealth History*, 10 (1981), p. 40: 'Rhodes' career was that of a colonial entrepreneur with political and sub-imperial ambitions for developing and stabilising the hinterland of the Cape and Natal. . . . There is [an] attempt on Rhodes' part to use the metropolitan office and the profitable accumulation of funds from marketing and stocking diamonds for strictly regional and local purposes in ways that were increasingly at variance with the interests of smaller and larger stockholders in Europe.'
41 R. Kubicek, *The Administration of Imperialism: Joseph Chamberlain at the Colonial Office* (Durham, NC, 1969), pp. 167–71.
42 P.T. Marsh, *Joseph Chamberlain: Entrepreneur in Politics* (New Haven, Conn., 1994), p. 413.
43 C&H, I, pp. 209–25, sort out the attitudes of British industrial and financial interests to Chamberlain's proposal. Also see the definitive work on Chamberlain's career on this point: Marsh, *Chamberlain*, pp. 596–7.

By 1911, Canadians and Australians collaborated from positions of some strength when it came to dealing with the structures and emissaries of British imperialism. The degree of autonomy they enjoyed in that relationship was a function of political disengagements through responsible government. But several other factors contributed as well. The way their economies had become integrated into an international system fostered economic development. Their social classes controlled and decided upon the transfer of capital and technology much more extensively than in other colonial situations where expatriates made the running.[44] This locally inspired transfer allowed for economies that could provide inputs for staple production and substitutes for imports. Even South Africa, with much of its domestic economy marginalized and its staple-led industry dependent on foreign capital, pursued a programme of economic nationalism.

The three settler Dominions examined here have been included in a number of recent comparative studies which have probed their relationship with British imperialism in the late nineteenth century.[45] Two of them, Australia and South Africa, as noted previously, were examined by Denoon as part of a comparative study of particular relevance to a study of the work before us. Cain and Hopkins, with an approach that is metropolitan based, are inclined to accept what the official mind thought was or should be happening abroad.[46] And the conclusions reached stress peripheral dependence. Where the approach has been to factor in the dynamics of settler societies, in terms of both class and capital formation, conclusions arrived at emphasize peripheral autonomy and locally stimulated expansionary forces. Denoon, for example, in stressing the need to fathom the workings of dominant local social classes, concludes that these discovered that 'British dominance was . . . compatible with a wide autonomy and considerable prosperity'. Accepting their assessment of the relationship, he concludes that 'the external dependency of these societies remained essentially a matter of self-regulation, although the machinery became increasingly complex and subtle'.[47] Regulating one's dependency may seem to be a contradiction in terms. But from the vantage point of Montreal and Toronto, or Melbourne and Sydney, or Cape Town and Johannesburg, Westminster,

44 Cf. D. Headrick, *The Tentacles of Progress: Technology Transfer in the Age of Imperialism, 1850–1940* (New York, 1988), pp. 380–4, who makes the point that peoples in the tropical empires of Europe seldom controlled industrial technologies transferred, to the disadvantage of their development.
45 Cf. Denoon, *Settler Capitalism*; Platt and di Tella, *Argentina, Australia and Canada*; K.A. MacKirdy, 'Conflict of loyalties: the problem of assimilating the Far Wests into the Canadian and Australian federations', *Canadian Historical Review*, 33 (1951); and D.K. Fieldhouse, 'For richer, for poorer?', in P.J. Marshall (ed.), *Cambridge Illustrated History of the British Empire* (Cambridge, 1996), pp. 108–46.
46 Cf. the distinction made between motives and causes by R. Robinson in his 'Explanation' in the 2nd edn of *Africa and the Victorians* (London, 1981), pp. ix–xxiii, and the important critique by A.G. Hopkins, 'The Victorians and Africa: a reconsideration of the occupation of Egypt, 1882', *Journal of African History*, 27 (1986), p. 391, where 'it is argued . . . that the causes of intervention lay in the metropole rather than on the periphery'.
47 Denoon, *Settler Capitalism*, pp. 223, 229.

Whitehall and the City were providing very good service. The metropole had enabled the peripheral settlement empire polities to serve themselves.

Cain and Hopkins's construction of metropolitan economic elements is particularly engaging because these are developed in an analysis that pays a good deal of attention not only to Britain's political dynamics but also to its social and regional characteristics. When it comes to positioning the periphery, in this case the settlement empire, in their analysis, the task is not done with the same consistency and thoroughness. The colonists' objectives and their equivalent of the official mind is then not sufficiently articulated to grasp the full range of actions and attitudes of the imperial relationship.

CHAPTER 5

British financial imperialism after the First World War

ANGELA REDISH

This chapter examines British financial imperialism in the twentieth century from the vantage point of the provocative hypotheses put forward by Cain and Hopkins in *British Imperialism*.[1] As described in more detail in chapter 3 of this volume, their central hypothesis is that the financial sector accounted for a considerable share of the economic growth of the British economy, and was the driving force behind British imperialism. They argue that 'gentleman capitalists' (perhaps a more accurate term than 'gentlemanly capitalists') controlled economic policy (and specifically imperial policy) and ensured that it served the ends of the service (especially financial) sector rather than the industrial sector. In the second volume a major sub-thesis is that imperialism was far more vital in the inter-war period than the conventional wisdom asserts, and that the gentlemen capitalists retained control of policy-making.[2] Cain and Hopkins argue that the introduction of central banks and of financial orthodoxy in the countries of the empire, as well as the development of the Sterling Area, reflected the strength of imperialism, and specifically financial imperialism, in the inter-war period. They conclude (C&H, II, p. 265) by arguing that the 'gentlemanly capitalists' maintained control over economic policy in the post-Second World War period and oversaw the demise of the empire, a demise that was in part determined by the declining relevance of the empire for the strength of sterling.

An appraisal of these hypotheses must begin with an evaluation of the definition of imperialism, and I begin by discussing the Cain and Hopkins definition, its applicability in the twentieth century, and its ability to generate testable hypotheses. I then examine the key policies of inter-war financial imperialism, drawing primarily on the Canadian experience, and briefly

---

1 P.J. Cain and A.G. Hopkins, *British Imperialism*, Vol. I: *Innovation and Expansion, 1688–1914*; Vol. II: *Crisis and Deconstruction, 1914–1990* (both London, 1993), hereafter cited as C&H, I/II.
2 'Britain remained a dynamic power, . . . [with a] . . . strikingly successful record in upholding British interests throughout the world' (II, pp. 3–4).

discuss Cain and Hopkins's treatment of the immediate postwar period. My analysis leads me in part to challenge Cain and Hopkins's conclusions; but I do not question their mastery of the source materials, nor of the political and economic history of the British Empire.

THE NATURE OF FINANCIAL IMPERIALISM

Cain and Hopkins define imperialism by stating (I, p. 43) that it 'involves an incursion, or an attempted incursion, into the sovereignty of another state', typically justified by a belief in the incursor's ideological and material superiority.[3] This intervention may or may not be successful, and it may or may not include the collaboration of colonial residents. Cain and Hopkins contrast and compare imperialism to an alternative policy regime (or counterfactual world) characterized by the mutual compromises that identify economic interdependence based on equality. Yet rarely is this counterfactual analysis made explicit, implying that the specific contribution of imperialist policies is often hard to identify. Specification of a counterfactual is always hard, and the problem with this one is its vagueness and the difficulty one might have in operationalizing it. For economists, the usual counterfactual is a 'perfectly competitive market system', which makes tractable, as Lance Davis has shown, major questions such as how far did 'imperialism' give the British, or some classes in Britain, advantages they would not have received under a free market system?

As Lance Davis (this volume) notes, Cain and Hopkins's definition of imperialism implies that the imperialist has some advantageous source of coercive power, either explicitly, through military intimidation, or implicitly, through colonial collaboration.[4] Military power would give the imperialist the leverage to extract resources in excess of those that would be obtained under a market system either through use of direct policies such as taxation and purchasing policies or by enabling industries (financial or goods) to have a monopoly in colonial markets and thereby to earn returns in excess of the market level.

Collaboration might occur if a colonial political elite existed and hoped to share in the excess returns at the expense of the rest of the colonial population, or because collaboration would be for the general public good of the colony. The latter is particularly relevant to the issue of financial imperialism. Cain and Hopkins argue that the main objective of the British imperialist was to expand opportunities for British investors. Unlike the goods trade, where exchange is simultaneous, the essence of debt contracts is that the lender promises to repay at some *future* time. In domestic lending a web of institutions has arisen to raise the probability that borrowers will repay their debts, or, at the very least, will not borrow fraudulently. These institutions, which

3 Cf. their argument (p. 263) that imperialists in China justified their intervention by reference to the 'duties and burdens of the civilizing mission.'
4 'An empire without coercion is hardly an empire at all.'

may infringe on an individual's sovereignty, nonetheless have the advantage that they enable the borrower to obtain funds. Thus, at least *ex ante*, these institutions and contractual arrangements are in the borrower's interest; and, of course, the borrower need not borrow if he/she finds the conditions too onerous.

In the international sphere, particularly prior to the Second World War, there were no such institutions. If the debtor could not commit to repay, then there would be no loan; and the more credible the commitment, the lower the risk premium and, also, the interest rate on the loan. There are a variety of ways whereby a creditor can ensure repayment, the easiest of which may be to lend to those who will want to borrow in the future (a 'repeated game' in economists' parlance) – then the threat of 'denying future loans' may be sufficient incentive to guarantee payment of the current one. Now, an alternative source of commitment to repay might require the borrower to surrender some sovereignty. This might be imperialistic, but it would not necessarily be exploitative since the colony as well as the imperial government would gain, in the sense of being better off than under a free market system.

Let me turn now to the question of the success of financial imperialism in the inter-war period. As Davis points out in Chapter 3 of the present volume, Britain's ability to enforce imperial policies by military force, at least in the self-governing Dominions (and certainly by the twentieth century), was virtually non-existent. Furthermore, while studies of nineteenth-century Canada argue that a small collaborating landed elite (similar to Britain's 'gentlemanly capitalists') dominated mid-nineteenth-century policy-making,[5] there is little evidence of such an elite holding political power in the twentieth century. In his pioneering study of Canadian society, Porter found that only 16 per cent of the Canadian political elite between 1940 and 1960 came from families in which previous generations had occupied elite roles in any sphere.[6]

Where then was the source of the power for British imperialism in Canada? Cain and Hopkins do not clarify this, and their careful examination of the inter-war experiences of a variety of countries reinforces the more traditional view among economic historians that Britain was on the defensive in this period. This should not come as a surprise. With the important exception of the dependent empire, a central source for Britain's power over the debtor nations was her ability to refuse future credits. Her net debtor position after 1914 removed that source of power and gave new financial power to the Dominions.

---

5 See especially Baskerville (1990) and Piva (1990–1). For a more sceptical analysis, arguing that such a view 'distorts the complexities of colonial politics and ignores the non-economic factors' in the relationship between Canada and Britain, see Buckner (1993), 17.

6 John Porter, *The Vertical Mosaic* (Toronto, 1965), p. 394. Expanding his analysis to include 'upper-class origins', Porter finds that 24 per cent of the political elite came from the upper class, in contrast to the economic elite, of whom about 50 per cent had upper-class origins. See Peter Newman, *The Canadian Establishment* (Toronto, 1975) for a detailed study of the economic elite.

CENTRAL BANKING

A significant fraction of the evidence used by Cain and Hopkins to demonstrate the ability of the City of London-based gentlemanly capitalists to manipulate policy revolves around the interrelated issues of debt default, exchange rates and central banks in the inter-war period. Specifically, London wanted the Dominions not to default on debt, to fix their exchange rates to sterling, to keep short-term balances in London, and to establish central banks along the lines of the Bank of England – independent of the government but with a conservative mandate, that is, a desire to follow the above policies.

Let me begin with the question of central banks. Cain and Hopkins argue (II, p. 66) that the Bank of England promoted the establishment of 'clones' of itself throughout the world. They mean clones in the sense of banks which had a monopoly over the issue of bank notes and which were simultaneously independent from the government and yet also the government's trusted financial advisor. The implication is that such institutions would be advocates of sound finance: that is, they would support membership in the Sterling Area and the avoidance of debt default.

There is considerable evidence of British attempts (mostly successful) to do this. At League of Nations conferences in Brussels (1920) and Genoa (1922) representatives of the British government advocated the establishment of central banks and cooperation between them. The declared motive was European worries about an imminent shortage of world gold. British and other delegates argued that only by centralizing reserves and using a reserve currency could the deflationary effects of such a shortage be prevented. In many respects this recommendation was the logical successor to the substitution of paper money for gold in domestic economies. Indeed, the delegates at the Brussels conference called for the establishment of an international central bank, a prelude to the establishment of the International Monetary Fund following the Second World War.[7]

The three relevant challenges to Cain and Hopkins here are, first, whether British involvement was critical in the establishment of central banks overseas; second, the extent to which such banks benefited Great Britain and exploited the empire countries; and third, the reasons why such countries would permit the presence of institutions that reduced their welfare. Let me address this issue by answering these questions in the case of Canada, and return below to what generalizations can be made from this special case.

In 1930 Canada was one of the few members of the world economy that did not have a central bank. In 1914 the Federal Reserve system was established in the US, and in the 1920s similar central banking systems were set up in Chile, Columbia, Peru and Ecuador.[8] By 1930 only Canada, Italy, Argentina

---

7 Barry Eichengreen, *Golden Fetters* (Oxford, 1992), p. 155.
8 C.H. Kisch and W.A. Elkins, *Central Banks* (London, 1930), p. 8. As Cain and Hopkins note, the South American banks were set up largely at the instigation of the US and by the missionary work of Kemmerer. Whether this was to establish a dollar bloc to offset British influence is not dealt with in the book.

and Ireland remained without a central banking institution. It must be remembered, of course, that all these economies operated in a world of commodity money, the gold standard. Thus while today we think of central banks as essential national monetary institutions because they issue the legal tender of the country, even in the inter-war period the monetary base was gold.[9]

There were occasional early suggestions in Canada that a central bank would be a useful institutional innovation. For example, in 1914 (the same year that the Federal Reserve system was introduced in the USA), two prominent bankers advocated the establishment of a Canadian central bank. However, it was argued that the Fed was necessitated by the specific (bizarre) US banking institutions – unit banks and bank notes that were required to be backed by government securities, not the general assets of the banks. Again, in 1923, when the Home Bank failed, some Canadians argued for an institution to regulate banks and especially the note issue.[10]

In spite of this, the functions of a central bank were not totally lacking in Canada. The Finance Department operated a discount window of sorts (under an amendment to the Finance Act of 1923), and the government had a monopoly of issue of notes less than $5 (Dominion Notes). However, the chartered banks issued notes of higher denominations, and in 1930 bank notes represented 5 per cent of chartered bank liabilities and demand and time deposits represented 20 per cent and 47 per cent respectively.[11]

Little serious attention was paid to the question of establishing a central bank in Canada until the Depression in the early 1930s. In February 1932 Prime Minister Bennett raised the idea, and in March 1933 the government proposed a royal commission to 'consider the arguments for and against a central banking institution'. The appointment of Lord Macmillan (a well-known proponent of central banks) to chair the commission, together with the appointment of Sir Charles Addis, a former director of the Bank of England, as one of the five commissioners, suggests that the outcome was predetermined. In September 1933 the commission reported in favour of the establishment of a Bank of Canada; and in November 1933 the Prime Minister announced his intention of accepting the recommendation. The Bank of Canada thus began operations in 1934.

Did imperial policy play a crucial role in the establishment of the bank? The evidence suggests that the views of the British gentlemen capitalists were influential rather than critical. The royal commission appears to have been the brainchild of Prime Minister Bennett alone. In a now famous explanation for the establishment of the commission, he stated:

9 This is not the same thing as saying that gold was the dominant medium of exchange – central bank notes and demand deposits at private banks were frequently more widely used, just as today, when central bank liabilities (notes and deposits) form the monetary base but represent only a fraction of the money supply – in Canada 10 per cent of M2.
10 George S. Watts, *The Bank of Canada* (Ottawa, 1993), p. 6.
11 *Canada Gazette* (Ottawa, Feb. 1930).

I learned to my surprise that there was no direct means of settling international balances between Canada and London, that the only medium was New York, and the value of the Canadian dollar would have to be determined in Wall Street. I made up my mind then and there that this country was going to have a central bank because there must be some financial institution that can with authority do business for the whole of the Dominion with the other nations of the World. If Canada was to be financially independent there had to be a means of determining balances, of settling international accounts and a central bank would furnish this.[12]

There is additional evidence of the importance of nationalistic feelings in the 1930s and of a desire to create sovereign institutions.[13] The other influence, which became more obvious as the commission travelled across the country hearing evidence from witnesses on the state of the monetary system, was the need for a political response to the economic hardship of the Depression. Ironically, a central bank was advocated both by those promoting financial orthodoxy, such as bureaucrats and academic economists, and those favouring an unorthodox expansionist monetary policy, such as prairie populists (read debtors).[14]

Emphasis on the nature of the testimony before the royal commission probably overstates domestic influences, however. The make-up of the committee virtually preordained its findings, as suggested by the following comment by the president of the Canadian Bankers' Association in August 1933: 'Confidentially, I think it was decided before Lord Macmillan left London that some kind of a central organization should be established in Canada.'[15]

What about the ability of the bank to deliver benefits to the imperial power, possibly at the expense of the Canadian economy? I discuss below the roots of Canadian financial orthodoxy in the inter-war period, and here simply note that the Bank of Canada had little influence. In fact, the bank exercised surprisingly little influence on the economy. An econometric analysis by Bordo and Redish on the influence of the establishment of the bank demonstrates that it had 'virtually no macroeconomic impact'.[16] This conclusion is consistent with the governor's annual reports of his activities between 1935 and 1939. Graham Towers stated that there was no direct connection between the

---

12 Cited in Milton L. Stokes, *The Bank of Canada* (Toronto, 1939), p. 65.
13 For example, the national airline (now Air Canada) was established in 1937 and the forerunner of the Canadian Broadcasting Company was established in 1932. Donald Creighton, *Canada's First Century* (Toronto, 1970), p. 227.
14 The only group systematically opposed to the establishment of a central bank was the association of the large chartered banks.
15 Cited in Michael D. Bordo and Angela Redish, 'Why did the Bank of Canada emerge in 1935?', *Journal of Economic History*, 47/2 (June 1987), p. 417. Also, in August a newspaper report stated that eastern financial circles were taking it for granted that a central bank would be created and that the banks would lose their rights to note issue (Vancouver *Sun*, 11 Aug. 1933).
16 Bordo and Redish, 'The Bank of Canada', p. 414.

level of income and the stock of money; and that the level of the exchange rate reflected institutional arrangements and that the bank rate was 'not at present of any significance'![17]

This discussion of the establishment of the Bank of Canada represents only one data point, but it does highlight two areas where I would like to have seen more analysis by Cain and Hopkins. Firstly, it suggests that a greater role was played by decision-makers at 'the periphery', that is, by the nationals of the empire/Commonwealth countries broadly defined. While the gentlemanly capitalists of the City of London may have wanted a central bank in Canada, it was the Dominion government that was the crucial player. Secondly, I would like to have seen more discussion of, and explicit testing of hypotheses concerning, the political and financial channels whereby imperial policy benefited the imperial power at the cost of the periphery.

THE STERLING AREA

A considerable part of Cain and Hopkins's argument for the renewed vitality of inter-war imperialism relies on the significance of the Sterling Area, and they consequently discuss in great detail the policies taken to enhance the sterling bloc. Yet the weaker part of the case concerns the significance of the bloc. What did Britain get out of the sterling bloc? Again the appropriate measure is the counterfactual, and the relevant counterfactual is not described by Cain and Hopkins, nor is it easy to define.

I begin with the easier question of what the sterling bloc was. The bloc included a group of countries – most of the British Empire, Scandinavia, the Baltic states and Portugal, Iraq, Egypt and Siam. While several characteristics of sterling bloc countries are given – they used sterling as a reserve asset, and were 'heavily dependent on the British market' – the exclusion of Canada from the bloc implies that its defining characteristic was fixing the currency in terms of the pound sterling. How did this benefit Britain? Cain and Hopkins do not make this clear, and it is not obvious. Firstly, it would have helped to have data on series of exchange rates. The authors state that one of the bloc's triumphs was to force South Africa off gold (C&H, II, p. 133), but many countries went off gold and depreciated their currency before October 1931, and after October 1931 maintained a lower exchange rate with sterling than before 1929 (see Table 5.1 below).

Economists are divided on the potential impact of currency devaluation. Changes in nominal exchange rates (e.g. \$/£) will not change the real exchange rate (the nominal exchange rate multiplied by the domestic price level (£/gd), divided by the foreign price level (\$/gd)) if domestic prices rise by the amount of the devaluation, and in consequence the depreciation will not increase domestic competitiveness. Beenstock, Capie and Griffiths have argued

17 Bank of Canada, *Annual Report* (Ottawa, 1935), p. 16.

TABLE 5.1

EXCHANGE RATE BEHAVIOUR IN THE STERLING AREA

	Date of abandonment of gold standard	Exchange rate in Dec. 1932 (1929 = 100)
Australia	Mar. 1930	53.8
New Zealand	Aug. 1930	61.5
United Kingdom	Sept. 1931	67.4
Sweden	Sept. 1931	66.8
Denmark	Sept. 1931	63.5
Norway	Sept. 1931	63.0
Malaya	Sept. 1931	67.0
India	Sept. 1931	67.9
Canada	Oct. 1931★	77.6
Portugal	Oct. 1931	68.2
Finland	Oct. 1931	56.5
Siam	June 1932	67.9
Union of South Africa	Jan. 1933	100.0

★ Canada unofficially abandoned the gold standard in August 1929, but the exchange rate remained at the 1925 par until October 1931.
Source: League of Nations Economic Intelligence Service, Monetary Review (Geneva), 1936–37, p. 112; with the exception of Canada, see Federal Reserve Bulletin.

that such price increases occurred in Britain in the 1930s, while Eichengreen and Sachs dispute this result.[18]

While the sterling bloc as strictly defined may not have been a source of imperial success, perhaps a more widely defined bloc was. That is, imperial benefit or advantage might be measured by the extent to which empire countries followed financial orthodoxy, in the specific sense that they continued to repay their debts in the face of dramatic reductions in the incentives to do so. In the late nineteenth century financial imperialism particularly involved Britain's position as a net creditor, and imperial policy referred to making sure the loans were safe. The First World War changed market conditions in two fundamental ways: by impoverishing Britain it stopped the flow of repeat loans, thus removing one incentive to repay the old loans; and it simultaneously reduced British military power, reducing a second incentive. Thus British imperialist policy during the inter-war period involved trying to put out fires all over the globe, to convince countries to make repayments in the face of dramatically reduced incentives to do so.

Cain and Hopkins argue that Britain was more successful as a financial power during the inter-war period than others have given them credit for

18 M. Beenstock, F. Capie and B. Griffiths, 'Economic recovery in the United Kingdom in the 1930s', Bank of England Panel of Academic Consultants, Discussion Paper (1984); B. Eichengreen and J. Sachs, 'Exchange rates and economic recovery in the 1930s', *Journal of Economic History*, Vol. XLV no. 41 (Dec. 1985), pp. 925–46.

(II, p. 4). Yet that conclusion reflects an analysis of stocks rather than of flows of wealth; and the standard of measurement used is extremely vague. The alleged success is measured by the fact that 'Britain was the only true world power of consequence in the 1930s' (II, p. 6); that the Sterling Area was the 'most important international economic bloc' (ibid.); and that the size of British foreign investment was still large (for example, 'Britain remained the largest foreign investor in South America down to 1939' (II, p. 149)).

Yet all these characteristics reflect past glory, not continuing success. The 'sterling bloc' of the inter-war period was probably a smaller group of countries than those who had used sterling as a key currency during the prewar period; the high level of foreign investment reflected the prewar stock, not the inter-war flows which were slowly reducing British dominance. Finally, and I would argue critically, while Cain and Hopkins do show a number of concessions that were wrung by Britain from both the formal and informal empires in the twentieth century, the overall tenor of their discussion is how much the British had to give up in order to ensure debt repayment. Nowhere is this more evident than in the discussion of the Ottawa agreements. Cain and Hopkins state (II, p. 85) that the Dominions got more than Britain did out of the preferential system introduced under the Ottawa agreement in 1932. They attribute this to the need for the empire countries to be able to export goods in order to earn sterling to repay their debts. On the one hand this is very nice evidence on how the financial interests sacrificed the industrial interests for their own gain; on the other hand it militates against a conclusion that the metropolitan power was strong during this period. The British had to give concessions to the empire/Commonwealth countries if they wanted their debts paid.

FINANCIAL ORTHODOXY

While Canada was not a member of the sterling bloc, she was an empire country deeply indebted to Britain. In Canada, as in so many other countries during the Great Depression, there raged a fierce debate over the stance of government economic policy, and over financial orthodoxy in particular. From August 1929 there was a continuous debate about the possibility of 'printing money'.

The ability of the government to 'print money' in the absence of a central bank derived from the emission of Dominion Notes. These notes, as seen above, were issued by the government and were convertible on demand into gold, and all issues over $63.5 million were 100 per cent backed in gold.[19] After August 1929 the government *de facto* suspended the convertibility of these notes, opening the way for a monetary expansion. The primary advocates of such an expansion were western farmers, who relied on wheat exports for income. They argued that a depreciation of the dollar would not hurt them, and that much of the problem of the Depression reflected an insufficiency of

---

19 Issues up to $63.5 million were backed 25 per cent by gold.

money.[20] In addition, westerners viewed the tariff imposed in 1930 as a policy that benefited the east at the expense of the west, and believed that depreciation would offset that wrong. The opposition to monetary expansion came from both major parties and reflected a variety of forces, only partially related to imperialism.

The primary fear was that monetary expansion would lead to a currency debasement. In September 1930, in response to questions about increasing the unbacked portion of the money supply, Prime Minister Bennett stated:

> Unless the paper money of the country has behind it an adequate reserve of the only commodity that passes in the settlement of international exchanges, namely, gold, I would suggest that it is of very little value; and to the extent to which the reserve may be depleted or the ratio decreased by the issue of legal tender or of Dominion of Canada bills, to that extent is there a possibility of the money of this country becoming debased and not of par value in the countries of the world.[21]

But why would debasement be a bad thing for Canada? The prime minister argued that depreciation would 'be ruinous alike to the credit and to the future development of this country', while both the minister of finance and the prime minister warned of the possibility of a 'flight from the dollar' (without going into any details of the effect such an ominous event might have).[22] Yet the key was surely Canada's ongoing need to borrow in international markets. In the budget speech in 1932 the minister of finance emphasized that 'during the past year Canada was the only country that was able to borrow in the public markets of the US', a position he attributed strictly to 'the maintenance of sound financial and monetary policies'.[23]

In addition to the need for future borrowing, the incentive for the Canadians to depreciate was reduced by the amount of foreign debt that was payable in foreign currency or in gold.[24] Thus while the government would have earned seignorage revenue by printing money, they would have needed more Canadian dollars to buy the foreign exchange to pay interest on the debt.

Yet fear of the effect of depreciation on future foreign borrowing was only one of the factors accounting for the refusal to pursue expansionary monetary

20 These views culminated in the election of the Social Credit party, in Alberta in 1935. This party followed the views of Major Douglas, and began to issue a social dividend. However, the government continually had to buy up issues to prevent them from depreciating, and the dividends were ultimately declared *ultra vires* since printing money was under federal jurisdiction. See R. Craig McIvor, *Canadian Monetary Banking and Fiscal Development* (Toronto, 1961).

21 Canada, *Official Report on the Debates of the House of Commons*, 1st Session, 17th Parliament, p. 78.

22 Cited in Michael D. Bordo and Angela Redish, 'Credible commitment and exchange rate stability: Canada's interwar experience', *Canadian Journal of Economics*, 23 (Dec. 1990), pp. 357–80.

23 *House of Commons Debates* (Canada), 4th Session, 17th Parliament, p. 3205.

24 The government's concern was the gold debt held externally. Experience after the dollar had devalued by about 15 per cent in October 1931 shows that they would have paid off gold bondholders who were Canadian residents in Canadian dollars, arguing that the legal price of gold in Canada was unchanged at $20.67 per ounce.

policy. A second was the great uncertainty of the effectiveness of such policy. Both Bennett (Conservative prime minister from 1930 to 1935) and MacKenzie King (Liberal prime minister 1935–48) argued that they did not believe monetary expansion would reduce unemployment:

> If I thought for a single moment that to add, beyond $71 million of the present outstanding unsecured paper money of this country, another 25 or 30 or 40 millions of dollars would cure unemployment, would lift the Depression and would end all our troubles, I would have no more hesitancy in asking the House for it than I have in asking the House to pass any estimate that is submitted to it.[25]

> Did I believe that this [monetary expansion] would make matters any better, I am not afraid to say that I should be among those who would support it . . . This is a matter which is giving rise to a great deal of study on the part of the most thoughtful economists and the most earnest of social reformers and workers, and there is at the present time no general consensus of view which one can say is accepted.[26]

The final factor was the supremacy of Dominion financial interests in the decision-making process. Though Cain and Hopkins discuss the origins of the political power of the gentlemanly capitalists in the UK, they treat the colonial and empire economies and societies as more homogeneous. Yet a socio-economic class structure, similar in style if not in scale, permeated Canadian politics and power loci.

GENTLEMANLY CAPITALISTS AND THE STERLING AREA IN THE POSTWAR ERA

Although the title of Cain and Hopkins's second volume suggests that it will cover the period 1914–1990, the coverage is not even, with 84 per cent of the volume dedicated to the period up to and including the Second World War. The later period is therefore discussed in considerably less detail, although the theme is continued. Cain and Hopkins argue (II, p. 265) that the gentlemanly capitalists continued to control economic policy-making and oversaw the demise of the empire, while their central preoccupation was the 'preservation of sterling's role in financing international trade and investment'. In this way they see Britain's twentieth-century efforts to maintain her old imperial and global power as a success. The brevity of the discussion concerning the post-1945 years is disappointing, because the arguments for this period deserve, perhaps require, as much evidence as the arguments put forward for the 1920s and 1930s. The continued dominance of the gentlemanly capitalists is not as self-evident as the authors appear to claim. Cain and Hopkins note (II, p. 267) the to me surprising fact that even in 1970 83 per cent of Conservative MPs were public school boys (and their emphasis is on the words 'public school',

25 House of Commons, 3rd Session, 17th Parliament, p. 650.
26 House of Commons, 2nd Session, 17th Parliament, p. 2669.

not 'boys'), but this is far less relevant than the undisclosed backgrounds of the MPs of the Labour Party who held power between 1945 and 1951 and who revolutionized British economic institutions.

Again, the argument on the sterling bloc would have benefited from the more explicit investigation and analysis of an economic counterfactual. For example, the extent to which the dominance of sterling as the channel for international financial dealings was traceable to a 'path dependence', and would have continued in place simply owing to traditional institutional arrangements and the fact that the City was the most efficient market place, rather than to some new and more potent imperialistic government intervention in the inter-war period, is not clear.

Cain and Hopkins structure their analysis of the Sterling Area around two options that, they argue, Britain had to face: a convertible currency in a multi-lateral trading world dominated by the US, or an inconvertible currency and stronger imperial ties. They then attempt to explain why Britain chose the latter alternative for the first decade and then switched to a convertible currency in the late 1950s. The initial choice was in part determined by the debts incurred by Britain during the Second World War, many of which took the form of sterling balances owned by the colonies (II, p. 270). Britain could not afford the liquidation of these balances that convertibility would probably have implied. This choice of inconvertibility was initially opposed by the US, Britain's other major creditor, but the exigencies of the Cold War tempered that opposition (II, p. 272). Finally, Cain and Hopkins argue that the empire/Commonwealth was necessary for sterling because it generated both essential supplies and dollar earnings. The switch to a convertible currency in the late 1950s they attribute to (1) the decreasing ability of the empire to generate dollars; (2) the increasing military (and therefore financial) cost of empire; (3) the need to attach the poorly performing British economy to the rising stars in Europe and Japan; and (4) the assumption that sterling could compete with the dollar (II, p. 266).

This portion of the book is less tightly argued than earlier chapters, which is unfortunate given its more immediate relevance for contemporary Britain and world financial relations. To begin with, it is not obvious that the dual choice that Cain and Hopkins outline (between convertibility and US domination vs. inconvertibility and empire) really existed. In a recent analysis of Bretton Woods, John Ikenberry argues that there was a consensus between the Americans and the British on 'the desirability of currency stability and the convertibility of currencies'.[27] In 1944, under the Bretton Woods agreement, Britain agreed to re-establish a convertible currency; and in December 1945, in return for a large loan from the US, the British agreed to reinstitute convertibility in 1947. They proceeded to do so, precipitating an immediate run on sterling which led to a suspension of convertibility seven weeks

---

27 John Ikenberry, 'The political origins of Bretton Woods', in M. Bordo and B. Eichengreen (eds), *A Retrospective on the Bretton Woods System* (Chicago, 1993), pp. 155–82.

later.[28] There is little evidence, cited by Cain and Hopkins or elsewhere, to suggest that Britain chose inconvertibility at this time for reasons other than short-run expedience. It is also not clear why the gentlemanly capitalists, who in the 1920s had restored convertibility of sterling and in the 1930s had desperately wanted financial orthodoxy, would not see such policies as inimical to imperial interests.

STERLING AND DECOLONIZATION

The framework adopted by Cain and Hopkins implies an important link between decolonization and sterling; that is, as long as the colonies provided support for sterling they were maintained, but as they generated fewer pounds and became more vociferous in their calls for independence (that is, more expensive) they were less useful, providing an impetus for decolonization. The authors are clear that this is only one of many factors explaining decolonization, but they provide no statistics or formal evidence that would enable the reader to assess whether this was a central or peripheral concern.

The central point that emerges clearly from the imperial economic analysis of Cain and Hopkins is the significance of the debts incurred by Britain during the Second World War for the Bretton Woods system, the Cold War and decolonization. While the significance of the debts of the First World War for the inter-war economy and polity are now well established, the impact of the debt legacy of the Second World War has received much less attention from scholars.[29] Yet the significance of these debts for global policy draws attention to the *weakness* of Britain's post-Second World War position rather than buttressing an argument for the continuing strength of British imperialism.

CONCLUSIONS

Cain and Hopkins state that the subject of their book is the primary causes of imperialism, that is, the self-interest of gentlemanly capitalists, rather than its tools or results and impact. Yet a large part of their argument, especially in Volume II, in fact concerns methods and evaluations, some of which have been the focus of this paper. The two authors argue that twentieth-century British imperialism was stronger than the conventional wisdom would have us believe, and that imperial policy was primarily motivated by domestic concerns rather than being a reaction to events in the periphery. Imperial intervention, to be exploitative, must have relied either on British military power or on collaborating elites working in the external economies. Yet in twentieth-century Canada, and more generally in all the self-governing Dominions, neither source of power was available.

28 Charles Kindleberger, *A Financial History of Western Europe* (London, 1984), p. 430.
29 For the role of the First World War in the inter-war economy, see Eichengreen, *Golden Fetters*, and Peter Temin, *Lessons for the Great Depression* (Cambridge, Mass., 1989).

I would argue that the perceived strength of Britain, her existence as a world power, represented past strength rather than ongoing successes. There may be no smoke without fire, but it is difficult to tell from smoke alone whether the fire is still actively feeding or whether merely the glowing embers remain. The decline in Britain's status in world capital markets is critical. Before lending money, a potential creditor may have considerable bargaining power, but after the loan is made, the debtor may have assumed the power. Before the First World War Britain was a net creditor, but after the war imperial policy was on the defensive as the British needed to ensure that repayments would be forthcoming.

CHAPTER 6

British informal empire in East Asia, 1880–1939: a Japanese perspective[1]

SHIGERU AKITA

P.J. Cain and A.G. Hopkins's major two-volume work, *British Imperialism*, Volume I, *Innovation and Expansion, 1688–1914*, and Volume II, *Crisis and Deconstruction, 1914–1990* (both London, 1993), has attracted keen attention from Japanese scholars in the fields of British history, the history of the British Empire and Commonwealth, and Japanese colonial history. Among the admirable features of Cain and Hopkins's work are the time span covered (they concentrate on the period 1800–1970), the incorporation of modern British domestic history into the history of the worldwide British Empire using their own concept of 'gentlemanly capitalism', and the presentation of a grand synthesis about British imperialism. One important issue raised by Cain and Hopkins concerns the chronology of the duration of British imperial power. They argue that the British Empire did not decline as rapidly after 1914 as is usually assumed, and that there was a greater degree of resurgence in British global power after 1914 than most scholars had previously supposed, based upon Britain's competitiveness in the financial and service sectors, and especially the growing influence of the City of London. As for the usefulness of the concept of 'gentlemanly capitalism' for interpreting British expansion overseas, they argue that the newly transformed gentlemanly elite, centred on the financiers of the City of London and combined with their old allies in the landed aristocracies and the professions, exerted strong influences on imperial policy and British expansion overseas, and that Britain's economic interest underwent an important shift of emphasis from markets for exports (industry) to opportunities for finance and services. This shift reflected the

1 I wish to thank my colleagues, Professor W.R. Nelson, Professor T. Matsuda and Mr Y. Sugita of Osaka University of Foreign Studies, Professor Peter J. Marshall of University of London, and especially Professor K. Sugihara of Osaka University for their valuable comments on the earlier versions of this paper; and also Professor Y. Takeuchi of Nihon University for his critical comments and encouragement at the Round-Table Conference of the American Historical Association on the Cain/Hopkins thesis in San Francisco, Jan. 1994.

transformation of gentlemanly capitalism in Britain. I agree with this aspect of their new interpretations to a large extent, but wish to locate this transformation in the more general context of Asian regional economic development and changes in the modern world system.

Cain and Hopkins discuss how the evolution of Britain's continuing imperialist ambitions intersected with events in East Asia, and how this junction prompted significant changes in policy towards China, in chapter 10 of volume II of their work. The purpose of this short paper is to review their treatment of the British informal empire in East Asia in the light of recent Japanese research.

My arguments are twofold. First, Cain and Hopkins's books provide us with interesting comparative perspectives on the two 'island empires' of Great Britain and Japan. However, their London-centred hypothesis deals with China and Japan as secondary or subordinate players in East Asia, and does not pay much attention to the economic dynamism of East Asia. To redress this defect, I first refer to the interconnection or complementarity between the development of intra-Asian trade and the new British financial empire at the turn of the twentieth century.

Secondly, I cannot agree completely with Cain and Hopkins's interpretation of the 1930s with regard to the chronology of the duration of British imperial power in East Asia. Here I would like to take up the issues of the Chinese monetary reform of 1935 and British 'appeasement policy' towards Japan in the 1930s, and through an analysis of these two issues emphasize the importance of East Asian initiatives and of the United States rather than of Great Britain. In other words, it may be suggested that there emerged a sub-system within the modern world system in East Asia in this period which had an important impact upon the western powers, and especially on Great Britain. My review will concentrate on the period after the First World War, which is dealt with in volume II of the Cain/Hopkins study. This is because most Japanese historians would broadly agree with their new interpretation of the period down to 1911, presented in chapter 13 of volume I.

Before taking up these topics, it may be worth mentioning the pioneering work on British imperial history by a Japanese scholar, work which seems to me to have achieved part of the content of Cain and Hopkins's thesis independently, and somewhat ahead of their publication. In 1983 Minoru Kawakita, professor at Osaka University, published *Kogyoka no Rekishiteki Zentei – Teikoku to Gentleman (The Historical Foundation of British Industrialization: The British Empire and Gentlemen)* (Tokyo: Iwanami shoten), some three years before the appearance of Cain and Hopkins's first article in 1986. In his book Kawakita argued that the co-existence of 'gentlemanly rule' and the British Empire and their close relationship was largely responsible for the British commercial revolution in the mid-eighteenth century, and that they paved the way for industrialization in Britain. Kawakita's main concerns were confined to the historical foundation of British industrialization (the Industrial Revolution), and differed from Cain and Hopkins's emphasis in this respect. However, he did lead the way in presenting a new synthesis of eighteenth-century British history, and successfully revealed the interrelation between British expansion overseas and gentlemanly rule as the twin pillars of early modern British history. As far as the period of the old colonial system is concerned, therefore, Kawakita's work should be acknowledged as a major contribution, preceding the work of Cain and Hopkins.

'GENTLEMANLY CAPITALISM' AND THE DEVELOPMENT OF
INTRA-ASIAN TRADE

Let us now consider the topic of British economic penetration into East Asia at the turn of the century, which is dealt with by Cain and Hopkins in chapter 13 of volume I of their work. In this chapter they try to show that Britain's interest in China underwent an important shift of emphasis, from an initial concern with markets for exports from India and Britain to a preoccupation with opportunities for finance (C&H, I, pp. 423–4). I agree in part with this interpretation about the shift of economic interest to finance, but from a rather different perspective. In fact, the British export trade to China stagnated in the 1870s and 1880s, and after 1883 cotton yarn from India replaced British yarn in the China market. The export of Japanese cotton yarn to China also increased and exceeded that from India by 1913. However, it may be pointed out that this drastic change of the export trade in cotton yarn was the result of the development of intra-Asian trade, rather than any structural change in the British economy. Rigorous though the Cain/Hopkins analysis is, it tends to overlook the importance of intra-Asian trade at the turn of the century.

Here I would like to introduce new perspectives on Asian economic history put forward by several Japanese economic historians, including Kaoru Sugihara (Osaka University), Heita Kawakatsu (Waseda University) and Takeshi Hamashita (Tokyo University). These historians argue that the economic growth of Asian countries was led by intra-Asian trade, which had long historical origins but which began to grow rapidly around the turn of the century.[2] Sugihara summarizes the development of intra-Asian trade as follows:

> The engine of growth of intra-Asian trade was the emergence of the modern cotton industry in India and Japan, as it stimulated the cotton trade on many levels: exports of Indian raw cotton to Japan, exports of Indian and Japanese yarn to China, exports of Japanese cotton manufactures and 'sundries' to China, etc. Such a growth of the cotton trade led to international specialisation on an Asian grand scale, and opened up new market

---

2 Several symposia have been held on economic growth in modern Asia and intra-Asian trade. The following books summarize the results of these symposia: Takeshi Hamashita and Heita Kawakatsu (eds), *Ajia Koeki-ken to Nihon-Kogyoka, 1500–1900* [*The Commercial Networks in Asia and Japanese Industrialization, 1500–1900*] (Tokyo, 1991); Heita Kawakatsu (ed.), *Atarashii Ajia no Dorama* [*A New Drama in Asia*] (Tokyo, 1994); A.J.H. Latham and Heita Kawakatsu (eds), *Japanese Industrialization and the Asian Economy* (London and New York, 1994). Readers may also refer to the bibliographies on each scholar's work.

opportunities for primary producers. Rice producers in Southeast Asia were among those who responded most quickly to the new oportunities. Thus there emerged an Asian inter-regional division of labour with Japan and India as exporters of manufactured goods and importers of primary products on the one hand, and China and Southeast Asia as exporters of primary products and importers of manufactured goods on the other.[3]

Many Asian countries had linked their currencies with silver and had formed a relatively 'autonomous' silver-using area. The fall in the value of silver from the 1870s onwards encouraged exports of Asian primary products to Europe and restrained imports of European manufactured goods.[4]

However, to give credit to Cain and Hopkins, Western impact was also necessary for the development of intra-Asian trade. By the end of the nineteenth century most Asian countries (except for China) had adopted the gold or gold-exchange standard to facilitate imports of capital and manufactured goods from the West, especially from Britain. Japan's entry into the international gold standard in 1897 confirmed that Asia needed closer contacts with the West to develop its own inter-regional trade network. As Sugihara explains, 'most of the manufactured goods which served for the development of an infrastructure such as railways, ports (communication system) and cities were imported from the West, without which the intra-Asian trade would have been confined to a centuries-old junk trade'.[5] (See Table 6.1.) In these respects, Cain and Hopkins's analysis complements Japanese scholars' recent works on intra-Asian trade. Cain and Hopkins point out that the leading European import and export firms moved out of the old staple trades and became managing agencies concerned increasingly with services, notably shipping, insurance and banking, and with an array of activities connected to property and utilities in the Treaty Ports (C&H, I, p. 429). European firms came to recognize the continuing influence of indigenous Chinese merchants upon the import and export trades. In return, China could take advantage of services, especially overseas financial services, offered by British firms and banks to promote intra-Asian trade, although this meant financial dependence on the West. The growth of intra-Asian trade, which had emerged 'autonomously' in the 1880s and 1890s, was thus fuelled by the worldwide boom before the First World War, when it tended to deepen its financial dependence on European countries. In this sense, as Sugihara suggests, there was clearly a sense of complementarity between British financial interests and

3 Kaoru Sugihara, 'Ajiakan-Boeki no Keisei to Kozo [Patterns and development of intra-Asian trade, 1880–1913]', *Shakai Keizai Shigaku* [*The Socio-Economic History*], 51/1 (1985), pp. 146–7. Sugihara illustrates the pattern of Asian settlements, following S.B. Saul's diagram of the world pattern of settlements in 1910, and also presents a chart showing Asia's integration into the world economy. (See Figures 6.1 and 6.2)

4 Shinya Sugiyama, *Japan's Industrialization in the World Economy, 1859–99: Export Trade and Overseas Competition* (London, 1988). See also A.J.H. Latham, *The International Economy and the Undeveloped World, 1865–1914* (London, 1978); A.J.H. Latham and Larry Neal, 'The international market in rice and wheat, 1868–1914', *Economic History Review*, 2nd ser., 36 (1983).

5 Sugihara, 'Ajiakan-Boeki', p. 146.

TABLE 6.1

GEOGRAPHICAL DISTRIBUTION OF ASIA'S TRADE (£ MILLION)

		1883			1898			1913			1928		
		the West	Asia	Total	the West	Asia	Total	the West	Asia	Total	the West	Asia	Total
India	Ex.	44.45 (68)	17.02 (26)	65.85 (100)	42.71 (63)	20.93 (31)	68.15 (100)	95.74 (63)	41.70 (27)	152.69 (100)	136.41 (58)	64.38 (28)	233.86 (100)
	Im.	34.69 (85)	5.12 (13)	40.97 (100)	33.51 (75)	6.37 (14)	44.52 (100)	91.80 (75)	26.58 (22)	122.25 (100)	117.39 (59)	64.33 (32)	200.38 (100)
South-east Asia	Ex.	14.98 (58)	6.70 (26)	25.62 (100)	15.19 (39)	14.70 (37)	39.25 (100)	54.17 (52)	42.93 (41)	104.70 (100)	139.69 (53)	96.77 (37)	261.46 (100)
	Im.	13.54 (57)	8.35 (35)	23.66 (100)	15.95 (51)	14.17 (46)	31.05 (100)	46.56 (56)	32.44 (39)	82.98 (100)	94.15 (55)	58.04 (34)	170.50 (100)
China	Ex.	17.78 (76)	3.96 (17)	23.25 (100)	15.47 (60)	8.85 (34)	25.80 (100)	29.99 (56)	30.42 (49)	61.87 (100)	61.79 (43)	70.71 (50)	142.56 (100)
	Im.	8.55 (47)	9.29 (51)	18.02 (100)	13.46 (51)	12.51 (47)	26.62 (100)	48.59 (56)	36.53 (42)	86.14 (100)	68.87 (40)	96.16 (56)	171.57 (100)
Japan	Ex.	5.23 (80)	1.20 (18)	6.53 (100)	8.54 (51)	8.04 (48)	16.90 (100)	34.21 (47)	36.56 (50)	72.64 (100)	97.11 (42)	120.38 (53)	228.74 (100)
	Im.	3.70 (71)	1.52 (29)	5.23 (100)	14.69 (52)	13.53 (48)	28.36 (100)	35.00 (44)	42.00 (53)	78.82 (100)	104.59 (42)	138.35 (53)	260.18 (100)
Total	Ex.	82.44 (68)	28.88 (24)	121.25 (100)	81.91 (55)	52.52 (35)	150.10 (100)	214.11 (55)	151.61 (39)	391.90 (100)	435.00 (50)	352.44 (41)	866.62 (100)
	Im.	60.48 (69)	24.28 (28)	87.88 (100)	77.61 (59)	46.58 (36)	130.55 (100)	221.95 (60)	137.55 (37)	370.19 (100)	385.00 (48)	356.88 (44)	802.63 (100)

Source: K. Sugihara, 'Japan as an engine of the Asian international economy, c.1880–1936', Japan Forum, 2/1 (April 1990), p. 130.

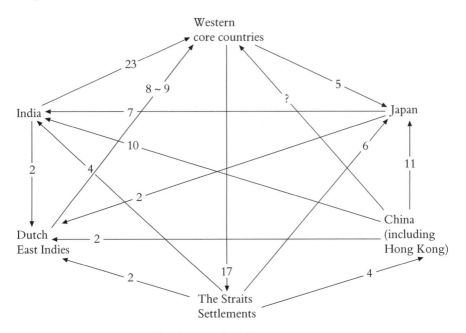

Figure 6.1 Asian pattern of settlement (£ million)
Source: Kaoru Sugihara, 'Patterns of Intra-Asian Trade, 1898–1913', in *Osaka City University Economic Review*, No. 16 (1980), p. 71.

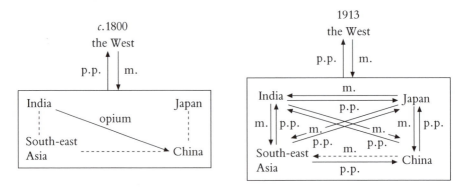

Figure 6.2 Patterns of Asia's integration into the world economy
Note: m. refers to manufactured goods and p.p. refers to primary products.
Source: Kaoru Sugihara, 'Patterns of Asia's Integration into the World Economy, 1880–1913', in Wolfram Fischer, R. Marwin McInnis and Jürgen Schneider (eds), *The Emergence of a World Economy, 1500–1914. Beiträge zur Wirtschafts- und Sozialgeschichte*, Band 33–2 (Franz Steiner, Wiesbaden, 1986), p. 719.

intra-Asian (cotton) trade. They went hand in hand in the more general sense that a rapid growth of intra-Asian trade was an essential condition for investment opportunities in railway construction, manufacturing and services.[6] However, in order to understand more fully the historical significance, as well as the limits, of the British financial presence in East Asia and its impact on the economic development of Asia, further research is needed into the interaction or complementarity between the financial or service sectors of the City of London and the development of intra-Asian trade around the turn of the century. Japanese industrialization in the early twentieth century benefited greatly from the huge loans issues in the capital market of London.[7]

In the case of China, it is important to highlight the connection between the growth of overseas trade and the long-term investments made by British expatriate firms, such as the Hongkong and Shanghai Bank, Jardine Matheson and Swires.[8] This, in turn, will lead to an assessment of the dynamism and rapid development of the Chinese economy in the late 1930s, which has been revealed in recent works and is also referred to by Cain and Hopkins.

THE CAIN/HOPKINS INTERPRETATION OF CURRENCY REFORM IN CHINA

In chapter 10 of volume II of *British Imperialism*, Cain and Hopkins present an original and stimulating line of argument about British policy towards China in the 1930s. They emphasize the importance of the changes that occurred in British foreign policy, especially the decision to cooperate with Chinese nationalist elements in 1926. This decision was even more radical: courting Chinese nationalists was a departure from a tradition of gunboat diplomacy which went back to the 1840s (II, p. 248).

Cain and Hopkins argue in addition for the continuity of Britain's priorities in China, which centred on securing payments on existing debts and creating the conditions for new investment. Affected by the global financial crisis, forging a new partnership led to fiscal and monetary reforms in China, although the most ambitious reform was the attempt to draw China into the emerging Sterling Area after Britain left the gold standard in 1931 (III, p. 253). This interpretation raises some extremely important historiographical questions. What we need to ask is, firstly, to what extent Britain played a role in Chinese

6 See Kaoru Sugihara, 'The economic motivations behind Japanese aggression in the late 1930s: perspectives of Freda Utley and Nawa Toichi', *Journal of Contemporary History*, 32/2 (1997), pp. 259–80.

7 Shigeru Akita, 'Gentlemanly capitalism, intra-Asian trade and Japanese industrialization at the turn of the century', *Japan Forum*, 8/1 (1996), pp. 51–65; Toshio Suzuki, *Japanese Government Loan Issues on the London Capital Market, 1870–1913* (London, 1994).

8 Mayako Ishii, '19 seiki-kohan no Chugoku ni okeru Igirisu-shihon no katsudo; Jardine, Matheson and Company no baai [Activities of British enterprise in China in the later half of the nineteenth century as seen in the documents of Jardine, Matheson and Company]', *Shakai Keizai Shigaku* [*The Socio-Economic History*], 45/4 (1979); Shinya Sugiyama, 'Marketing and competition in China, 1895–1932: the Taikoo sugar refinery', in *Papers Presented to the 11th International Economic History Congress, C47: Commercial Networks in Asia, 1850–1930* (Milan, 1994).

monetary reform in 1935–36, and secondly, what was the impact of this reform upon the struggles for predominance both in China itself and in East Asia more broadly?

Cain and Hopkins explain that the monetary reform in 1935 was forced by the silver crisis in China. The long decline in silver prices was reversed in 1931, when a rise in world demand began to draw silver out of China. For fear of the decline in the profitability of British investment, the British government decided to dispatch Frederick Leith-Ross, its chief economic adviser, to China in 1935, to recommend monetary reform, to take the Chinese monetary system off the silver standard, and also to secure British interests. However, recent joint research by Japanese scholars, entitled *Chugoku no Heisei-Kaikaku to Kokusai-kankei (Currency Reform in China (1935) and China's Relations with Japan, Britain and America)* (ed. Yutaka Nozawa; Tokyo: Tokyo Daigaku Shuppankai, 1981), suggests that Cain and Hopkins tend to place too much emphasis on the role that Britain played in this monetary reform.

First, let us consider the background or preconditions of the Chinese monetary reform. The US government had signed the London silver agreement in 1933 under pressure from American mining interests, and had begun to purchase silver bullion on the world market. The Silver Purchasing Act in 1934 encouraged the rise of silver prices, which caused the heavy outflow of silver from China. Within the space of six months, 200 million ounces of silver (about one-fifth of all silver holdings in China) flowed out of the country. There is no doubt that the silver crisis in China was caused primarily by the silver purchasing policy of the United States, and that the Chinese monetary reform in 1935 was strongly influenced by the economic and financial policies of the US government, rather than those of the British government.[9] (See Tables 6.2 and 6.3 below.)

The United States had also taken a keen interest in the Chinese market, and had sent the Kemmerer Commission of Financial Experts to Nanking in 1929 to recommend financial reform. The Kemmerer Commission's report advised the Chinese nationalist government to leave the silver standard and to adopt the gold exchange standard just before the Great Depression began in 1929.[10] After the publication of its report, three members of this commission, A.N. Young, O.C. Lockhart and F.B. Lynch, remained in China as financial advisers to the nationalist government. In the meantime, in close cooperation with American financial advisers, the Chinese nationalist government itself prepared for the currency reform under the leadership of two ministers of finance, T.V. Soong (1928–33) and H.H. Kung (1933–47).[11] Soong was

---

9 Yutaka Nozawa (ed.), *Chugoku no Heisei-Kaikaku to Kokusai-kankei* [*Currency Reform in China (1935) and China's Relations with Japan, Britain and America*] (Tokyo, 1981), Part II: Currency Reform and the Far Eastern Policies of Britain and America.

10 Arthur N. Young, *China's Nation-Building Effort, 1927–1937: The Financial and Political Record* (Stanford, Ca., 1971), ch. 7.

11 Ibid., chs. 7 and 8, esp. pp. 277–9.

TABLE 6.2
PURCHASE OF SILVER BY THE US DEPARTMENT OF THE TREASURY, 1934–39

Year	US new silver		Nationalized silver		Foreign silver		Gross amount	
	ounces (millions)	dollars paid (millions)	ounces (millions)	dollars paid (millions)	ounces (millions)	dollars paid (millions)	ounces (millions)	dollars paid (millions)
1934	21.8	14.1	110.6	55.3	172.5	86.5	304.9	155.9
1935	38.0	27.3	2.0	1.0	494.4	318.2	534.3	346.5
1936	61.1	47.3	0.4	0.2	271.9	150.3	333.4	197.9
1937	70.6	54.6	–	–	241.5	108.7	312.2	163.4
1938	61.6	42.2	–	–	355.4	156.9	417.1	199.1
1939	60.7	39.9	–	–	282.8	120.5	343.3	160.4

Source: Takeru Saito, 'Amerika Ginseisaku no tenkai to Chugoku [American silver policy and China]', in Yutaka Nozawa (ed.), *Chugoku no Heisei-Kaikaku to Kokusai-kankei [Currency Reform in China (1935) and China's Relations with Japan, Britain and America]* (Tokyo, 1981), p. 146.

TABLE 6.3

CHINA'S NET SILVER IMPORTS AND EXPORTS, 1926–41

Year	Imports	Exports	Cumulative	Estimates of smuggled exports	
				Bank of China	E. Kann
1926	64	–	565	–	–
1927	79	–	644	–	–
1928	129	–	773	–	–
1929	128	–	901	–	–
1930	81	–	982	–	–
1931	55	–	1037	–	–
1932	–	9	1028	–	–
1933	–	11	1017	–	–
1934	–	194	823	15	15
1935	–	45	778	174	113
1936	–	188	590	30	23
1937	–	301	289	–	–
1938	–	60	229	–	–
1939	–	20	208	–	–
1940	–	17	191	–	–
1941	–	2	189	–	–
Total	536	847	–	219	151

[Unit: millions of ounces of fine silver]

Source: Kenji Takita, 'Roosevelt Seikeu to Beichu-Ginkyotei [The Roosevelt administration and the Sino-American Silver Agreements]', in Yutaka Nozawa (ed.), *Chugoku no Heisei-Kaikaku to Kokusai-kankei [Currency Reform in China (1935) and China's Relations with Japan, Britain and America]* (Tokyo, 1981), p. 181; Arthur N. Young, *China's Nation-Building Effort, 1927–1937: The Financial and Political Record* (Stanford, Ca., 1971), pp. 190–2.

a westernized liberal who had studied economics at Harvard and was keen to attract outside expertise and funds for China's development (C&H, II, p. 252). His first major decision was to adopt the customs gold unit early in 1930, following the advice of the Kemmerer Commission. The next major decision was to abolish *tales* as units of account and unify the currency on the basis of the standard silver dollar in March 1933. The decisive break with silver came with the adoption of the flexible silver export duty in October 1934. This duty brought about abandonment of the free silver standard and led to variable managed exchange rates. It made almost inevitable a definite currency reform as soon as the public was psychologically ready and external conditions suitable. Thus, even before the Leith-Ross mission arrived in China on 21 September 1935, T.V. Soong and H.H. Kung had almost completed the planning of monetary reform, which included the centralized control of bank notes, the creation of a Central Reserve Bank, the nationalization of silver bullion possessed by foreign exchange banks and the adoption of a managed exchange standard.[12] The Chinese nationalist government merely consulted Leith-Ross, and got his warm assent. These facts seriously undermine the core of the Cain/Hopkins argument. Britain neither played a major role nor took strong initiatives in the initial stages of monetary reform.

What, then, were the major reasons for the success of the Chinese monetary reform? Cain and Hopkins emphasize the cooperation of the foreign exchange banks and particularly of the Hong Kong and Shanghai Bank, which played a vital part in helping to maintain the stability of the new system (II, p. 254). However, the telling facts are to be found mainly in the history of Chinese–American financial relations, rather than of Anglo-Chinese banking relations. The stability of the new Chinese currency system depended crucially upon the disposal or sale of nationalized silver bullion. The Chinese nationalist government realized this, and several times asked the US government to buy silver for deferred delivery in order to strengthen reserves. During the second half of 1935, the attitude of the US government changed, and as a matter of urgent necessity, H.H. Kung began on 8 October 1935 a new effort to sell silver to the United States.[13] They reached an agreement on 2 November 1935, only one day before the official announcement of the monetary reform.

The first Chinese–American Silver Agreement was signed on 13 November 1935, and the US Department of the Treasury purchased 50 million ounces of Chinese silver, which gave the Chinese government $32.5 million. Henry Morgenthau, the US Secretary of the Treasury, took a leading role in this negotiation in the hope that the new Chinese dollar might be linked to the US dollar and that the Chinese nationalist government could be placed under the financial influence of the United States. The US Department of the Treasury signed the second Chinese–American Silver Agreement on 18 May 1936, and purchased 123 million ounces of Chinese silver. The payment was made in US dollars and deposited at the Federal Reserve Bank in New York, which functioned as *de facto* final guarantor of the stability of the new Chinese managed exchange standard.[14] In June 1937 the Chinese nationalist government possessed $379 million of foreign exchange reserves, which consisted of pounds sterling (24.3 per cent), US dollars (19.5 per cent), gold (12 per cent) and silver (44.3 per cent). Between November 1935 and July 1937 the US Department of the Treasury purchased 192 million ounces of silver from China and paid nearly $100 million to provide vitally needed support for the currency reform.[15]

12 Kazuyoshi Hirano, 'Chugoku no Kinyu kozo to Heisei-Kaikaku [The financial structure of China and the currency reform]', in Yutaka Nozawa (ed.), *Chugoku*, ch. 2; Young, *China's Nation-Building Effort*, pp. 229–30.

13 Young, *China's Nation-Building Effort*, pp. 233–4.

14 Takeru Saito, 'Amerika Ginseisaku no tenkai to Chugoku [American silver policy and China]', in Yutaka Nozawa (ed.), *Chugoku*, ch. 4, p. 157.

15 Kenji Takita, 'Roosevelt Seiken to Beichu-Ginkyotei [The Roosevelt administration and the Sino-American Silver Agreements]', in ibid., ch. 5, p. 192; Young, *China's Nation-Building Effort*, p. 245.

According to the official statement concerning the second Chinese–American Silver Agreement, the new Chinese dollar was officially linked to neither the US dollar nor the pound sterling. However, it was US dollars and gold that provided China with the material foundations for successful monetary reform. The United States took full advantage of those opportunities to integrate China into the dollar bloc, and successfully strengthened its financial influence in China.[16] In return for such heavy financial reliance on the United States, China was able to consolidate its monetary grounds in the face of Japanese invasion. Especially after the outbreak of the Sino-Japanese War in 1937, Morgenthau bought further large amounts of silver. These wartime purchases came to a total of 362 million ounces, which realized $157 million. Altogether the Chinese Central Bank sold to the US Department of the Treasury 553 million ounces and realized $252 million.[17] Thus, it may be more appropriate to view the Chinese monetary reform not as an opportunity for making China effectively a member of the Sterling Area, but as the first step towards American predominance over China. Cain and Hopkins totally overlook the UK–US financial rivalry in China; and they overemphasize Britain's power and the role and impact of its leading financial agent, Sir Charles Addis (Britain's chief representative to the Second China Consortium, adviser to the Governor of the Bank of England and the London manager of the Hong Kong and Shanghai Bank). Cain and Hopkins also tend to minimize the growing potency of American imperialism in East Asia at the expense of Britain before the Second World War. Against the picture of the growing power of the United States and Japan, together with the growth of Chinese nationalism and her economic development, recent research by Japanese scholars tends to play down the image of a resurgent British informal empire in the 1930s, instead suggesting the formation of a multi-polar balance of power in East Asia.[18]

BRITISH APPEASEMENT POLICY TOWARDS JAPAN

Finally, we need to re-examine the fragile nature of Anglo-Japanese diplomatic relations in East Asia in the 1930s. Cain and Hopkins place a high value

16 Toshio Iyotani, 'Sekai-kyoko ka ni okeru Chugoku Heisei-Kaikaku [The currency reform in China during the Great Depression]', in *Keizai Ronsou* [*The Journal of Economics*], Univ. of Kyoto (1977), 120–3/4.

17 Young, *China's Nation-Building Effort*, pp. 245, 280 and App. 15: Silver sales from 1934 to 1941.

18 For important works on the growing role of Japanese financiers in this period, see Taichiro Mitani, 'Kokusai Kinyu Shihon to Ajia no Senso: Shumatsuki ni okeru Taichu Yongoku Shakkandan [International finance capital and the war in Asia: the final phase of the four-power international consortium to China]', *Nenpo Kindai Nihon Kenkyu* [*Annual Report of Modern Japanese Studies*], 2 (1980); *idem,* 'Japan's international financiers and world politics, 1904–31', *Proceedings of the British Association for Japanese Studies* (1980). For the international relations in East Asia before 1931, see Harumi Goto, *Japan and Britain in Shanghai, 1925–1931: After Alliance* (London and New York, 1995); Takeshi Matsuda, *The Limits of Dollar Diplomacy: A History of the New Chinese Banking Consortium, 1917–1931* (Johns Hopkins University Press, forthcoming, 1999).

on the growing success of Britain's new economic and financial policy towards China in the 1930s, and state that it was a powerful consideration in the decision to confront Japan (II, p. 258). But does their interpretation really correspond to the realities of Britain's attitude towards Japan in the 1930s? In the light of recent Japanese scholarship, it may be necessary to modify the provocative Cain/Hopkins interpretation of diplomatic relations in East Asia to a considerable degree. As seen from the diplomatic correspondence that followed the establishment of a puppet state in Manchuria by Japan in 1931, the British Foreign Office continued to pursue a policy of cooperation or peaceful co-existence with Japan over China. This attitude can be called an 'appeasement policy' towards Japan. The British government regarded Japanese control of Manchuria as a local dispute, not as a threat to British interests in China. The publication of the menacing Amau Statement in 1934 did not provoke strong reactions from British officials, and Britain continued to pursue a policy of maintaining the status quo, or what might be called an opportunistic policy with regard to China's predicament. Cain and Hopkins argue that this approach ran parallel to the Treasury's view that the stability of sterling required a low-cost defence policy, which meant making concessions to Japan in the Far East (II, p. 257). At a Cabinet meeting in March 1934, Neville Chamberlain proposed the signing of the Anglo-Japanese Non-Aggression Pact, and attempted a rapid rapprochement with Japan in order to relax the mounting tensions between the two countries. These included a naval dispute, a trade war in British Empire markets and disagreements over Chinese affairs.[19] In the midst of so friendly and yielding an attitude towards Japan, the Leith-Ross mission was dispatched to China by way of Canada and Japan. Leith-Ross arrived in Tokyo on 6 September 1935 and soon proposed his ingenious scheme on Chinese affairs, which was fully endorsed by Neville Chamberlain. Cain and Hopkins say that he devised a banker's solution to the problem of containing Japan which involved giving her Manchuria and compensating China by offering her a loan on favourable terms (II, p. 258). In fact, he proposed a £10 million Anglo-Japanese joint loan to the Chinese nationalist government, using the Japanese puppet state in Manchuria as bait. This proposal aimed at subtly reconciling Japan's territorial claims in China with the monetary reforms of the nationalist government. This incredible concession meant a formal recognition of Japan's stake in Manchuria by the British government, and is certainly deserving of the label 'British appeasement of Japan'. At that time, however, the Japanese government had completed the first stage of its original monetary reforms in Manchuria, just the day after the announcement of the currency reform in mainland China. It is important to note that Japan succeeded in incorporating Manchuria into its yen bloc, and that it also tried to extend its influence to north China, setting up another two local puppet governments and encouraging smuggling along

19 Chihiro Hosoya, '1934 nen no Nichi-Ei Fukashinkyotei Mondai [An attempt for a rapprochement in Anglo-Japanese relations in the mid-thirties – the question of the Anglo-Japanese Non-Aggression Pact]', *Kokusai Seiji* [*International Politics*], 58 (1977).

the north China coast. In addition, the Japanese government insisted that Britain should recognize its predominant status and influence in East Asia.[20] Within this context of what has been called an 'East Asian version of the Monroe Doctrine', there was little scope for the Japanese government to cooperate with Britain over currency reform in China. Thus the Japanese government was reluctant to consider the Leith-Ross proposal, and the Chinese government likewise refused to consider it.[21] However, before returning to Britain, Leith-Ross visited Japan again in June 1936, and on the advice of Neville Chamberlain searched for the possibility of Anglo-Japanese financial cooperation in China. But all of these efforts were in vain.

Cain and Hopkins contend that there occurred a change in the British attitude towards Japan after 1935. They argue that when the scheme for recognizing Japan's position in Manchuria failed in 1935, Britain began to adopt a firmer line. The outbreak of the Sino-Japanese War in 1937 is said to have confirmed Britain's attitude and stiffened her resolve (II, p. 258). However, this interpretation runs contrary to the British government's attitude towards Japan after 1937. In fact, Great Britain was reluctant to impose an embargo to contain Japanese military expansionism in 1937, and it continued its appeasement policy towards Japan until June 1941. In April 1939 a Chinese puppet official of the Japanese-supported administration was assassinated in the British concession at Tientsin. And in June 1939 the Japanese military implemented a thorough blockade of the concession, an act which brought Britain and Japan nearer to conflict than at any previous time in the twentieth century.[22] Under these circumstances, the British government issued a statement on 22 July 1939, recognizing that the Japanese forces in China 'have special requirements for the purpose of safeguarding their own security and maintaining public order in regions under their control, and that they have to suppress or remove any such acts or causes as will obstruct them or benefit their enemy'.[23] At this critical juncture, the focus of British foreign policy decision-making shifted sharply towards problems in Europe. On 31 April 1939 the Prime Minister declared that Britain would guarantee the security and independence of Poland in the event of German invasion. Furthermore, in order to deter the military threat of Germany, Britain tried to get diplomatic support and the promise of cooperation from Rumania, Greece, Turkey and

---

20 Shigeo Nishimura, 'Zhang Xueliang seiken-ka no Heisei-Kaikaku [Currency reform in Manchuria under the rule of Zhang Xueliang]', *Toyoshi Kenkyu* [*Study of Oriental History*], Univ. of Kyoto, 50/4 (1992); Hideo Kobayashi, 'Heisei-Kaikaku wo meguru Nihon to Chugoku [Japan, China and the currency reform]', in Yutaka Nozawa (ed.), *Chugoku*, ch. 7.

21 Sumio Hatano, 'Leith-Ross no Kyokuto homon to Nihon [Leith-Ross's mission's visit to the Far East and Japan's response]', *Kokusai Seiji* [*International Politics*], 58 (1977); *idem*, 'Heisei-Kaikaku eno ugoki to Nihon no Taichu Seisaku [The making of the currency reform and Japanese policy towards China]', in Yutaka Nozawa (ed.), *Chugoku*, ch. 8.

22 Peter Lowe, *Great Britain and the Origins of the Pacific War* (Oxford, 1977), pp. 72–102; *idem*, 'Britain and the opening of the war in Asia, 1937–41', in Ian Nish (ed.), *Anglo-Japanese Alienation, 1919–1952: Papers of the Anglo-Japanese Conference on the History of the Second World War* (Cambridge, 1981), ch. 5.

23 *Documents on British Foreign Policy, 1919–1939*, 3rd ser., 9 (London, 1955), p. 313.

especially the USSR. However, the attempted political/military negotiations with the Soviet Union came to an impasse, and the crisis over Danzig (Poland) became more acute. Adherence to an appeasement policy towards Japan in East Asia was thus related to British policies towards Nazi Germany and Fascist Italy in Europe and in the Mediterranean.[24]

Behind the continued pursuit of the appeasement policy towards Japan there existed a definite weakness or fragility in the British military and naval presence in East Asia, as documented in many excellent works on the diplomatic history of this period.[25] Neville Chamberlain clearly perceived this military and naval weakness, and pursued a rapprochement between the two 'island empires' of Great Britain and Japan. The appeasement policy towards Japan in the mid-1930s, which was a prelude to the Munich Conference in 1938, stands as a stark revelation of the military and naval weakness of Britain and her empire in East Asia.

In addition to this military incapacity, the British could not even fulfil their promise of railway loans to China. As Cain and Hopkins state, in 1937 Addis persuaded members of the (Second International) Consortium to allow a substantial new railway loan to be issued in London (C&H, II, p. 254). In May 1937 the Chinese nationalist government urged Britain to finance a £10 million loan for the stability of the new Chinese currency as well as for the increase of railway loans. The issue of these loans was planned by Britain primarily to roll back American financial penetration into China after the monetary reform. The outbreak of the Sino-Japanese War and the sterling crisis of 1937–38 prevented the plan from reaching fruition.[26] This small episode reveals that Britain's weakness in East Asia at this critical stage of international politics lay not only in its military and naval capabilities, but in its financial capacity. The central argument of Cain and Hopkins, namely the significance of the power of the British service sectors emanating from the City of London, underestimates the importance of geopolitical factors and of naval and military strength in the formulation of Britain's foreign policy in East Asia.

24 Yuta Sasaki, *Sanjyu-nendai Igirisu Gaiko-Senryaku: Teikoku Boei to Yuwa no Ronri* [*The Strategy of British Foreign Policy in the 1930s: The Defence of the British Empire and the Logic of Appeasement*] (Nagoya, 1987).
25 Yoichi Kibata, 'Nitchu-Senso Zenshi ni okeru Kokusai-kankyo – Igirisu no Tainichi Seisaku, 1934 nen [Anglo-Japanese relations in 1934]', *Kyoyo-Gakka Kiyo* [*Bulletin, Dept. of Liberal Arts, Univ. of Tokyo*], 9 (1976); idem, '1930-nendai ni okeru Igirisu no Higashi-Ajia Ninshiki [British view of East Asia in the 1930s]', in Akira Fujiwara and Yutaka Nozawa (eds), *Nihon-Fashizumu to Higashi-Ajia* [*Japanese Fascism and East Asia*] (Tokyo, 1977); idem, 'Nitchu-Senso Zenya ni okeru Igirisu no Tainichi Seisaku [British policy towards Japan on the eve of the Sino-Japanese War]', *Ronshu* [*Bulletin, Tokyo Univ. of Foreign Studies*], 29 (1979); idem, '15 nen-Senso to Igirisu [The background of British policy towards the Japanese aggression in China]', in *Rekishigaku-Kenkyu* [*Historical Journal*] (annual special number, 1979). See also Ann Trotter, *Britain and East Asia, 1933–1937* (Cambridge, 1975); Stephen L. Endicott, *Diplomacy and Enterprise: British China Policy, 1933–1937* (Manchester, 1975).
26 Yoichi Kibata, 'Leith-Ross Shisetsudan to Eichu-kankei [The Leith-Ross mission and Anglo-Chinese relations]', in Yutaka Nozawa (ed.), *Chugoku*, ch. 6.

CONCLUSION

In this paper I have suggested the complementarity or interrelatedness between intra-Asian trade and 'gentlemanly capitalism' in East Asia, and I have considered British policy towards China in the 1930s, with special reference to the Chinese monetary reform in 1935 and Britain's appeasement policy towards Japan. From this critical review of the Cain/Hopkins thesis, it becomes clear that we should re-evaluate the struggle for British hegemony in East Asia during the 1930s in the context of an already dominating Japanese presence combined with the rising power of the 'Pax Americana'. We also need to place a greater emphasis on the UK–US economic rivalry in assessing the extent of any genuine resurgence of British global power. Furthermore, in order to reappraise the nature of the British appeasement policy, it is essential to take into account Britain's ambivalent attitude towards Japan, which reflected the weakness of British strategy in East Asia. The adoption of an appeasement policy in itself seems to suggest the limits of British hegemony on a global scale. It may be argued that Cain and Hopkins's new interpretation of the British roll-back strategy in the 1930s, especially in China, is too Anglocentric, and that what is needed are comparative studies of British, American and Japanese policies and strengths in East Asia. In the case of East Asia, the development of intra-Asian trade and the emergence of a sub-system within the modern world system in Asia conditioned and in some respects determined the ways in which Britain and the United States were able to extend their economic influences. It is imperative to take these perspectives into account in reinterpreting the British 'informal empire' and British expansion overseas in general during the twentieth century.

CHAPTER 7

Gentlemanly capitalism and the Raj: British policy in India between the world wars

MARIA MISRA

Peter Cain and Antony Hopkins argue that the case of India must lie at the centre of any credible account of the development of the British Empire, and in chapter 10 of *British Imperialism* volume I and chapter 8 of volume II they apply their model to the problem of the Raj. As described elsewhere in *British Imperialism*, Cain and Hopkins argue that the history of the empire, its acquisition, governance and loss were strongly related to the peculiar anatomy of the British state, and they stress that from the middle of the nineteenth century onwards the British imperial government was single-minded in its pursuit of 'Gladstonian' fiscal orthodoxy, with an emphasis on 'gentlemanly' financial and commercial, rather than industrial, interests.[1]

Cain and Hopkins argue that from its inception in the eighteenth century to its demise in 1947 the Raj served primarily the interests of the south-eastern commercial, financial and older landed groups which dominated the state and ensured that it remained committed above all to sound finance. In the later nineteenth century the Raj, by developing India as an agricultural commodity exporter through British investment in infrastructure, both provided safe opportunities for bondholders and also enabled India to contribute to the British balance of payments by exporting to non-British markets. India also provided prestigious employment opportunities to social elites from the south-east of England (C&H, I, pp. 323–9, 338–48). The Raj sought to do this inexpensively and in a way least likely to promote social disorder by collaborating with Indian landed elites (C&H, I, pp. 329, 331–2). The placation of British industrial interests, and in particular the creation of export markets for

---

1 P.J. Cain and A.G. Hopkins, *British Imperialism: Innovation and Expansion, 1688–1914* (London, 1993), pp. 19, 24, 41–6 and ch. 4. Referred to hereafter as C&H, I.

Lancashire textiles, was a coincidence rather than the primary objective of government policy.[2]

BRITISH POLICY IN INDIA BETWEEN THE WORLD WARS

In the inter-war period, Cain and Hopkins argue, the Raj continued to be concerned primarily with financial orthodoxy, although the main objective of the state was now to secure repayment of Indian debts and to ensure that India would not become a charge on British taxpayers or a threat to the stability of British finances.[3] This explains the course of British policy, both economic and political: firstly, the Raj now developed import-substituting Indian industry to save foreign exchange, at the expense of British manufacturing interests (C&H, II, pp. 186, 191); secondly, it formulated its approach to Indian nationalism in order to prevent nationalists from interfering with the repayment of debt. It tried to promote conservative and moderate Indian politicians who would accept these financial objectives and to exclude those who would not (II, pp. 173–4, 183, 193). When the British did give power to Indians, they always tried to retain control over financial policy (II, pp. 182, 192). Cain and Hopkins even imply that the British were willing to give India independence only when these debts had been repaid (II, p. 174). Therefore, throughout the inter-war period financial orthodoxy was the reigning ideology; the financial interests of bondholders had less of a direct influence on policy than they did before the war, but, in general, the interests of the nineteenth-century Raj persisted into the twentieth century (II, p. 173). The 'gentlemanly' attitudes of disdain for industry, the ideal of the 'leisured amateur' and the commitment to laissez-faire economics informed by Christian notions of moral probity, which had been so influential in the nineteenth century, also survived into the twentieth (II, pp. 177–9).

The Cain/Hopkins analysis is elegantly expressed and tightly argued. Their emphasis on the importance of financial considerations in the formulation of British policy towards India accords with a great deal of recent research and is an important corrective to the belief, still common in the historiography, that the main determinants of British economic policy were British manufacturing interests.[4] Cain and Hopkins relate economic interests to ideological issues in a refreshing way, arguing that economic policy has to be understood in the

2 Cain and Hopkins write: 'An assessment of the benefits derived by British exporters from the possession of India needs to be related to the aims and ambitions of India's rulers, both in Britain and in the sub-continent. Seen from this perspective, the Lancashire lobby appears to have been far less powerful than Marx supposed; its successes were achieved largely because its aims were congruent with those of India's rulers' (I, pp. 335–6).
3 P.J. Cain and A.G. Hopkins, *British Imperialism: Crisis and Deconstruction, 1914–1990* (London, 1993), pp. 172–3. Referred to hereafter as C&H, II.
4 See, for example, A.K. Bagchi, *Private Investment in India, 1900–1939* (Cambridge, 1972); R.K. Ray, *Industrialisation in India, 1914–47: Growth as Conflict in the Private Corporate Sector* (Delhi, 1979); A.K. Sen, 'A pattern of British enterprise in early Indian industrialisation, 1854–1914', reprinted in R.K. Ray (ed.), *Entrepreneurship and Industry in India, 1800–1947* (New Delhi, 1992).

context of prevailing values and ideas, not simply in terms of business interests.[5] However, this paper will argue that in certain areas they overstate their
case, and it will discuss three issues: the relationship between economic interests and the state; the nature of the state's economic policies and ideology; and
the relationship between political and economic motivation in inter-war policy.

For Cain and Hopkins, the British state in the nineteenth century acted
broadly in the interests of financial and commercial groups, and this 'constituency of southern investors, and its institutional representatives in banking and
shipping, fell in readily behind the flag of empire and gave full support to
policies of free trade and sound money' (C&H, I, pp. 338–9). By these representatives they presumably mean the managing agency houses, diversified business groups which were based in India but had offices in Britain and, while
having some industrial as well as commercial and financial interests, had close
relationships with banks and were increasingly moving away from industry.[6]
They certainly refer to the close relationship between Lord Inchcape, the
senior partner in MacKinnon MacKenzie & Co., and the government of
India. Inchcape may be taken as one of the archtypal 'gentlemanly capitalists',
who allegedly included the strongest supporters of imperial policy.[7] Even
when there is no evidence of direct lobbying by business, the two authors
imply that close social and cultural links helped to promote indirect influence
on policy.[8] In the twentieth century, they suggest, the relationship between
private business and the state was less direct and there was no 'conspiracy of
bondholders', but they argue that 'private investors' were still served by government policy, although only as a consequence of the pursuit of sound state
finance (C&H, II, p. 173).

HOW GREAT WAS THE POLICY-MAKING INFLUENCE OF
BRITISH FINANCE CAPITALISM?

An examination of the history of the relationship between Raj officials and the
managing agencies suggests, however, a more complex picture. Firstly, these
firms did not always share a common commitment to financial orthodoxy
and free trade, and, perhaps because they were associated with a diverse set of
financial, commercial and industrial interests, they had difficulty achieving unity

5 They write: 'This vision does not merely qualify a crude, materialist interpretation of the imperial purpose, whether couched in political or economic terms, but suggests, more interestingly,
ways in which principle and interest were joined' (C&H, II, p. 179).
6 For more detailed studies of these business groups, see B.R. Tomlinson, 'Colonial firms and the
decline of colonialism in eastern India, 1914–47', *Modern Asian Studies*, 15/3 (1991), pp. 455–86;
S. Chapman, *Merchant Enterprise in Britain from the Industrial Revolution until World War I* (Cambridge, 1991); M. Misra, *Business, Race and Politics in British India, c.1860–1960* (Oxford, 1988).
7 Cain & Hopkins, I, 340–1.
8 For example, they say of the National Bank of India: 'By 1900 . . . the bank had become part of
the City hierarchy and had developed ties with Whitehall and the Indian Civil Service which led
to seats on the Board of Directors for a number of retired officials' (C&H, I, p. 340). Of the inter-
war ICS they say: 'they tended to despise industry as well as to fear the spread of its influence . . .
they had a closer affinity with invisible income' (C&H, II, p. 177).

of opinion on a range of economic issues, from the currency question and the level of the rupee exchange to the tariff issue.[9] Their main associations, the Bengal and the Associated chambers of commerce, declined to offer any views to the Government of India on these matters. The expatriate-dominated Bengal chamber of commerce refused to give a collective opinion on the question of tariffs in India because they were so controversial.[10]

More generally, these firms were not particularly successful lobbyists, either collectively or individually, and Lord Inchcape is a peculiar case. Their primary ideological attachment seems to have been to the principle of extreme business autonomy, and they often deliberately eschewed opportunities to draw closer to the state for fear of permanently eroding that autonomy.[11] Inchcape's *sub rosa* links with officialdom were, if anything, viewed with distaste by other expatriate businessmen. One, Henry Gladstone, son of the prime minister and head of the firm Gillanders, Arbuthnot & Co., denounced Inchcape's activities in the harshest terms.[12]

There is also little evidence of the strong cultural and social links between state and business which, it is implied, underwrote an unspoken alliance between gentlemanly capitalists and gentlemanly officials (C&H, I, p. 177). Indeed, by 1914 it would seem that far from sharing a common set of values, officials and business groups in India were very much at odds with one another. To some extent this appears to have been because officials were abandoning Cain and Hopkins's gentlemanly values, which stressed the importance of social background and favoured amateurishness, and were adopting a more professional ethic based on recruitment by intellectual merit.[13] The differences between the two groups were most starkly illustrated during the enquiry into Civil Service reform, held in 1913. Expatriate business witnesses to this enquiry were wholly opposed to the government's proposals to make to the Indian Civil Service (ICS) recruitment even more dependent on intellectual ability through examination; they continued to advocate the importance of non-professional qualities such as 'character', and they stressed recruitment by interview selection and recommendation. The president of the Bengal chamber of commerce complained that 'even the present system

9 See for example the evidence of the Bengal chamber of commerce to the 1898 Indian Currency Committee, which makes it clear that there was no agreement on what kind of exchange regime the Indian government should adopt: *Appendix (Evidence) to the Report of the Indian Currency Committee, 1898* (Calcutta, 1898), pp. 62ff. A more detailed examination of these issues may be found in Misra, *Business, Race and Politics*, chs 1, 6.

10 Bengal Chamber of Commerce to the Indian Fiscal Commission, *Evidence to the Indian Fiscal Commission, 1921–22* (New Delhi, 1923), p. 250.

11 Misra, *Business, Race and Politics*, chs 6, 7.

12 H.N. Gladstone to A. d'A. Willis, 30 Nov. 1922, from the archive of Ogilvy, Gillanders & Co., MSS Glynne/Gladstone, file 2609.

13 In 1913 and again in 1924 major commissions of enquiry were held into recruitment and training for the ICS. The Report of the 1913 Public Services Commission recommended further reliance on examination and less on interview in ICS recruitment. It also proposed further professionalization of training. See *Report of the Indian Public Services Commission, 1913* (Calcutta, 1913).

of recruitment appears to me faulty because it attaches too much importance to book-learning'.[14]

Behind this division over methods of recruitment lay a more general difference between businessmen and officials over the values most suitable in an imperial elite. As the director of the Bank of Bengal stated in 1913:

> I do not think they are . . . drawing recruits for the ICS from the right class of boys in England. I think that you want boys who have been brought up from childhood in families where there have been two or three generations of education and culture . . . I think that you have to draw them from a certain class.[15]

On the other side, ICS officials increasingly charged the managing agents with amateurishness and lack of professionalism in business. This was particularly evident in the report of the Indian Industrial Commission 1916–18, which criticized firms for focusing their recruitment on generalists and ignoring the benefits of specialized business training:

> During the course of our tours the necessity for special schools and colleges of commerce was frequently brought to our notice by Indian witnesses, who were, in many cases, men of considerable practical experience. On the other hand, British [business] witnesses, expressed grave doubts as to the utility of such institutions. . . . We are inclined to think that the British evidence we have received is not based on a sufficiently wide examination of the circumstances.[16]

More generally, there is a great deal of evidence that these divisions over values led to social tensions between businessmen and officials. Another business witness to the 1913 Public Services Commission complained that there had been

> a marked change for the worse in the character of ICS recruits . . . I think that in respect to their [social position and manners] a deterioration has occurred.[17]

Another, writing in the 1930s, complained:

> I cannot help thinking that these ICS people who go in to dinner ahead of me are the same wretched people who put up little bungalows around my place in Hampshire.[18]

14 N.C. McLeod, *Appendix to the Report of the Indian Public Services Commission, 1913*, vol. III, p. 443.
15 J.C. Shorrock, ibid., pp. 253ff.
16 *Report of the Indian Industrial Commission, 1916–18* (Calcutta, 1918), para. 174, p. 133. The official members of the 1913 Public Services Commission also expressed surprise at the managing agencies' refusal to recruit technical specialists to managerial posts: see the *Appendix to the Report of the Indian Public Services Commission, 1913*, vol. IV, p. 192.
17 Evidence of E.J. Holberton, *Appendix to the Report of the Indian Public Services Commission, 1913*, vol. III, p. 449.
18 Cited in D.C. Potter, *India's Political Administrators* (Indian edn 1997), p. 64.

This distaste was mutual. Percival Griffiths, writing of inter-war Bengal, stressed that this distance and snobbery between official and British business-men was very pronounced:

> One aspect of our aloofness was our attitude towards the British business-men, who were rather disparagingly known as box-wallahs [travelling sales-men]. That was a very, very strong attitude. Indeed I remember myself, when, from time to time, the heads of big British houses came to my district, while I was polite to them, I was apt to regard them with a great deal of suspicion, with very much more suspicion than I would regard the ordinary Indians. . . . It [Calcutta] was a city of gulfs. Nobody knew any-body at that time . . . outside their own particular sphere. The civil-service didn't hob-nob with the British businessman . . . Clubs were separate.[19]

These attitudes, combined with many businessmen's 'die-hard' opposition to the state's strategy of political concessions to Indian opinion, led to an increasingly sour relationship between expatriate business and the state. In-deed, it would not be an exaggeration to argue that the attitude of these businessmen contributed to the failure of British political strategy in India between the wars.[20] As Cain and Hopkins have noted, a central element in the Raj's response to the challenge of a radicalized mass nationalism in inter-war India was to woo the increasingly important Indian business elite (C&H, II, p. 193). Yet a series of political initiatives ranging from increasing Indian business representation in the reformed assemblies to the encouragement of joint Indian–British business political parties was rejected by much of the expatriate business community, much to the irritation of officialdom.[21] By the 1930s it is clear that the state took very little interest in assisting these British businessmen in securing their long-term future in India. This position was emphasized by London officials when, in 1937, the political spokesman for expatriate firms based in Bengal was told by the India Office that

> the European business community have made a great mistake if they think that [under the new Constitution] their commercial position will be pro-tected by the Governors or Governor General.[22]

THE QUESTION OF THE SUPPOSEDLY LIMITED INFLUENCE OF
BRITISH MANUFACTURING INTERESTS

If it is difficult to show a close relationship between managing agencies and the state, can it also be said that British industrial interests exerted no

---

19 P. Griffiths, oral memoir, IOLR, MSS Eur., (R), T 31 (1981). There is much memoir material in the records of the India Office Library which confirms this point; one businessman recalled that on the eve of the First World War social distinctions in India between business and official groups 'was much sharper than it was in society at home': N. Carrington, *Personal Memoir*, IOLR, MSS Eur., C392, 124 (1978).
20 Misra, *Business, Race and Politics*, chs 5, 7.
21 Ibid., ch. 7.
22 Reported by E. Benthall to T. Chapman-Mortimer, 13 Dec. 1937, MSS Benthall, Box 2.

influence, as Cain and Hopkins suggest? This issue has attracted a vast amount of scholarly attention and continues to be controversial. A number of historians, such as Tomlinson and Dewey, agree that this interest was systematically eroded after the First World War, as the state was forced to sacrifice free trade to the raising of revenue and financial stability. They cite in evidence the steady increase of protective tariffs in India, the development of import-substitution industries in India, and the failure of advocates of imperial preference.[23] There is clearly much to these arguments, as the influence of Lancashire exporters did decline when their interests diverged from the interests of the state in revenue. However, it does not necessarily follow from this that British manufacturing interests had no influence over policy-making in India. Basudev Chatterji and Partha Gupta have both recently published well-documented analyses of Lancashire politics which suggest that these manufacturers still had allies and were able to secure some policy concessions.[24] Although it is true that tariffs on British goods increased steadily throughout the 1920s, cotton was given some respite in 1922 when, unlike general tariffs, which were raised to between 11 and 20 per cent, cotton duties stayed at 7.5 per cent. In 1930 an element of imperial preference was introduced for duties on cotton piece-goods,[25] while in 1931, when the general tariff rate was raised to 25 per cent, certain classes of British industrial goods, such as machinery, railway plant and rolling stock, were admitted at significantly lower rates and it was luxury goods that were hit hardest.[26] Chatterji argues that these concessions were in part the result of successful lobbying by the Federation of British Industry, which he suggests was an increasingly influential counterweight to City influence and which developed strong links with the Conservative Party and particularly the Conservative Research Bureau.[27]

DIVISIONS IN THE ATTITUDES AND IDEOLOGIES OF BRITISH GOVERNMENT ADMINISTRATORS

It is therefore important not to exaggerate the influence of 'gentlemanly' interests on the state. To some extent these objections are accepted by Cain and Hopkins for the inter-war period, when they argue that ideology was more

23 B.R. Tomlinson, *The Political Economy of the Raj, 1914–47* (London, 1979), pp. 60–2; C. Dewey, 'The end of the imperialism of free trade: the eclipse of the Lancashire lobby and the concession of fiscal autonomy', in C. Dewey and A.G. Hopkins (eds), *The Imperial Impact: Studies in the Economic History of Africa and India* (London, 1978).
24 B. Chatterji, *Trade, Tariffs and Empire: Lancashire and British Policy in India, 1919–1939* (New Delhi, 1992); P.S. Gupta, 'State and business in India in the age of discriminating protection', in D. Tripathi (ed.), *State and Business in India: A Historical Perspective* (New Delhi, 1987), pp. 123–216.
25 The newly introduced duties applied at the rate of 15 per cent to British and 20 per cent to non-British cotton piece-goods. S. Sarkar, *Modern India, 1885–1947* (2nd edn, London, 1989), p. 285.
26 Tomlinson, *Political Economy of the Raj*, p. 62.
27 Chatterji, *Trade, Tariffs and Empire*, pp. 11–12, 142.

important than economic lobbies in driving imperial policy.[28] However, this raises the question of whether there was such a coherent and consistent commitment to 'Gladstonian' economic principles on the part of the state as the state existed throughout the late nineteenth and first half of the twentieth centuries.

To begin with, in the case of India there are problems with Cain and Hopkins's adoption of a strongly 'metropolitan' view owing to the fact that even before the 'transfer of power' the Government of India in Delhi was becoming increasingly autonomous from London. On account of the growing tensions between the two bodies it is difficult to speak of a single 'state' policy.[29] In the inter-war period the creation of powerful provincial governments created a further decentralization of authority. There were also, of course, significant political differences between persons within Indian government administration at each level.

Another issue which Cain and Hopkins were not able to treat in depth concerns divisions between businessmen and the Indian state, but also personal and ideological differences between government officials on issues pertaining to government involvement in Indian economic development. While, in general, London sought to extract as much benefit from the Indian connection for as little expenditure as possible, from at least the viceroyalty of Lord Curzon (1899–1905) some Delhi officials became interested in developing the Indian economy, and in particular Indian industry, for its own sake. Curzon famously castigated British businessmen for their failure to develop Indian heavy industry and so started a tradition of state incentives to the Indian iron and steel industry.[30] There is also some evidence that the cotton duties of 1896 were intended primarily to promote Indian industry.[31]

28 For example: 'financial management was for them [British officials] an instrument of Christian rule, the balanced budget was the realisation of a state of spiritual harmony, and taxation was a powerful force for moral progress as well as a means of funding the Raj' (C&H, II, p. 179).
29 J.M. Brown, 'Imperial facade: some constraints upon and contradictions in the British position in India, 1919–35', *Transactions of the Royal Historical Society*, 26 (1976), pp. 35–52.
30 On the evolution of state aid to the Indian iron and steel industry, see D.M. Wagle, 'Imperial preference and the Indian steel industry, 1925–39', *Economic and Social History Review*, 34/1 (1981). The classic account of the view that British officials in India did adopt a mildly interventionist ideology regarding Indian industrialization is given by C. Dewey, 'The Government of India's "new industrial policy", 1900–1925: formation and failure', in C. Dewey and K.N. Chaudhuri (eds), *Economy and Society: Studies in Indian Economic and Social History* (New Delhi, 1978). There is a growing literature which supports this view. See, for example, T.D. Rider, 'The tariff policy of the Government of India and its development strategy, 1894–1924' (PhD thesis, University of Minnesota, 1971), who concludes that Raj officials were 'development-oriented'; G.G. Jones, 'The state and economic development in India, 1890–1947: the case of oil', *Modern Asian Studies*, 13/3 (1979), pp. 353–75; W.D. Macpherson, 'Economic development in India under the British crown, 1858–1947', in A.J. Youngson, *Economic Development in the Long Run* (London, 1972); N. Tyabji, *Colonialism, Chemical Technology and Industry in Southern India, 1880–1937* (New Delhi, 1995), pp. 16–32.
31 Henry Fowler, Secretary of State at the India Office in 1894–95, admitted that there was 'an element of protection in the duties' which he introduced on cotton in 1895. See H.C.G. Matthew, *The Liberal Imperialists: The Ideas and Politics of a Post-Gladstonian Elite* (Oxford, 1973), p. 164.

A commitment to develop Indian industry emerged in a particularly strong fashion at the provincial level. This was not only because of the increasing involvement of Indian ministers in provincial policy after the 1919 government reforms; even before this certain provincial bureaucracies were moving away from Gladstonian orthodoxies and laissez-faire. The most famous example is that of Madras, where Alfred Chatterton, the first 'Director of Industrial and Technical Inquiries', pioneered a programme of industrial development initiated by the state.[32] In 1916 the Government of India signalled a major shift in its approach to economic policy when it established the Indian Industrial Commission under the auspices of the Munitions Board. As Tomlinson has noted, the commission was influenced by the widely held view that the post-war era would be marked by economic warfare in which only those states whose governments were willing to plan for autarchy would survive.[33] The commission's report of 1918 was a detailed and sophisticated programme for Indian industrialization. The role of the state in the provision of social infra-structural investment, technical education, industrial banks and the supply of financial and entrepreneurial assistance was strongly emphasized. Impressed by the work of the Munitions Board, the report insisted that it was essential for these plans to be implemented centrally, and the Munitions Board was converted into a Department of Industries in 1921.[34]

As Cain and Hopkins correctly point out, this ambitious plan was never fully implemented; and they go on to suggest that it foundered mainly owing to the re-emergence of fiscal orthodoxy and retrenchment in 1919–21.[35] This may be questioned. It is doubtless true that some officials in Delhi would have welcomed a return to orthodoxy (as some politicians and officials did in London). However, given the continuing interest in industrial policy in official circles throughout the inter-war period, it seems more likely that political expediency rather than the re-emergence of orthodox economic ideology led to the failure of this programme, as has been persuasively argued by Clive Dewey. Particularly important was the need to transfer real power to the new Indian provincial assemblies, which undermined the idea of a central Department of Industries with power to coordinate and initiate provincial policy.[36] Even so, the programme was only partially abandoned and Delhi officials continued to show interest in state involvement in Indian industrialization. So, although the Indian Tariff Board may not have been as radical in conception as some might have hoped, it did grant significant protection to nearly a dozen new industries during the inter-war period. Finally, as Tomlinson

32 Dewey, 'India's "new industrial policy"', pp. 221–2.
33 Tomlinson, *Political Economy of the Raj*, pp. 58–60.
34 Ibid. See also Dewey, 'India's "new industrial policy"', pp. 215–18.
35 They argue: 'Given the prevailing monetary orthodoxy, there could be no big push for development' (C&H, II, p. 185).
36 Dewey, 'India's "new industrial policy"', pp. 240–3.

observes, even though these hesitant steps may not have constituted a long-term integrated policy of protection, they nevertheless provided genuine assistance to infant industries in India.[37]

Cain and Hopkins do acknowledge the emergence of official interest in Indian industrialization in this period (although, in my view, they underestimate its importance), and they try to reconcile this with their general model of interpretation by suggesting that it was compatible with the state's overriding concern with India's financial obligation to Great Britain. With agriculture in crisis and substantial revenues alienated to the new provincial governments, they argue, the British had to promote industry if India was to be in a position to maintain its remittances (C&H, II, pp. 185–6, 191). However, there is evidence that Delhi's interest in promoting industry predates the crisis in state revenues and had more to do with military concerns during the First World War.[38] By 1917 officials were increasingly aware that India's lack of a heavy industrial base was undermining its war effort. So the viceroy, Lord Chelmsford, told George V:

> We are, of course, handicapped by our inability to procure machinery and by the necessity of establishing industries which should have been set up in pre-war days. For this we have to thank the ill-judged parsimony and the now discarded *laissez-faire* policies of those days.[39]

Similarly, the Report of the Indian Industrial Commission of 1918 censured the British managing agency houses for their

> lack of enterprise. They have been inclined to develop commerce rather than industries and have thus been less helpful than they might have been . . . in clearing the way for continuous industrial progress. . . . Important industrial [opportunities] have been almost entirely neglected, partly through ignorance of the country's raw materials, but mainly because commercial firms have prospered too well along conservative and stereotyped lines to trouble about underdeveloped industries with uncertain prospects.[40]

Following the First World War the Delhi government and, on occasion, the London government established numerous committees and commissions, on industry (1916–18), foreign capital (1924), banking (1931), labour (1929–31), the Indian Companies Act (1934–36), and various Tariff Board enquiries, mostly dominated by officials and official witnesses, who went out of their way to condemn the weak interest in industrial innovation shown by British

---

37 Tomlinson, *Political Economy of the Raj*, p. 62.
38 Dewey, 'India's "new industrial policy"', pp. 218–22; B.R. Tomlinson, *The Economy of Modern India, 1860–1970* (Cambridge, 1993), pp. 127–30.
39 Lord Chelmsford to George V, 21 July 1917, in Chelmsford Papers, vol. 1.
40 *Report of the Indian Industrial Commission*, para. 77, p. 510.

firms in India and their excessive preoccupation with financial and commercial activities.[41] Taken together, the reports of these various enquiries suggest, at least, a challenge to laissez-faire ideas. They tended not only to stress the importance of industrialization in India, but also to advocate at least a degree of state involvement in the process.[42] There were also signs of an incipient corporatism in the Indian Labour Commission's report, which called for worker training and state involvement in industrial relations. Similarly, the government became a strong advocate of 'rationalization' in the ailing jute and cotton textile industries.[43] The Government of Bengal insisted that British jute mills embark on policies of amalgamation and reorganization under government guidance if the industry wished to receive price support.[44]

By the early 1930s it is clear that a number of prominent officials favoured a more radical approach to policy, such as George Schuster, the Finance Member of the Council of India (1928–34), and Arthur Clow, the Labour and later Commerce member of the council from the late 1920s to the mid-1930s.[45] Schuster, for example, was convinced that 'the world is moving towards a stage where economic planning by governments is becoming more and more necessary'.[46] In 1932 he urged the adoption by the Government of India of something like a five-year plan and proposed the establishment of an Economic Advisory Committee. Eventually an Economic Sub-Committee of the Viceroy's Executive Council was established to coordinate departmental action, and later a new permanent statistical and economic intelligence unit was established as the first stage in a proposed 'economic census' of India. Schuster also authorized the establishment of a Civil Aviation Authority, supposedly based on Keynesian notions of trying to 'pump-prime' a depressed economy with state spending on capital projects.[47] Schuster had moved so far from laissez-faire principles that he believed that even if there was little that government could do to assist the internal economy, it should at least be seen

41 See ibid; *Report of the Foreign Capital Committee, 1924* (New Delhi, 1924); *Report of the Indian Central Banking Enquiry Committee, 1931* (New Delhi, 1931); *Report of the Royal Commission on Indian Industrial Labour, 1931* (London, 1931); *Report of the Enquiry into the Indian Companies Act, 1934–6* (New Delhi, 1936).

42 For the continued interest in interventionism exhibited by these reports, see Misra, *Business, Race and Politics*, chs 5, 6.

43 For an account of the incipient corporatism of official approaches to labour policy in inter-war India, see R. Chandavarkar, *The Origins of Industrial Capitalism in India: Business Strategies and the Working Classes in Bombay, 1900–1940* (Cambridge, 1994).

44 Misra, *Business, Race and Politics*, ch. 6.

45 Their interest in state involvement in Indian industrial development may be traced in their books. See G. Schuster, who noted, in his 'Indian economic life: past trends and future prospects', *Journal of the Royal Society of Arts*, 83 (1935): 'Governments in these days have got to accept a far greater responsibility for guiding the economic life of their countries'; A. Clow, *The State and Industry: A Narrative of Indian Government Policy in Relation to Industry under the Reformed Constitution* (Calcutta, 1928). In ch. 10 Clow comments that 'the policy of the Government of India is to make their purchases . . . for the public services in such a way as to encourage the industries of the Country'.

46 Schuster, 'Indian economic life'.

47 Tomlinson, *Political Economy of the Raj*, pp. 89–90.

to be trying. Clearly this was not the view of all officials in India, and Schuster was replaced in 1934 by the ultra-orthodox John Grigg.[48]

Even so, these trends accelerated during the Second World War, and it is clear that Raj officials' interest in planning went further than what was simply required for an effective war effort. In 1943 the Reconstruction Committee of the viceroy's council was established, and in 1944 a Department of Planning and Development was set up with the explicit aim of coordinating departmental and business opinion on future economic development and to think about issues of 'coherent state economic management'.[49] In 1945 Delhi issued the famous Industrial Policy Statement, which anticipated thorough-going state intervention in the form of state-owned industries as well as the planning and regulation of the private sector.[50]

The most dramatic illustration of the emergence in Delhi of a concern for Indian economic development for its own sake, and not merely as an adjunct of imperial needs, is the clash between Delhi and London over government responses to the depression in 1931. Viceroy Willingdon and the entire imperial council of ministers in Delhi threatened to resign if India was not allowed to decouple her currency from the pound and devalue the rupee, calling for Britain to lend India £100 million to help reflate the prices, cut interest rates and boost exports. As Tomlinson has noted, the desire by the Government of India to counteract the deflationary impact of retaining the rupee's link to sterling was not merely designed to promote the recovery of Indian agricultural exports and thus fund the sterling debt and home charges. It was also motivated by a desire to help the internal Indian economy and to promote political stability.[51]

CLASHES BETWEEN DIVERGENT ECONOMIC PHILOSOPHIES

Despite this gesture, the Government of India was defeated, and so, where there was a clear conflict of interest between British financial interests and those of the Indian domestic economy, London, representing financial orthodoxy, won. However, it would be inaccurate to conclude that London's policy was monolithic and always determined by fiscal concerns. During the discussions of the Indian Industrial Commission in 1916–19, a number of London and Delhi officials attempted to have imperial preference for British export industries built into any plans to give India fiscal autonomy. Officials sympathetic to Austen Chamberlain, Bonar Law and other British tariff reformers saw this as a way of securing the Indian market for emerging British manufacturing interests such as the car and industrial chemicals industries.[52] During the preliminary discussions surrounding the introduction of the new Indian

48 Ibid., p. 90.
49 Tomlinson, *The Economy of Modern India*, pp. 166–7.
50 Ibid.
51 Tomlinson, *Political Economy of the Raj*, pp. 85–7, 125–6.
52 Gupta, 'State and business in India', pp. 172–3.

political reforms in 1918, the leading politicians at the India Office, Edwin Montagu (the secretary of state), Lord Islington (the under-secretary of state) and T.W. Holderness (the under-secretary of state) all urged that the preferential treatment of British industrial imports be formalized.[53] There is further evidence of continuing concern with British industrial rather than financial interests in the debates surrounding the 1922 report of the Indian Fiscal Commission. Malcolm Hailey noted that the reception of this report in London would be influenced by the fact that

> the Cabinet has at present one outstanding preoccupation, namely the unemployment position in England . . . Any pronouncement of policy on our part will be viewed first and foremost in the light of that outstanding problem in Great Britain.[54]

While these groups were ultimately unsuccessful in entrenching imperial preference in India's new economic and political institutions, their defeat was as much a result of the power of the advocates of industrial interests in India as that of the supporters of free trade.

The continuing commitment among London officials to the development of British industry is also evident in the 1930s, particularly during the discussions surrounding the introduction of the second great instalment in twentieth-century political reform, the Government of India Act of 1935. The conservative and authoritarian elements in this act, particularly on the fiscal side, have not always been sufficiently emphasized. The 1935 legislation entrenched a series of officially sanctioned financial and commercial safeguards for British economic interests in India. It also removed the freedom of the provincial Indian legislatures to insert clauses in favour of Indian capital or ownership in cases of new industries receiving government aid, which they had been exercising under the 1919 reforms.[55] The commercial safeguards, in particular, were viewed as necessary to prevent any future Indian government from discriminating against new British entrants into the Indian economy. It was felt that such safeguards were vital, given the increasingly strident economic nationalism of Congress rhetoric which called for the reservation of key Indian industries exclusively to Indian capital.[56]

Ironically, while a more conventionally 'liberal' economic ideology was revived in India with the appointment of John Grigg in 1934, the mid-1930s saw new thinking in London on India's role as an imperial market. Interest in Indian industrial development became a feature of policy-making in both the India Office and the Board of Trade. Officials in these departments became interested in placing the economic relationship between Britain and India on new foundations in order to assist the long-term development of new British

---

53 Ibid., pp. 164–6.
54 Ibid., pp. 176–7.
55 Ibid., pp. 191–4.
56 Misra, *Business, Race and Politics*, chs 5, 7.

industrial interests.[57] They acknowledged that the old foundations of Indo-British trade, according to which India's role was as a primary commodity exporter and importer of basic manufactures from Britain, could no longer be sustained. However, they did not conclude, as Cain and Hopkins seem to imply, that divergence between the two economies was therefore inevitable; rather, they came to see India as a potential market for more advanced industrial products, but believed that to realize this potential a strategy of government intervention was required, designed to develop further the Indian economy and raise purchasing power. A memorandum prepared for the Board of Trade by the trade commissioner for India during the early stages of the 1939 Anglo-Indian Trade Agreement explained: 'Where Indian industries exist, more abundant capital would enable them to buy more expensive British machinery . . . informal collaboration between the two governments and industrialists to this end is highly desirable.'[58]

POST-SECOND WORLD WAR POLICY TRENDS:
POLITICAL VERSUS ECONOMIC CONSIDERATIONS

This new thinking about India's economic relationship with Britain continued into the Second World War. From an early stage it is clear that elements within the British government were anxious to find ways of preserving Britain's long-term interests, both financial and industrial, in the Indian market against American encroachment. Officials and politicians in the India Office, and particularly R.A. Butler, the Under-Secretary of State for India, argued that it was essential to secure the goodwill of Indian business groups in order to preserve India as a market for British exports. To this end they were even willing to see the sacrifice of British expatriate firms, if that was the price Indian business demanded. Butler, in a long memorandum entitled 'Post-War Economic Questions in India', suggested that if America and Britain were to maintain their economic superiority over Germany, Japan and the USSR they would have to find large new markets 'ripe for development'. While America would, he concluded, have China, Britain would have to retain influence in India.[59]

This vision of an industrializing India as a market for British capital goods was also propagated by Ernest Bevin.[60] By 1945 the Board of Trade was assiduously cultivating Indian business missions in London in the hope of persuading them to place orders in Britain rather than in the US.[61] Clearly, these good intentions were soon overtaken by Britain's severe financial crisis at the end of the war, but it is equally evident that at the highest level policy-

57 Ibid., ch. 6.
58 Note on 'The Indian Trade Agreement', prepared by the Trade Commissioner for India, in papers of the Conservative Party Research Bureau (CRB), 19 Jan. 1937.
59 R.A. Butler, Memorandum, 'Indian post-war economic questions', 10 Sept. 1941 (CRD), R.A. Butler Papers, 3/2.
60 P.S. Gupta, *Imperialism and the British Labour Movement, 1916–34* (London, 1975), p. 282.
61 Misra, *Business, Race and Politics*, chs 7, 8.

makers continued to see India as an important market for British industry. Indeed, India remained one of Britain's top three markets for chemicals, ships and textile machinery and an important market for iron and steel, electrical goods and machinery into the 1960s.[62]

Thus, it is important not to exaggerate official fiscal orthodoxy or to over-simplify the nature of state economic policy. At times during the period, particular groups within the state were interested in an interventionist policy which promoted industrial development in India and Britain, and not merely for financial reasons. From the late 1920s, in particular, ideas of planning and corporatism became increasingly fashionable, even among state officials in London but particularly in India.

It could also be argued that Cain and Hopkins's attempt to stress the state's financial orthodoxy not only neglects other currents of economic thought but overlooks other, non-economic, imperatives and leads to an impression of British government motivation which is unconvincingly narrow. A particularly important consideration affecting imperial policy in this period was the need to manage nationalism, a factor which Cain and Hopkins mention, but which they argue was ultimately secondary to financial considerations (C&H, II, p. 173). However, this is perhaps to overstate the case, and in some cases imperial fiscal orthodoxy had to give way to political imperatives.

It is difficult to support the conclusion that it was primarily financial considerations that informed British strategy towards Indian nationalism, and, in particular, that the political reforms of 1919 and 1935 made concessions to Indian opinion.[63] The devolution of substantial financial assets in the form of revenues from land, irrigation, excise and stamps to the new provincial assemblies established in 1919, leaving Delhi with considerably fewer revenues from income tax, salt and opium, undoubtedly contributed to the ongoing financial problems of the Raj throughout the 1920s, and surely suggests that by this time the government in Delhi, at least, had given precedence to political stability in India over fiscal exigencies.[64] This is also suggested by the

---

62 Tomlinson, *Political Economy of the Raj*, p. 166.

63 For a useful overview of the Indian political context to the inter-war constitutional reforms, see J.M. Brown, *Modern India: The Origins of An Asian Democracy*, 2nd edn (Oxford, 1994), pp. 197–209, 264–93; B.R. Tomlinson, 'India and the British Empire, 1880–1935', *Indian Economic and Social History Review*, 12/4 (1976), pp. 337–77. There is a very large literature on the origins and nature of the constitutional reforms of inter-war India. It is generally agreed that the old 'Whig' interpretation of these reforms as the beginning of decolonization on the part of the British is unconvincing. The reforms are now seen as a means by which a balance could be struck between imperial interests (of which financial stability was only one aspect, alongside military and trade considerations) and increasingly powerful Indian political interests. Tomlinson argues that different aspects of the 'imperial commitment' took priority at different times. He suggests that it was only really during the 1931 currency crisis that the relationship between British and Indian financial stability was the paramount concern. He also argues that the increasing success of nationalist politics forced greater and greater concessions at the expense of the 'imperial interest' throughout the period (Tomlinson, 'India and the British Empire', p. 339).

64 As Tomlinson comments, 'For the reforms to work Indian politicians had to be given increased financial resources ... These arrangements cost the centre Rs 10 Lakhs' (Tomlinson, *Political Economy of the Raj*, p. 112).

decision in 1923 to transfer the financing of the Indian Army, in certain circumstances, from the Indian to the British taxpayer.[65]

It is further unconvincing to suggest that British attitudes towards Indian political interests were primarily determined by these groups' views of state financial policy and debt, as Cain and Hopkins suggest.[66] As a case in point, British hostility towards the Indian National Congress was not primarily determined by Congress's threat to renege on India's debt obligations abroad: Congress adopted this stance only in 1930, long after British hostility towards nationalism had become entrenched.[67] Conversely, many of the groups which the British identified as potential allies adopted highly unorthodox attitudes towards state finance. Indian industrialists, whom they assiduously courted, continued stubbornly to demand rupee devaluation, government subsidies, steep tariffs and a politically controlled central bank in the late 1920s and 1930s.[68] Some even supported Congress's threat to default on public debt.[69] Many of the Indian princes, who were seen by the British as the foundation of the 1935 constitution, were also fiscally unorthodox. Some of the larger states, such as Mysore, Hyderabad and Travancore, developed rather imaginative economic plans in the inter-war period, involving state-owned industry, state-directed investment and other forms of industrial subsidy.[70] The Government of India's choice of collaborators was therefore informed by a number of considerations, amongst which a predisposition to fiscal orthodoxy does not seem to have been essential. Rather, notions of racial fitness, aristocratic rights, communal balance and latterly even of 'positive discrimination' in favour of oppressed castes underlay the British choice of political collaborators, the particular combination being determined by the balance of forces in any particular province.[71]

65 In 1920 the viceroy refused to countenance further imperial demands for the use in the Middle East of additional Indian Army battalions at India's expense, warning that it would cause 'a complete breakdown in the political situation in India' (see ibid., pp. 114–17).

66 They argue: 'The choice of political alliances in India was determined largely by the need to promote groups that would support the government's fiscal and monetary policies' (C&H, II, p. 173).

67 Repudiation of public debt first appeared as Congress policy at the Lahore Congress of December 1929; it was later adopted by Gandhi in his eleven-point ultimatum to Irwin made on the eve of the Civil Disobedience campaign in early 1930. C. Markovits, *Indian Business and Nationalist Politics, 1931–39: The Indigenous Capitalist Class and the Rise of the Congress Party* (Cambridge, 1985), p. 71.

68 Sarkar, *Modern India*, pp. 279–86; Markovits, *Indian Business*, pp. 68–78.

69 G.D. Birla, *Path to Prosperity: A Plea for Planning* (Allahabad, 1950), p. 192.

70 For further details of industrialization initiatives in some of the princely states, see Tyabji, *Colonialism*, pp. 30–4, 122–31; B. Hettne, *The Political Economy of Indirect Rule: Mysore, 1881–1947* (New Delhi, 1978); V. Ramakrishna Reddy, *An Economic History of Hyderabad State* (New Delhi, 1987).

71 There is a rapidly burgeoning historiography on this subject. A good synthetic overview of the issues can be found in T. Metcalf, *Ideologies of the Raj* (Cambridge, 1994), epilogue. For more detailed studies of how the Raj came to choose its collaborators, see D. Washbrook, 'Economic depression and the making of "traditional" society in colonial India, 1820–1855', *Transactions of the Royal Historical Society* (1993), and D. Gilmartin, *Empire and Islam: Punjab and the Making of Pakistan* (Berkeley, Ca., 1988).

Cain and Hopkins's inference that financial concerns also determined the timing of British withdrawal from India is also questionable and requires documentary rather than circumstantial evidence to support it. The authors suggest that it was the conversion of India's longstanding debt to Britain into a British debt to India of £1.3 billion during the Second World War (as a result of British debt obligations accrued for the use of Indian resources during the war) that made it possible and, indeed, desirable to leave the sub-continent in August 1947.[72] This is a neat argument and may well be true. However, it has yet to be shown in official sources that the debt situation directly influenced policy-makers during the negotiations over the timing of the transfer of power. It is clear that by 1942, before the complete repayment of the debt, the British had decided to leave India;[73] it is likely that the accelerated timing of their withdrawal had more to do with the rapidly deteriorating law and order situation in India in 1946–47 than with calculations about public debt.[74]

CONCLUSION

Cain and Hopkins's work on India, and on the British Empire more generally, is a powerful defence of the primacy of economic – and especially fiscal – forces in imperial policy. However, their attempts to explain everything, including British responses to nationalism, in financial terms pushes the argument too far and diminishes the impact of their insights on economic policy. When discussing economics, they clearly identify a central feature of British economic policy towards India and British economic policy more generally. However, in arguing that Gladstonian economic orthodoxy was overarching, they neglect frequent and forceful challenges to these ideas. Indeed, an analysis of the attitudes of dissenting officials suggests a positive hostility to many of these values after the First World War. Similarly, they exaggerate the dominance of 'gentlemanly capitalist' interests and values. Ultimately, Cain and Hopkins's financial interests do seem to have gained the upper hand, but, inevitably in a synthetic analytical work of this kind, they have not had the opportunity to show with detailed reference to particular episodes why they became dominant and why alternative economic ideologies were relatively

72 They write: 'The main obstacle to political independence remained India's indebtedness . . . When, as a result of the war, the financial and monetary imperatives which had long underpinned the imperial mission were removed, the imperial presence quickly followed' (C&H, II, p. 200).
73 See extracts from the Cripps' Offer 1942, in C.H. Philips and B.N. Pandey (eds), *The Evolution of India and Pakistan, 1858–1947* (London, 1962), pp. 370–3.
74 The decision to accelerate British withdrawal by cutting short constitutional negotiations in 1946 seems to have been the feeling that the only real alternative was the stationing of large numbers of British troops on the sub-continent for several years in order to contain the growing communal lawlessness. As Cripps told the Commons, 'it is certain that the people of this country – short as we are of manpower – would not have consented' and that such a move 'would be politically impracticable, from both a national and an international point of view' (quoted in V.P. Menon, *The Transfer of Power in India* (Bombay, 1968), p. 346).

weak. Cain and Hopkins have opened the way for scholars, stimulated by their arguments, to examine the conflicts between these interest groups and the intellectual and cultural context in which they took place. This will contribute further to our understanding of the peculiar nature of the British state and its imperial and economic policies.

CHAPTER 8

Gentlemanly capitalism and empire in the twentieth century: the forgotten case of Malaya, 1914–1965

NICHOLAS J. WHITE

Malaya[1] (or south-east Asia more generally) did not feature in Cain and Hopkins's vast synthesis. Lack of space and time dictated such economies, but the authors were following in a long tradition of collective amnesia.[2] Imperial historians, when discussing the colonial empire over the last three centuries, have more often than not neglected the Malaya region, concentrating instead on Africa and India.[3] In this essay, Malaya is taken as a 'testing ground' for 'gentlemanly capitalism' and empire in the twentieth century from the First World War to 1965, when Singapore was expelled from the independent Federation of Malaysia. Cain and Hopkins were indeed unfortunate not to discuss Malaya. On the one hand, the first section of this paper suggests that their case-studies of dependent empire in India and Africa together with their analysis of decolonization broadly fit the British presence in south-east Asia. On the other hand, my discussion then moves on to modify the 'gentlemanly capitalism' approach in three ways: firstly, problems are identified with Cain and Hopkins's characterization of the government–business relationship in Malaya; secondly, it is argued that Cain and Hopkins have paid too much attention to the role of the 'metropole' to the detriment of autonomous developments in the 'periphery'; and thirdly, it is demonstrated that Britain's Malayan

1 The term 'Malaya' is used here to mean the Malay States and the Straits Settlements of Penang and Melaka (without Singapore). Events in Singapore will only be discussed when they have a direct bearing on developments 'up country' in the Malayan peninsula.
2 P.J. Cain and A.G. Hopkins, *British Imperialism: Innovation and Expansion, 1688–1914* (London, 1993), p. 8n. Referred to hereafter as C&H, I.
3 The 'tradition' of neglect was established by J.R. Seeley in his *The Expansion of England* (1883). When Malaya is mentioned, it is often only in passing relative to the space afforded India and Africa: e.g. T.O. Lloyd, *The British Empire, 1558–1983* (Oxford, 1984); C.A. Bayly, *Imperial Meridian: The British Empire and the World, 1780–1830* (1989); R. Hyam, *Britain's Imperial Century, 1815–1914*, 2nd edn (1993); B. Porter, *The Lion's Share: A Short History of British Imperialism, 1850–1983*, 2nd edn (1984).

empire in the twentieth century served a multiplicity of interests, and not primarily those of 'gentlemanly capitalists'.

Britain's formal presence in the Malaya region dates from 1786, when a British settlement was founded on the island of Penang in the Straits of Melaka to promote trade between India and China through the establishment of a naval base. In 1819 Sir Stamford Raffles – an agent of the East India Company – occupied Singapore, and Melaka was acquired from the Dutch five years later. In 1826 these commercial entrepôts were federated as the Straits Settlements, and in 1867 the Settlements were transferred from the Government of India to the Colonial Office. The British 'forward movement' (or 'new imperialism') in the mainland Malay States began in 1874 with the signing of the Pangkor Engagement with the chiefs of Perak. In return for the institution of 'government by advice', the Anglo-Malay treaties bound HMG to recognize the sovereignty of the sultans and the autonomy of their states. In 1896, the four states which had accepted British advisers were federated and administered by a resident-general in the administrative capital, Kuala Lumpur. The five Unfederated Malay States jealously defended their 'independence' and stayed outside this centralized structure. By 1914, British paramountcy had been established in the Malayan peninsula; although the region comprised three different administrative systems. It is generally agreed that this territorial expansion was a 'reluctant imperialism' dictated by the need to defend traditional strategic – as opposed to new commercial – interests, namely the sea-lanes between India and China which were regarded by British policy-makers as a national interest and which were threatened by internal instability and international rivalry.[4] Malaya was not expected to fulfil any grand imperial, economic role; she was merely an afterthought of empire and little more than a strategic appendage to the 'jewel in the crown'.

Yet the British, by a typically unplanned act of serendipity, had stumbled upon a treasure chest, as Malaya became financially and commercially important in the twentieth century. By the inter-war years, the region was the recipient of large-scale British capital investment in primary production. European (principally British) dredges were used to recover tin ore. With the exponential growth in Western consumption of canned food from the Boer War onwards, Malaya emerged as the world's largest tin producer. In addition, British business took full advantage of Malaya's favourable soil and climatic conditions, large tracts of uncultivated land, and stable colonial administration, for the growth of rubber trees on large-scale plantations. By the 1930s Malaya was producing over half the world's rubber. Advantages

---

4 For a convincing overview, see N. Tarling, *The Fall of Imperial Britain in South-East Asia* (Singapore, 1993), chs 2–3.

of geographical location between India and China also facilitated the mass immigration of estate and mine labour to lay the basis of the peninsula's plural society. Malaya (with Singapore) achieved a level of prosperity and economic sophistication unrivalled in the tropical empire.

Large British merchant firms – known as agency houses – which had established themselves in Singapore from the first half of the nineteenth century promoted and controlled much of Malaya's primary production. The Straits merchants' expert knowledge of local investment opportunities was fed back to the City of London, where syndicates were formed and companies floated.[5] By virtue of their local expertise, the agency houses were granted managerial and secretarial functions, thus maintaining control of plantation and mining companies they did not necessarily own. A highly incestuous form of colonial capitalism thus came to dominate the Malayan export economy by 1914.[6] Through interlocking directorships, a limited number of directors in the City (often agency house executives) controlled vast mining and estate assets. In turn, the British 'investment groups' were linked through directorships to the British exchange banks, which exercised a virtual monopoly over the financing of the export trades. Shipping, insurance and the import trade were also handled by the big British firms. This classic cluster of interdependent interests was further cemented in the City by Malayan commercial associations, such as the Rubber Growers' Association (RGA) formed in 1907 and the Malayan Chamber of Mines (MCM) formed in 1918. By the First World War, as in other parts of the tropical empire, closely interconnected interests in the City (rather than in provincial industry) had played the central role in luring Malaya into the 'imperial enterprise'.[7]

In support of Cain and Hopkins, British imperialism clearly had not reached its peak in Malaya by 1914. As in Africa, administrative expansion continued after the First World War with the appointment of more and more Europeans to the growing State bureaucracies.[8] In addition, the commercial division of the peninsula between the British houses continued with the promotion of plantations through to the 1930s. In the tin industry, the competitive advantage of British firms over the Chinese was completed by 1920 with the widespread introduction of capital-intensive, bucket-dredging recovery techniques. British mining supremacy was also aided in the 1920s by the emergence of the London Tin Corporation (LTC) and its subsidiary in Malaya, Anglo-Oriental,

5 For a good summary of the development of British capitalism in Malaya, see J.-J. van Helten and G. Jones, 'British business in Malaysia and Singapore since the 1870s', in R.P.T. Davenport-Hines and G. Jones (eds), *British Business in Asia since 1860* (1989).
6 J. Puthucheary, *Ownership and Control of the Malayan Economy* (Singapore, 1960).
7 C&H, I, pp. 338–50, 356–62. It remains doubtful, however, that financial and commercial interests were the engine behind imperial expansion in the Malay States. British investment was the consequence, not necessarily the cause, of colonial rule. See C.N. Parkinson, *British Intervention in Malaya, 1867–77* (Singapore, 1960); C.D. Cowan, *Nineteenth-Century Malaya: The Origins of British Political Control* (1961); W.D. McIntyre, *The Imperial Frontier in the Tropics, 1865–75* (1967); E. Chew, 'The reasons for British intervention in Malaya', *Journal of South-east Asian History*, 6 (1965); K. Sinclair, 'Hobson and Lenin in Johore', *Modern Asian Studies*, 1 (1967).
8 J.S. Sidhu, *Administration in the Federated Malay States, 1896–1920* (Kuala Lumpur, 1980).

which rationalized production through more efficient management and more productive equipment. Furthermore, the City of London maintained control over the marketing of Malayan production. Once the outstanding trading centre for rubber, London lost its pre-eminence during the inter-war years to New York and Singapore on account of the vast consumption of natural rubber by the USA and the increasing tendency to ship direct from Malaya. Nevertheless, rubber-trading expertise remained based in London, centred on the Rubber Trade Association (RTA) established in 1913. The speculative futures trade in tin was regulated by the London Metal Exchange (LME). The LME retained its control over the world tin market after both world wars and beyond since 'tin production and smelting also remained in British hands, and the convenience of the LME for merchants and financiers was well-established and outweighed the fact that the UK was no longer the main market'.[9]

As was the case with Africa and India, Malaya owed much of its economic development to a British financial and service sector monopoly.[10] Indeed, Britain's Malayan territories appeared to offer little for the industrialist. Like Britain's African colonies, Malaya was run as an open economy where tariffs were designed 'primarily to raise revenue rather than to encourage discrimination or protection' and where colonial administrations were 'generally successful in balancing their budgets' (C&H, II, p. 206). Again as with British Africa, financial policy was tightly controlled by London. The Malayan currency boards issued currency through the agency of the exchange banks and kept reserves in London. The Straits and Malayan dollars were held at parity with sterling and were freely convertible. The sterling exchange standard thus allowed Malaya to link its currency with that of the UK, easing the payment of debts and the transfer of capital. British banks in Malaya invested surplus funds in London, and the Malayan banking system was closely based on the London money market.[11] Here, it would seem that the 'Treasury and the Bank of England were intimately associated with the City and the expatriate banks, which, in turn, were joined to the colonial administration by holding the government account and by acting as agents of the Currency Boards'.[12] British finance and commerce's pivotal role in Malaya was also aided by the ethics of her colonial administrators. The Malayan Civil Service (MCS), like its Indian and African counterparts, remained distinctly anti-industrial in its 'gentlemanly' outlook. Malaya's communal functionalism – with European managers of plantations and mines presiding over largely Indian and Chinese workforces – balanced demands for economic development against the desire to preserve what were regarded as idyllic, 'indigenous' Malay rural communities.

9 J. Crabtree, G. Duffy and J. Pearce, 'The Great Tin Crash: Addendum 2', in K.S. Jomo (ed.), *Undermining Tin: The Decline of Malaysian Pre-eminence* (Sydney, 1990), pp. 31–3.
10 P.J. Cain and A.G. Hopkins, *British Imperialism: Crisis and Deconstruction, 1914–1990* (London, 1993), pp. 198–9, 203–4. Referred to hereafter as C&H, II.
11 W.G. Huff, *The Economic Growth of Singapore: Trade and Development in the Twentieth Century* (Cambridge, 1994), pp. 18–19.
12 C&H, II, p. 207.

TABLE 8.1

BRITISH MALAYA: PERCENTAGE DISTRIBUTION OF EXPORTS BY AREA, 1934–38 AND 1947–50

Country or area	Annual average, 1934–38	1947	1948	1949	1950
United Kingdom	13	16	14	12	14
Rest of Sterling Area	12	16	16	22	17
United States	40	34	27	26	27
Canada	2	4	3	2	2
Non-sterling OEEC countries	14	10	15	16	18
Indonesia	5	10	10	8	6
Rest of world	14	10	16	14	16
Total	100	100	100	100	100

Note: Figures include data for Singapore, but basic trends for the Malayan peninsula should not be obscured.
Source: Adapted from Tables 162–3 in US Economic Cooperation Administration Special Mission to the UK, *The Sterling Area: an American Analysis* (London, 1951), p. 388.

At the same time, minimal government assistance to business – save for providing an Adam Smith-style framework of law and order – was favoured.[13]

In further defence of Cain and Hopkins, Malaya's true financial significance to the metropolitan economy was realized only after 1914. Prior to the First World War, the Colonial Office had usually allowed the Malayan administration a substantial degree of autonomy in economic decision-making. But with the outbreak of war in Europe, the metropolitan government swiftly imposed destinational controls on strategic raw materials via the Rubber and Tin Exports Committee in London to secure against supplies reaching Germany and its allies. By the end of the war it was clear that the 'decisive say' in Malayan economic policy now lay with London.[14] Furthermore, through the troubled 1920s and 1930s Malaya came to be seen by policy-makers in London as increasingly significant for upholding the exchange value of sterling. The peninsula had established a massive surplus trade with the USA. As Tables 8.1 and 8.2 illustrate, in the period 1934–38 the US supplied on average just 2 per cent of Malaya and Singapore's imports and took a generous 40 per cent of the region's exports in return. In contrast, the UK received only 13 per cent of Malayan production, while supplying 16 per cent of the region's imports.

13 P.J. Drake (ed.), *Money and Finance in Malaya and Singapore* (Kuala Lumpur, 1966), pp. 177–8, 210; R. Heussler, *British Rule in Malaya: The Malayan Civil Service and Its Predecessors, 1867–1942* (Oxford, 1981); J. de Vere Allen, 'Malayan Civil Service, 1874–1941, colonial bureaucracy–Malayan elite', *Comparative Studies in Society and History*, 22 (April 1970), pp. 149–78; J. Butcher, *The British in Malaya, 1880–1941: The Social History of a European Community in Colonial South-east Asia* (Kuala Lumpur, 1979).
14 J.H. Drabble, *Malayan Rubber: The Interwar Years* (Kuala Lumpur, 1991), pp. 143–5.

Nicholas J. White

TABLE 8.2

BRITISH MALAYA: PERCENTAGE DISTRIBUTION OF IMPORTS BY AREA, 1934–38 AND 1947–50

Country or area	Annual average, 1934–38	1947	1948	1949	1950
United Kingdom	16	19	19	21	18
Rest of Sterling Area	16	23	23	27	24
United States	2	10	12	6	3
Canada	1	2	1	1	1
Non-sterling OEEC countries	5	5	4	6	6
Indonesia	31	19	20	17	27
Rest of world	29	21	21	22	21
Total	100	100	100	100	·100

Note: As Table 8.1.
Source: As Table 8.1.

Malaya's economic value thus transcended any Marxian role as a market and source of raw materials for British industry. In intervening in the rubber and tin markets (in the form of price stabilization and export restriction schemes) from the 1920s, the imperial government was primarily concerned with maintaining Malaya's dollar-earnings as opposed to her industrial potential.[15]

It might appear that a mutuality of interest between government and business connected with Malaya had emerged by the inter-war years. The influence of commercial interests on policy-making is seemingly brought out by the blocking of proposals for political reform in the Malay States. During the 1920s and 1930s several attempts were made, in the interests of efficiency, to draw together the diversity of governments in British Malaya – the four protected Federated Malay States (FMS), the five protected Unfederated Malay States (UMS) and the colony of the Straits Settlements. Economies and rationalization were to be effected through decentralizing the FMS government and thus bringing it into line with the UMS. The broad aim was to 'increase and strengthen the links between all components of Malaya'. Decentralization was intended as a 'prelude to effective recentralisation'.[16] These proposals were generally opposed by the commercial community. Business leaders and investors had a vested interest in securing the status quo since the FMS administration's much-vaunted cost-effectiveness and political stability had ably assisted economic growth and modernization in the peninsula. The opposition of the commercial community 'on the spot' was channelled back to the City. Here, what might be identified as a 'gentlemanly capitalist' network was

15 Ibid., pp. 157–8, 300; *idem, Rubber in Malaya, 1876–1922. The Genesis of the Industry* (Kuala Lumpur, 1973), pp. 194–9. Hillman, 'Malaya and the international tin cartel', *Modern Asian Studies*, 22 (1988), p. 247.
16 A.J. Stockwell, *British Policy and Malay Politics During the Malayan Union Experiment, 1942–1948* (Kuala Lumpur, 1979), p. xiv.

mobilized. The 'arch-opponent' of reform was the Association of British Malaya (ABM), whose membership was made up of ex-civil servants and City directors. The views of the ABM were 'chiefly moulded and shaped by [Sir] Frank Swettenham, the architect of the FMS system and a director of numerous Malayan companies after retirement'. In addition, links with Parliament were exploited. The Conservative MP and government whip, George Penny (later Viscount Marchwood), was a leading tin smelter.[17] 'In all this the commercial interests gained a receptive ear from British officials because upon them depended the realisation of the government's central goal of economic development in Malaya.'[18] By the late 1930s, plans for political reform had been effectively abandoned.

Malaya's economic significance for both City and imperial government was undiminished after the Second World War.[19] Despite the moral blow inflicted by the fall of Singapore to the Japanese in February 1942, metropolitan wartime planners framed a reinvigorated and progressive 'raj'. In many ways this constituted the 'new imperialism'. In the political and constitutional realm, the Malayan Union scheme was intended to create an administratively

17 Yeo Kim Wah, *The Politics of Decentralization: Colonial Controversy in Malaya, 1920–9* (Kuala Lumpur, 1982), pp. 272–3, 338–40; see also K.K. Ghosh, *Twentieth Century Malaysia: Politics of Decentralization of Power, 1920–1929* (Calcutta, 1977), pp. 173–4, 177–9, 242–9; R. Emerson, *Malaysia: A Study in Direct and Indirect Rule* (New York, 1937, and Kuala Lumpur, 1964), ch. vii. Swettenham, Sir Frank Athelstane (1850–1946): Edu: St Peter's School, York; Cadet Straits Settlements, 1871; Deputy Commissioner with Perak Expedition, 1875–6; British Resident, Selangor, 1882; British Resident, Perak, 1889–95; Resident-General, FMS, 1896–1901; Governor, Straits Settlements, 1901–4. Marchwood, 1st Viscount, 1945 (formerly Frederick George Penny) (1876–1955): Edu: King Edward VI Grammar School, Southampton; senior partner Fraser & Co., Singapore; managing director Eastern Smelting Co., Penang, before becoming director of the firm in London and director of the parent firm, Consolidated Smelters, in the 1920s; MP (Cons.) Kingston-upon-Thames, 1922–37; Parliamentary Private Secretary to Financial Secretary to War Office, 1923; Conservative Whip, 1926–37; Lord Commissioner of the Treasury, 1928–9 and 1931; Honorary Treasurer of the Conservative Party, 1938–46.
18 Yeo, *Politics of Decentralization*, p. 340.
19 The economic aspects of the Japanese occupation of Malaya (1941–45) are a sadly neglected area, and, surprisingly, Cain and Hopkins devote little space to the Second World War in the empire generally. The engine behind the Japanese occupation of south-east Asia was resource-driven. In Malaya, however, the Japanese did not systematically exploit available resources. One set of limitations was the disruption of communications, the devastation of shipping, and the general havoc on estates and mines wrought by the invasion. Moreover, Japanese plans placed emphasis on Malaya's coal and iron rather than on its rubber and tin. Many former plantations were given over to food programmes. On their reoccupation, the British were pleased to find that Malaya's two main industries were not as badly damaged as wartime planners had feared. Unlike in Burma, the British did not return to Malaya after military conquest, and thus installations were not subject to the destruction of a retreating Japanese army. Many rubber planters discovered that their trees benefited from a period out of production, while the tin dredges dismantled by the Japanese had been of small capacity and outdated. Much of pre-war production needed only renovation rather than complete reconstruction. See A.J. Stockwell, 'Southeast Asia in War and Peace: The End of European Colonial Empires', in N. Tarling (ed.), *The Cambridge History of Southeast Asia: Volume Two: The Nineteenth and Twentieth Centuries* (Cambridge, 1996), pp. 355–6. Arkib Negara Malaysia, Kuala Lumpur, BMA INTELLIGENCE 506/30, 'Appreciation of the economic position of Malaya under the Japanese', n.d.; Public Record Office, Kew, London (hereafter PRO), CO 852/606/2, 'General report of the Rubber Inspection Committee, 11 December 1945'; CO 852/623/1, 'Report of the Tin Inspection Committee, October–November 1945'.

efficient, defensible constitutional unit whilst providing the framework for a multi-racial Malayan citizenship.[20] Malays, fearful of being suffocated by the Indian and Chinese immigrant communities, rallied around their rulers in protest against the Malayan Union, with the result that in 1948 the states returned to protected status. A Federation of Malaya was created which preserved state autonomy under a federal central government; yet British objectives were satisfied in that the essence of the Malayan Union – a strong central government and financial stability – was preserved in the federal constitution.[21] In the economic sphere a parallel reordering was envisaged which would streamline Malaya's export industries and thereby maximize dollar earnings.[22] Under the pressures of reconstruction, these schemes were also abandoned.

But the reoccupation of the peninsula from the autumn of 1945 witnessed a fresh invasion by an army of technocrats. For the first time Malaya had a peninsula-wide economic secretariat whose role was regarded as much more dirigiste than pre-war administrations. This new level of official economic intrusiveness was also reflected in the economic experts and the local representatives of UK ministries, who were attached to the coordinating commissioner-general's office in Singapore from 1948. As in tropical Africa and, informally, in the Middle East, this 'second colonial occupation' represented an enlarged metropolitan appetite for Malaya's fruit (C&H, II, pp. 275–81). Britain's other principal possession in south-east Asia, Burma, had attained independence outside the Commonwealth in 1948. But this unceremonious withdrawal was in some senses an imperial rationalization, since Burma's India-bound exports were not dollar earners. Malaya's huge sales of rubber and tin to the USA, on the other hand, made her economically vital to a heavily indebted and overextended postwar Britain.[23] As Tables 8.1 and 8.2 show, the Malaya region's balance of trade surplus with the dollar area was less pronounced than before the war. Yet the imperial financial crises of August 1947, September 1949 and November 1951 brought to the fore Malaya's imperial economic role. 'Malaya's dollar earnings were too important to lose.'[24]

Decolonization in Malaya thus emerged as a strategy for preserving Britain's interests in a changing international and local environment.[25] In this the

20 A.J. Stockwell, 'Colonial planning during World War II: the case of Malaya', *Journal of Imperial and Commonwealth History*, 2 (May 1974), pp. 333–51; C.M. Turnbull, 'British planning for post-war Malaya', *Journal of South-east Asian Studies*, 5 (Sept. 1974), pp. 239–54; A. Lau, *The Malayan Union Controversy, 1942–8* (Singapore, 1991), pp. 28–97.

21 A.J. Stockwell, 'British imperial policy and decolonisation in Malaya, 1942–52', *Journal of Imperial and Commonwealth History*, 13 (1984), pp. 70–1.

22 N.J. White, *Business, Government, and the End of Empire: Malaya, 1942–57* (Kuala Lumpur, 1996), pp. 65–8.

23 R.B. Smith, 'Some contrasts between Burma and Malaya in British policy in south-east Asia, 1942–46', in R. B. Smith and A.J. Stockwell (eds), *British Policy and the Transfer of Power in Asia: Documentary Perspectives* (1988), pp. 46–8, 68–72.

24 Stockwell, 'Imperial policy and decolonisation', p. 78.

25 A.J. Stockwell, 'British imperial strategy and decolonisation in south-east Asia, 1947–57', in D.K. Bassett and V.T. King (eds), *Britain and South-east Asia*, Hull: Centre for South-east Asian Studies, occasional paper 13 (1986); Tarling, *Fall of Imperial Britain*, ch. 6. The decolonization epoque in Malaya has been comprehensively documented with an excellent editor's overview in

British were remarkably successful. The Emergency – as the war against the mainly Chinese communist guerillas from June 1948 was known – effectively anaesthetized the radicals who might have divorced Malaya from the British economy, and who might have drawn dangerously on Malaya's massive sterling balances.[26] The alliance of communal parties led by Tunku Abdul Rahman which won the elections for internal self-government in July 1955 proved able 'collaborators'. In this sense, Malaya epitomizes the Cain and Hopkins model of decolonization: 'the purpose of the exercise was to transfer power to friendly rather than hostile nationalists' and 'in this way, Britain hoped to keep the Commonwealth "sterling-minded"' (C&H, II, pp. 288–9). Like Kwame Nkrumah in Ghana, the Tunku and his ministers agreed to respect the rules governing the sterling area, and independence ensued in 1957. In contrast to Burma, British investment remained intact after *merdeka* (independence), and Malaya remained an export-oriented and primary-producing 'open' economy to the 1970s.[27] In addition, the British proved partially successful in their long-term aim of federating Malaya with Britain's other south-east Asian possessions.[28] Despite little evidence of support for a Malaysian federation amongst the peoples of Borneo, the former crown colonies of North Borneo and Sarawak were encouraged by the British to unite with the mainland in 1963.[29] Between 1963 and 1966, British forces assisted Malaysia in a limited and undeclared war with Indonesia – known as Confrontation – to defend this zone of political and financial stability.[30] Singapore temporarily fulfilled British wishes by joining the Federation in 1963, only to be expelled in 1965. Nonetheless, the drawn-out (and ultimately failed) efforts to unify Malaya and Singapore were not necessarily disastrous for British financial interests in the region. Susan Strange has suggested that the emergence of a Malayan central bank with limited powers which did not fundamentally depart from the old colonial monetary system was due to Britain's efforts as a 'marriage counsellor' between the two territories. Monetary independence thus lagged far behind political independence due to the 'difficulties of reconciling the interests of the parties'. Malaya dispensed with the currency board only in 1967, following the divorce of Singapore from Malaysia.[31]

A.J. Stockwell (ed.), British Documents on the End of Empire series B, volume 3, *Malaya* (3 parts, 1995).

26 A. Short, *The Communist Insurrection in Malaya, 1948–1960* (1975); R. Stubbs, *Hearts and Minds in Guerilla Warfare: The Malayan Emergency, 1948–1960* (Singapore, 1989).

27 White, *Business, Government, and the End of Empire*, pp. 144–8.

28 Stockwell, 'Imperial policy and decolonisation', pp. 70–1; J.H. Pullé, 'The management of political change: British colonial policy towards Singapore, 1942–54', PhD thesis, University of London (1991), p. 29.

29 The Sultan of Brunei, however, was not prepared to share the oil riches or sovereignty of his small state with his Malay cousins and did not join the Federation.

30 J.A.C. Mackie, *Konfrontasi: The Indonesia–Malaysia Dispute, 1963–1966* (Kuala Lumpur, 1974).

31 S. Strange, *Sterling and British Policy: A Political Study of an International Currency in Decline* (1971), pp. 96–103, cited in C.R. Schenk, 'The Origins of a Central Bank in Malaya and the transition to independence, 1954–59', *Journal of Imperial and Commonwealth History*, 21 (May 1993), pp. 409–31.

At the same time, it could be argued that Malaya was becoming progress-ively less significant for Britain's financial and commercial needs. As Cain and Hopkins have argued, the colonial empire's disintegration was not simply the product of nationalist pressures or metropolitan undercapacity. Rather, global economic trends had already emerged in the mid-1950s which sug-gested that the Sterling Area had served its purpose. The City now had more to gain from a new and wider financial world which transcended formal and informal empires. '[B]y moving with the nationalist tide, Britain hoped to benefit from informal ties with the Commonwealth while simultaneously promoting sterling's wider, cosmopolitan role' (C&H, II, pp. 266, 285–91). The imperial government continued to regard Malaya's dollar earnings as a valuable asset. But the decline of natural rubber and tin as commodities in world trade, the improvement in Britain's balance of payments position, and new economic strategies in the metropole which looked to Europe and North America began to reduce the economic significance of the region during the 1950s. The mythical 'Golden Khersonese' was losing some of its glitter. Metro-politan financial reassessments were most visibly evinced in the development of a synthetic rubber plant in the UK which came on stream in 1958. This project had been approved in Whitehall as early as 1951 when the Treasury and the Board of Trade accepted that British manufacturers could no longer be denied supplies of synthetic rubber if British export competitiveness was to be sustained in hard currency markets.[32] These were considerations which made Britain's 'disengagement' from the region that much easier, even for Conservative governments with longstanding Malayan business links. In the Malayan case, it would seem that 'calculations about the means of maintaining Britain's position as a major financial centre are a vital and underestimated part of the explanation of rebuilding the empire and then of transferring power' (C&H, II, pp. 290–1).

Cain and Hopkins's thesis would indeed appear to be substantiated by this broad sketch of British imperialism in twentieth-century Malaya. However, as we shall now see, viewing the Malayan scene from wider perspectives reveals a multi-layered mosaic of relations between government and business, interactions between 'metropole' and 'periphery', and preoccupations with non-financial interests.

THE GOVERNMENT–BUSINESS RELATIONSHIP

As I have argued elsewhere, a potential flaw in the 'gentlemanly capitalist' approach is the tendency to 'assume that both government and business were homogeneous institutions with clearly-defined monolithic goals'.[33] In Lon-don, Malaya's growing imperial significance after 1914 meant that influential departments such as the Treasury (as well as the quasi-official Bank of England)

---

32 White, *Business, Government, and the End of Empire*, pp. 190–4.
33 N.J. White, 'Government and business divided: Malaya, 1945–57', *Journal of Imperial and Commonwealth History*, 22 (May 1994), p. 252.

had burgeoning concern with the region's affairs. This might suggest that Malayan interests in the City could exercise considerable influence on government. In practice, however, the mish-mash of policy-making in Whitehall often resulted in wishy-washy compromises or masterly inactivity in which the leverage of 'gentlemanly capitalists' is hard to isolate. In the formulation of international rubber policy in the inter-war years, John Drabble reminds us that 'there were divergencies over policy between the colonial and metropolitan government, and between the various offices in the latter (Colonial Office, Treasury, Cabinet, etc.)'.[34] In this complex policy-making arena, the imperial government largely constituted a separate interest group with its own agenda, little concerned with protecting British financial interests. During the central episodes relating to policy on rubber export restriction before the Second World War, Whitehall made the crucial decisions autonomously with imperial trading advantages in mind rather than concern with any sectional interest in the City or elsewhere.[35]

The situation was no more clear-cut in the post-1945 era, as illustrated by the insurance issue during the communist insurrection. Malayan interests in London pressed for a government-guaranteed insurance scheme given the uncertainties generated by the Emergency. The Bank of England, at least, did show sympathy for these pleas: the RTA exploited its links with Threadneedle Street, and the financier Anthony de Rothschild approached the deputy-governor of the Bank. The leading rubber trader and Tory MP, Walter Fletcher, lobbied Labour's Treasury team. This might be taken as the 'gentlemanly capitalist' web in action. It does support the view that there was a broad unity of purpose between Malayan interests in the City and the Bank of England. Yet, as was frequently the case, this nexus was not the principal policy-maker or arbiter. The Treasury took an independent view. Despite pressure from the Bank and the obvious dollar-earning interest involved, the Exchequer was overstretched in other theatres and therefore was not prepared to release imperial funds for a high-risk proposition in Malaya. The reluctant Colonial Office was mobilized. But the Colonial Office (in partnership with the local government that would be footing the bill) succeeded in complicating and delaying the issue. No guarantee scheme was implemented in Malaya.[36] Evidently, the Bank and the City did not always get their way. Moreover, this variety of governmental viewpoints in London modifies the Cain and Hopkins hypothesis. 'Gentlemanly capitalism' conjures up a somewhat bowdlerized image of the policy-making process.

Furthermore, it is hard to identify a Malayan 'united front' operating in the City. Any 'gentlemanly capitalist' complex was 'undermined by divisions and rivalries between individuals, corporations and industrial sections'.[37] For example, the City directors who oversaw the Malayan tin industry were bifurcated

34 Drabble, *Malayan Rubber*, p. 140.
35 Drabble, *Rubber in Malaya*, pp. 192–5; *idem, Malayan Rubber*, pp. 147–99.
36 White, *Business, Government, and the End of Empire*, pp. 116–18.
37 White, 'Government and business divided', p. 254.

into two opposing camps from the 1920s onwards. On the one side were the long-established 'Cornish' tin mining companies that had 'played a pioneering role' in technology transfer to the Malayan tinfields; on the other side was the emergent 'international' sector in the guise of the LTC in dredging and Consolidated Smelters in smelting. These conglomerates operated on a global scale and had close connections with international finance capital. They tended to side with Whitehall and welcomed the opportunities for forward planning and rationalization presented by the international control schemes and buffer stocks of the 1930s. Yet the other substantial sector of the industry in Malaya, the Cornish (who dominated the MCM), bitterly opposed restriction on the grounds that it denied opportunities for profit maximization and seemed to benefit the expanding international sector.[38] These historical divisions between 'interventionists' and 'free-marketeers' re-emerged in the 1950s. For Whitehall, the International Tin Agreement (finally ratified in 1956) was a means of defending the pound and securing invisible earnings from Malaya whilst, concurrently, defeating economic radicalism in the 'periphery'. The official view was broadly supported by the rationalized sector of the industry, which again welcomed the chances for long-term planning. But the smaller-scale, Cornish firms remained intransigent in their desire for short-term profit maximization.[39] This lack of homogeneity amongst British capital interests again calls into question Cain and Hopkins's thesis.

One also has to question the social cohesiveness of Malayan business–government circles. It is hard to pin down an interchangeable elite or 'old-boy network' which shared the same educational and cultural backgrounds. Those like Sir Frank Swettenham who moved from administration to commerce were the exception, not the rule. Whilst Whitehall mandarins and colonial bureaucrats were generally Oxbridge products, the majority of Malaya's commercial leaders were 'privately educated', self-made men.[40] 'Gentlemanly capitalists' were thin on the ground. The principal rubber baron in London from the 1930s was John Hay (1883–1964; Sir John after 1939), managing director of the premier agency house, Guthrie & Co., from 1930 until 1963, chairman of numerous rubber and tin firms in the Guthrie empire, and a director of one of Malaya's exchange banks, the Mercantile, from 1941. Born of penurious Fife parents, Hay had entered a draper's shop at the age of seventeen, winning an accountancy diploma at night school before gaining a position in the accounts department of Guthrie's London office. In the manner of Cecil Rhodes, perhaps Hay was an archetypal 'gentleman in the making' (C&H, I, p. 357). But his mercurial temperament and lowly Scottish background did not endear him to officialdom.

38 Hillman, 'International tin cartel', p. 329.
39 PRO, CAB 134/225, EPC (50) 35, 'Proposed International Tin Agreement. Memorandum by the President of the Board of Trade, 13 March 1950'; CAB 134/848, EPC EA (53) 89, 'Tin. Memorandum by the Colonial Secretary and the Minister of Materials, 18 July 1953'; White, *Business, Government, and the End of Empire*, pp. 151–2.
40 The term 'privately educated' in *Who Was Who*, etc. indicates an inferior or limited schooling.

It is true that government often relied on key individuals like Hay for informal advice on commodity matters. Hay did develop a close working relationship with the Colonial Office mandarin Sir John Campbell, 'becoming virtually an integral part' of the department during negotiations on international restriction during the 1930s.[41] Yet this cordiality between mandarin and rubber baron soon broke down. Far from accepting Hay as a 'gentleman', Campbell described in 1937 how Sir John had made him feel like 'the toad beneath the harrow who knows exactly where each prick-point goes!'[42] Other 'ungentlemanly capitalists' with limited schooling, like Sir Sydney Palmer, had made their names in the 'periphery', progressing from planter to estate manager before elevation to the metropolitan boardroom.[43] The leading tin smelter, Viscount Marchwood, had an illustrious career in the Conservative Party, but he was a grammar-school boy who had not gone to university and who had likewise made his fortune in Malaya and not the City.[44] In Malaya itself, there existed a similar cultural chasm between official and unofficial. As Anthony Burgess, a Malayan education officer during the 1950s, pointed out, within the white man's club it was clearly understood that the 'hairy legs and shorts of the visiting planter should not be juxtaposed to the pressed linen slacks of the government man'.[45] Malaya's planters were hardly the social equivalent of Kenya's 'gentleman farmers' (C&H, II, p. 219).

Moreover, on key Malayan issues business leaders and public servants were frequently at loggerheads. Government often had no hesitation in pursuing its own autonomous agendas. This is clearly illustrated by the decision to end rubber restriction in 1928. In the early part of that year, the leading rubber barons in the City wished to see the Stevenson scheme gradually phased out over a three- or four-year period to avoid disastrous market instability and a competitive struggle for labour. The imperial government, however, took a very different view. The Cabinet sub-committee which reported in April 1928 recommended that restriction should end in November because the scheme was being progressively undermined (and thus British dominance threatened) by the non-participation of the Dutch in Indonesia, where a great expansion in output and new planting of rubber had taken place, particularly on indigenous smallholdings. At the same time, the continuance of restriction discouraged efficient estate management and technical innovation, and encouraged American manufacturers to increase their consumption of reclaimed rubber, thereby reducing Malaya's market share. The report was accepted by Cabinet. But the

41 Drabble, *Malayan Rubber*, p. 184.
42 Cited in ibid., p. 333n.
43 Palmer, Sydney Bacon (1890–1954), Kt 1949: Edu: Privately. Rubber planter in Perak from 1909; director of various local estate interests and own firm of visiting agents; planting member Perak State Council, 1932–42; FMS Federal Council, 1934–42; President United Planting Association of Malaya, 1935–36, 1938, 1940–42, 1946–48; member, Advisory Council Malayan Union, 1946–47; Federal Legislative Council, 1948–49. Retired from Malaya to take on directorships of sterling rubber companies in the City; RGA chairman, 1952–53.
44 See biographical note in n. 18 above.
45 Review of Butcher, *British in Malaya*, reproduced in *Homage to Qwert Yuiop: Selected Journalism, 1978–1985* (1986), p. 65.

rubber producers and traders in London could not accept the official reasoning: a storm of criticism, a slump of rubber prices, and a massive drop in the market value of rubber stocks and shares ensued.[46] Likewise in 1946, the London planters 'strongly deprecated' their 'cavalier treatment'[47] Whitehall when an artificially low, Ministry of Supply monopsony price of 10*d.* per pound was imposed on Malayan rubber essentially to appease American policymakers. The imperial government was in the process of negotiating massive loans from the US and wished to avoid controversy at all costs. Here, Whitehall clearly valued American largesse more than she treasured Malaya's dollar earnings or the interests of British investors in south-east Asia.[48]

Indeed, disputes between government and commerce in Malaya seemed to multiply in the decolonization era. During the reconstruction of the peninsula Britain's postwar capital shortage, compounded by the Treasury's tight control of overseas expenditure, local priorities in a period of acute shortage, and destabilizing political developments in Malaya sought to progressively alienate business from government and frustrate any partnership in postwar economic development.[49] There was limited collusion in facing up to radical subversion and aggression on plantations and mines. Cain and Hopkins have claimed that the harmony of interests between officials and boxwallahs in primary-producing territories like Malaya ensured that after 1945 'coercion tended to be the first resort of policy' (C&H, II, p. 280). This was not strictly the case. From 1946 planters and miners were actually frustrated by government inaction. The declaration of the Emergency in June 1948 did not bring immediate satisfaction as deputations and delegations in both London and Kuala Lumpur demanded stronger and more effective action than government was willing or able to provide.[50] At the same time, the costs of counter-insurgency fell increasingly on the profit and loss accounts of individual British companies.[51] For a short period from February 1952, with the partnership of General Templer (as civil–military supremo in Malaya) and Oliver Lyttelton (as Tory Colonial Secretary in London), things seemed to improve for the business community. But Malayan budget deficits forced security cutbacks from 1954 which provoked the return of former anxieties.[52]

There was an equally limited consensus on political change and constitution-making. The Malayan Union scheme was regarded by business leaders as a dangerous departure from pre-war orthodoxy with its potential to provoke unrest and its prospect of eventual decolonization. This was overturned in favour of the more evolutionary Federation of Malaya. But government nurturing of nationalist leaders from 1950 onwards was regarded by commercial men as suicidal given the recent expropriation of foreign investments

46 Drabble, *Malayan Rubber*, pp. 162–9.
47 Ibid., p. 169.
48 White, *Business, Government, and the End of Empire*, pp. 77–9.
49 Ibid., ch. 2.
50 PRO, CO 717/172; CO 537/5979; CO 537/7265; CO 1022/39.
51 PRO, CO 537/7265; T 220/281–2.
52 *Manchester Guardian*, 13 April 1955, 'Anxiety in Malaya'.

in Indonesia and Burma. Government, however, ignored such warnings and took a quite different view: precisely the way to avoid the extremes of economic nationalism was to bring on moderate Malayan politicians.[53] The Alliance was recognized as a moderate force by officials and commercials alike; yet business leaders doubted the independent government's long-term ability to contain communal tension and radical nationalism, provide an efficient administration or remain in power.[54] On issues of economic development, British capital in Malaya may have found a new significance sheltered under the Sterling Area, especially in the years 1947–51. But the interventionist tendencies of the 'new imperialism' were far from welcomed by Malaya's rugged individuals brought up on the laissez-faire tenets of the old colonialism.[55] For British business, the wind of change in Malaya was a particularly chill one.

A postwar shortsightedness on the part of the 'exposed' planting and mining industries might perhaps be expected. But even the more cosmopolitan exchange bankers in London (with their apparent close ties with the Bank of England and the Treasury) were distanced from, and dissatisfied with, government actions. In the 'liberation' of Malaya a prime concern for the British banks was the recovery of debts paid to the Japanese liquidators during the war. Debtor–creditor legislation, however, favoured non-liquidated Asian banks and infuriated the City exchange bankers. A central problem for the British liquidated banks was that provisions concerning duress and coercion made it possible for debtors to avoid paying the real value of their debts by pleading that payments to the Japanese liquidator were forced by coercion.[56] During the 1950s William Cockburn, London general manager of the Chartered Bank and chairman of the Eastern Exchange Banks Association, was to be further disillusioned by policy-makers. He castigated the Treasury for its slow settlement of war damage compensation payments, he refused to subscribe to long-term local government loans because of political uncertainty in Malaya, and he feared tinkerings with currency legislation against the background of the 'agitation for independence'.[57] The bankers' difficulties hardly reveal a postwar 'gentlemanly code' amongst government and City applied to 'development and decolonisation abroad' (C&H, I, p. 36).

THE ROLE OF THE PERIPHERY

Another potential cause of friction was the increasingly autonomous role of the colonial government in Malaya. This brings us to our second charge

53 PRO, CO 537/7265; FO 371/93010, FZ 1016/64; CAB 134/497, MAL C (51) 1, 26 July 1951.
54 Inchcape Archives, Guildhall Library, London, Borneo Co. Ltd, MS 27259/4, BCL 43, Donald to Malcolm, 1 April 1957 and enclosures; PRO, CO 1030/438, 'Talk to RGA, 1 April 1957 by Sydney King (RGA Special Representative in Malaya)'.
55 White, 'Government and business divided', pp. 261–4.
56 P. Kratoska, 'Banana money: consequences of the demonetization of wartime Japanese currency in British Malaya', *Journal of South-east Asian Studies*, 23 (March 1992), pp. 322–45.
57 Bank of England Archive, Threadneedle Street, London (hereafter BoE), OV 65/4, copy of letter from Cockburn to Sutherland, Singapore Manager, 13 Oct. 1950; PRO, CO 717/186/5, Cockburn to Bourdillon, 8 Aug. 1951; BoE, OV 65/4, Cockburn to Jackson, 19 July 1951.

against the 'gentlemanly capitalist' model: Cain and Hopkins would seem to exaggerate the role of metropolitan financial impulses in dictating colonial policy. Even before the Second World War, the colonial regime was no mere tool of London. From 1914 to the Singapore débâcle of 1942, the imperial government did take command of Malayan economic policy. Yet this still does not mean that the 'periphery' was divorced from decision-making. John Hillman's work on the tin control schemes of the 1930s emphasizes the 'extensive process of negotiation and consultation between London and Malaya'. London 'would not act without the approval of the FMS government' or 'without industry support'. Nothing was actually forced on Malaya. It was instead the failure of sectors of the Malayan industry to adjust to the new international economic order which perpetuated 'the myth' that cartelization was centrally imposed on Malaya.[58] After 1945, the local administration was a more assertive, intrusive and interventionist animal which was far from the passive instrument of Whitehall or the City. This tendency was reinforced after 1951 with the introduction of the proto-ministerial member system, the overlordship of General Templer, and the appointment of Oscar Spencer as the Federation's Member for Economics. Spencer, in particular, epitomized the new breed of colonial official who came to see Malaya's future as lying in the creation of an autonomous, Keynesian 'national economy'. Typical here were the rubber replanting schemes of the 1950s which placed greater emphasis on local Asian producers to the detriment of British estate interests. Malayan agriculturalists were to be bolstered through government-assisted replanting programmes. The redistribution of resources (replanting was to be financed from additional export taxes) from the British estates to Asian, mainly Malay, plantations was regarded as unjust by the City-based rubber barons. Their bitter opposition resulted in compromise in 1952, but a much more effective scheme was introduced in 1955 in which the objections of Sir John Hay et al. were ignored.[59] Malayan economic policy was increasingly pulling away from Britain just as British economic policy was pulling away from Malaya. A more and more participatory regime in Kuala Lumpur could not neglect Asian economic interests.

Moreover, implicit in the Cain and Hopkins model of decolonization is a degree of metropolitan control which is probably unrealistic. Whilst it is true that the British withdrawal from Malaya was not solely determined and timed by the 'revolt of the periphery', it is equally the case that the favourable outcomes of decolonization were not exclusively the result of managed change from London. As Catherine Schenk has shown in her study of the origins of Malayan central banking, the delay in achieving monetary independence did not arise primarily from British imperial, delaying tactics. Rather, local politicians and officials were autochthonously reluctant to carry the full burden of

58 Hillman, 'International tin cartel', p. 246.
59 M. Rudner, 'Malayan rubber policy: development and anti-development during the 1950s', *Journal of South-east Asian Studies*, 7 (Sept. 1976), pp. 235–59; White, *Business, Government, and the End of Empire*, pp. 201–9.

financial *merdeka* given their canny and shrewd appreciation of the triple limits imposed by the historic integration of the mainland economy with Singapore, the immature domestic financial system and, not least, the international fixed exchange rate system which still prevailed in the 1950s.[60] Far from being bamboozled or coerced by the metropole, this scenario suggests a dynamic independent of City, Whitehall or Westminster mediation. The Alliance government recognized the need for a slow adjustment to domestic control of the economy 'if the longer-term welfare of the newly independent Malaya was to be achieved'.[61] The local political scene was fortuitous for the British and it largely managed itself. Crucial on commercial and financial matters was the role of Chinese entrepreneurs in the Malayan Chinese Association (MCA) which diluted the economic pretensions of Malay political leaders. The price of the Malay aristocracy's pact with the *towkays* was a free enterprise economic policy, a partnership of local and foreign capitals, a 'sound economy' and balanced budgets.

Any analysis of Malayan political economy in the twentieth century must indeed take account of the role of Chinese capital as well as of the City of London. The benefits of strong Chinese family, dialect and community networks proved as powerful as anything unleashed by 'gentlemanly capitalism'. By the Pacific war, leading Malayan Chinese rubber merchants had developed trade and credit networks independent of British commerce and finance, and they were largely responsible for Singapore's emergence as a service centre for south-east Asia as a whole.[62] The leading Chinese financial institution was the Oversea-Chinese Banking Corporation (OCBC) headed by the rubber millionaire Lee Kong Chian. Formed in 1932, and recovering remarkably rapidly in the postwar era, by the mid-1950s OCBC was on a par with the British banks in Malaya.[63] Chinese entrepreneurs were increasing their political influence through the MCA, which was established in 1949. The MCA's leader, Tan Cheng Lock, was a director of OCBC and the 'British' agency house, Sime Darby & Co. The leader of the Chinese tin miners, H.S. Lee, became the Federation's first finance minister in 1956. Indeed, by independence, British economic interests in Malaya were more and more dependent on the political connections of these Chinese business leaders.

Furthermore, with the benefit of hindsight there is a danger of assuming that the advantageous end-results of Malayan devolution were expected or predicted at the time by British officials and commercials. We have already mentioned the apprehensions of British business leaders regarding independence for the Federation in 1957. The early years of Malaysia were no more

---

60 Schenk, 'Origins of a central bank'.
61 Heng Pek Koon, *Chinese Politics in Malaysia: A History of the Malaysian Chinese Association* (Singapore, 1988), pp. 207–9, 428.
62 W.G. Huff, 'The development of the rubber market in pre-World War II Singapore', *Journal of South-east Asian Studies*, 24 (Sept. 1993), pp. 285–306.
63 D. Wilson, *Solid As A Rock: The First Forty Years of the Oversea-Chinese Banking Corporation* (Singapore, 1972); R. Brown, 'Chinese business and banking in south-east Asia since 1870', in G. Jones (ed.), *Banks as Multinationals* (1990).

comforting or certain. Surveying the scene from the City or Whitehall in the 1960s, it was by no means clear that the British had presided over a magisterial transfer of power. There was every possibility that Malaysia would descend into the political maelstrom consuming other parts of south-east Asia. As independent Singapore left the Federation in August 1965, the consequences were far from clear. The 'whole structure of decolonization in the region, based on the creation of Malaysia, seemed in jeopardy'. Few would have expected that firstly, the rump Malaysia would hold together and would remain a pro-Western capitalist state; secondly, that Singapore would not become a satellite of Beijing on Malaysia's doorstep; or thirdly, that the moderate Suharto would replace Sukarno in Indonesia, thereby bringing about a swift end to Confrontation in August 1966.[64] This imponderability again emphasizes the autonomy of local developments from metropolitan control or censure. In this Daedalian environment, the delineations between 'metropole' and 'periphery' were becoming increasingly fuzzy. The locus of corporate decision-making was correspondingly shifting from City head offices to local experts 'on the spot'.[65]

BRITAIN'S EXTRA-FINANCIAL INTERESTS

If the 'metropole' was not always the key actor in Malayan dramas, it is also clear that the peninsula was perceived as serving a multiplicity of functions and interests for Britain. The City did not necessarily have the most clamorous voice in Malayan affairs. Cain and Hopkins have claimed that, notwithstanding the emergence of the large corporation in British industry after the First World War, the industrial interest continued to exercise 'little influence upon the distribution of power' and a token 'determining effect upon economic policy'. Despite the growth of corporatism after 1945, the manufacturing lobby was 'no more successful in steering policy . . . than they were before'. The City remained top dog (C&H, II, pp. 20, 291n). Yet in devising the tin and rubber control schemes of the Depression years there existed a broad concern for British industry. As Hillman tells us, 'it was evident that there was a fundamental problem affecting all primary commodities, a chronic tendency to oversupply and consequent sagging incomes to producers. This was in turn considered a weakness for the international capitalist system as a whole since it reduced demand for *manufactures*'.[66] By the 1950s industrialists had considerable influence over policies which affected Malaya. In November 1951 Sir Clive Baillieu, chairman of the Dunlop Rubber Co. (Britain's largest rubber manufacturer), persuaded the Minister of Materials, Viscount Swinton, of the merits of synthetic rubber production in the UK. The London rubber

---

64 P. Edwards, 'When decolonisation almost came undone: the separation of Singapore and Malaysia, August 1965'. Paper read at the Australia and the End of Overseas Empire Conference, Institute of Commonwealth Studies, London, April 1994.
65 White, *Business, Government, and the End of Empire*, p. 50.
66 Hillman, 'International tin cartel', p. 242. The emphasis is mine.

barons were kept in the dark about the work of the interdepartmental White-hall committee which considered the matter at the end of 1951.[67] The genesis of this industry in the later 1950s effectively marked the downfall of Malayan rubber as a leading commodity in world trade. RGA protests to HMG about the importation of 70,000 tons of synthetic rubber into the UK in 1956 and 80,000 tons in 1957 fell on deaf ears.[68] This was part of Whitehall's wider strategy to assist the export competitiveness of British industry. After 1953, metropolitan economic policy became more and more focused on stimulating British industrial exports to the dollar area to achieve a balance of trade. The relaxation of import controls was designed to encourage production for export by giving industry access to cheaper raw materials. Freer trade was naturally facilitated by the free convertibility of sterling from 1955.[69] The multilateral world trading system and the global role for sterling benefited British industry as much as they profited the City.

On a much wider footing, it is by no means clear that key Malayan decisions were taken for exclusively economic (whether financial or industrial) reasons. The stalling of political reform in the 1920s and 1930s is a case in point. Nicholas Tarling has suggested that the objection of 'gentlemanly capitalists' was not the principal factor determining the abandonment of decentralization. The 'Malayan interest' in the City was not potent enough to influence colonial policy in a decisive way. Rather, Britain's assessment of the international situation in Pacific Asia as a whole was the overriding concern of policy-makers. British confidence in Far Eastern stability, particularly by the 1930s, was limited. The rise of Japanese militarism was compounded by British doubts concerning her capacity to reinforce the Singapore base and fears that the Americans might quit the Philippines. A 'business-as-usual' policy therefore would 'demonstrate a confidence in the future . . . while an attempt at change would risk failure and show weakness'.[70]

Indeed, Malaya's politico-strategic role – independent of economic considerations – should not be underestimated. Malaya and Singapore played vital roles in Britain's regional hegemony, relations with the Australasian dominions and ultimately the Cold War. Conceived in 1921, the Singapore naval base was intended to provide Australasia's outer defence. Despite the military disaster of 1941–42 and the Attlee government's swingeing, cost-cutting designs in the immediate postwar years, Malaya's role as a frontline state in the battle to win Asia away from communism increased its strategic importance by the late 1940s and early 1950s.[71] The British also hoped that a regional

---

67 White, *Business, Government, and the End of Empire*, pp. 190–1.
68 Ibid., p. 195.
69 C.R. Schenk, *Britain and the Sterling Area: From Devaluation to Convertibility in the 1950s*, (London and New York, 1994), chs 3, 5.
70 Tarling, *Fall of Imperial Britain*, pp. 123–4; see also N. Tarling, *Britain, Southeast Asia and the Onset of the Pacific War* (Cambridge, 1996), pp. 55–8.
71 J. Neidpath, *The Singapore Naval Base and the Defence of Britain's Far Eastern Empire, 1919–41* (Oxford, 1981); W.D. McIntyre, *The Rise and Fall of the Singapore Naval Base, 1914–42* (1979); K. Hack, 'South-east Asia and British strategy, 1944–51', in R.J. Aldrich (ed.), *British Intelligence*

defence complex based upon Malaya (and hence outside the USA's Asian sphere) 'might revitalise Britain's influence within the American-dominated western alliance'.[72] Indeed, just as Malaya's economic importance was fading, the country's strategic value was enhanced in the light of the Geneva settlement for Indo-China and the subsequent formation of the South-East Asia Treaty Organisation during 1954.[73] For this reason, it was just as essential to secure the Anglo-Malayan Defence Agreement in 1957 as Malaya's continued membership of the Sterling Area. Any 'gentlemanly capitalist' interpretation of twentieth-century Malaya is liable to downplay the region's position in Britain's wider Far Eastern strategies. In this regard, it is not clear that economic disengagement (whether by British 'industry', 'finance', or some combination of the two) is a satisfactory mono-causal explanation of decolonization in Malaya. If thoroughgoing financial and commercial reappraisal were taking place in London from the mid-1950s, as Cain and Hopkins claim, British actions in the 1960s are puzzling: the extension of the Anglo-Malayan Defence Agreement coinciding with a growing British desire to join the EEC would seem somewhat contradictory. 'Indeed, Britain's increasing commitment to military operations in the Borneo territories came at the same time as the first unsuccessful British attempts to join the European Community.'[74] Throughout the first half of the 1960s, metropolitan policy-makers remained firmly committed to retaining the Malaysia region as a British sphere of influence. It was not until January 1968, following the exceptional circumstances induced by the great sterling crisis of November 1967, that the 'Great Britain' wing of the Labour Cabinet was finally isolated and discredited. Britain's 'East of Suez' role was abandoned, and the decision to accelerate the withdrawal of forces from Malaysia and Singapore was announced.[75] In the Malayan case, the 'gentlemanly capitalist' approach seems too neat, too ordered and ultimately too rational to explain the multiple, unexpected and conflicting pressures acting on British policy-makers.

CONCLUSION

On the whole, 'gentlemanly capitalism' seems to pose more problems than it solves for historians of twentieth-century imperialism and decolonization. In the first part of this essay it was suggested how the Cain and Hopkins model

---

Strategy and the Cold War, 1945–51 (1992); M.H. Murfett, *In Jeopardy: The Royal Navy and British Far Eastern Defence Policy, 1945–51* (Kuala Lumpur, 1995).

72 Stockwell, 'Imperial strategy', p. 88.

73 Stockwell, *Malaya*, Part I, p. lxxiv; and see PRO, CO 1030/67, Lennox-Boyd to Head, 9 Feb. 1955, Enclosure: CO memorandum 'United Kingdom aims in Malaya, and means by which they might be achieved, with special reference to defence', reproduced in Stockwell, *Malaya*, Part III, Document 343, pp. 95–9.

74 A. Sharma, *British Policy Towards Malaysia, 1957–67* (New Delhi, 1993), pp. 141–2.

75 The process was to be completed by the end of 1971; previously in July 1967 eventual withdrawal was foreshadowed in 1975. For a stimulating discussion involving many of the participants in the defence reviews of 1964–68, see P. Catterall (ed.), 'Witness seminar: the East of Suez decision', *Contemporary Record*, 7 (Winter 1993), pp. 612–53.

might help explain the Malayan case from 1914 to 1965: the development of export industries dominated by British finance; the incestuous nature of British capitalism in Malaya; the support given to British commercial hegemony by the colonial administration; the significance of Malaya to British monetary stability; Malaya's undiminished financial role for the UK after 1945 followed by Britain's successful management of colonial nationalism which coincided with the growing disjunction between metropolitan economic policy and Malayan primary production. However, in examining this framework more closely a number of difficulties emerge. In explaining government–business relations the concept of 'gentlemanly capitalism' tends to oversimplify the complex divisions between and within commerce and officialdom. It suggests a social cohesiveness between official and unofficial that is hard to establish. Furthermore, it throws a blanket over a host of disagreements between business and government on numerous key Malayan questions. On interactions between 'metropole' and 'periphery', 'gentlemanly capitalism' underestimates the autonomous role played by the colonial administration in Kuala Lumpur. It implies an unrealistic degree of metropolitan control over the process of decolonization, and it points to an almost superhuman predictive capacity on the part of British policy-makers.

Finally, Malaya served a variety of British interests in the twentieth century which were not exclusively those of 'gentlemanly capitalists'. Industry was not always more marginal than finance or commerce in Malayan affairs. Moreover, key decisions were taken for political, diplomatic and military reasons, independent of financial considerations. The Cain and Hopkins theory is not completely without its uses, for it is clear that the economic value of Malaya to Britain continued in the period 1914–65 to represent more in its contribution to finance and commerce than to industry;[76] yet 'gentlemanly capitalism' remains insufficient as an all-embracing explanation of Britain's dialogue with Malaya in the twentieth century.

76 A point made by Bayley for the empire of the late-eighteenth and early-nineteenth centuries. *Imperial Meridian*, p. 253.

The theory and practice of British imperialism

P.J. CAIN AND A.G. HOPKINS

INTRODUCTION

We must begin by expressing our appreciation of the time and care taken by the contributors to this volume, whether in agreeing or disagreeing with our interpretation of British imperialism. The problem, as they have recognized, is far greater than our collective contribution towards solving it. In trying to understand why such a small island should have created and sustained such a large empire, none of us can hope for more than a plausible outcome, even of our best efforts. Illumination is a rare bonus; a definitive solution is not on the agenda. We also acknowledge that those who choose to attack large-scale historical problems must expect their efforts to be scrutinized and criticized. One of the considerable merits of the preceding essays is that they have been constructive, even where they have been critical. In helping to carry the debate forward, they have also demonstrated its importance and interest for a new readership.

Our response is written in a complementary spirit. Spacious subjects need to be opened up to new ideas rather than shut down by scholarly introversion. Now that the history of imperialism and empires is beginning to enjoy a revival, having been out of fashion for some time, there is a particular obligation to ensure that its renewed vitality is conveyed to a new generation of readers. We propose therefore to identify and comment on the major issues raised by the contributors rather than to take refuge in excessive detail. In defending our interpretation, where we feel that defence is justified, we shall also try to avoid the charge that fixed positions accompany closed minds.

Two large themes suggest themselves: one concerns the domestic roots of imperialism, and the concept of gentlemanly capitalism in particular; the other deals with the definition of imperialism and its forms of expression overseas. Baldly stated, these are vast and virtually unlimited topics, so it is important to recognize that the essays in this volume deal with aspects of them and not the totality, and that our response will be similarly confined. The first theme is discussed primarily by Green, whose focus is on policy and on the period 1880–1914, though direct links between the gentlemanly order and imperial (and colonial) policy can be found elsewhere, especially in the contributions by Kubicek, Redish, Misra and White. The second theme, the definition and expression of imperialism, is addressed directly by Davis's challenging essay, and is taken up with equal vigour by other contributors: Kubicek, Redish, Misra and White explore the subject within the formal, constitutional empire; Gough and Akita consider its application to two areas of informal influence. Here, too, the present discussion has necessary limits: it deals mainly with the late nineteenth century onwards (and is particularly strong on the period after 1914), and it omits, of necessity, some important regional studies (as indeed did *British Imperialism*). We should also add here that we are glad to see that so much emphasis has been placed on discussing British economic imperialism in the white settler colonies, later the Dominions. This is a subject that has been neglected for many years, and one that, in our judgement, should be at the centre of the debate about the nature of British economic imperialism. We are pleased, too, by the consideration given to the period after the First World War, since one of our original aims was to suggest that the inter-war years deserve far more attention than they have received from specialists on the history of imperialism.

We shall treat these issues within the contexts defined by the contributors to this volume. This allows scope for a wide-ranging discussion, though not one that covers all themes, periods, and regions. However, the bibliography that follows this essay provides a means of enquiring further not only into the matters discussed here, but also into the new debate on the nature and causes of British imperialism generally.[1]

GENTLEMANLY CAPITALISM AND BRITISH POLICY

In returning to the domestic roots of policy, we were reacting against two influential approaches. One, known as the 'excentric' or 'peripheral' thesis,[2] sought to locate the causes of imperialist expansion on the frontier rather than at the centre of the imperial power. The other, associated primarily with diplomatic history, treated international and imperial policy as being the product of Top People whose actions could be isolated from the power structure that produced them.[3] In returning to the metropolis, however, it was also

1 Our own reflections on this wider literature will appear in a separate essay in due course.
2 Ronald Robinson, 'Non-European foundations of European imperialism: sketch for a theory of collaboration', in Roger Owen and Bob Sutcliffe (eds), *Studies in the Theory of Imperialism* (1972), ch. 5.
3 Among many examples, see Ronald Robinson and John Gallagher with Alice Denny, *Africa and the Victorians: The Official Mind of Imperialism* (1961; 2nd edn 1981). We are not suggesting that these studies are anything other than valuable; simply that their value arises within limits that do not encompass the whole of the problem.

necessary to avoid the temptation of trying to resuscitate traditional Eurocentric theories that had come to the end of their useful life.

The notion of gentlemanly capitalism attempted to redefine the nature of
power in British society. It did so by offering a view of Britain's long-run
development that emphasized the importance of finance and services, and by
suggesting how this pattern of modernization was linked to social and political institutions and to cultural *mores*. In a rather sweeping criticism of this
endeavour, it has been suggested that we failed to 'develop a conception of the
state'.[4] To the extent that we were unable to present a full account of power
and authority in British society during the last three centuries, the criticism
carries weight. Had an appropriate conception of the state been to hand, we
would have grasped it with gratitude and relief. Alas, this was not the case.
Given that our primary obligation was to cover the world, it was not possible
for us to do more than indicate how gentlemanly interests took hold of and
reshaped the British state before placing their imprint on international policy.[5]

The great merit of Green's essay is that, in seeking to amplify our understanding of the forces that moulded policy, it has a direct bearing on the
problem of the nature of the British state. His analysis bears out, with more
authority than we could command, the main lines of the interpretation we
pieced together from the sources available in 1993. Green confirms the importance of the growth of the financial and service sector, provides evidence of
the emerging alliance between aristocratic and financial interests, and supports
the view that its agents had a profound influence on international economic
policy. His differences with us, as we see them, are primarily those of emphasis within a broad framework of agreement. They arise, in our view, from
his assessment of the concept of gentlemanly capitalism and of the influence of
its agents on policy. However, since what we regard as a degree of ambival-
ence in Green's treatment arises from our own statement of the concept, we
welcome the opportunity to clarify our original presentation. It was certainly
too compressed, and in consequence it may also have been opaque at points
where it ought to have been transparent.

Taking the conceptual issue first, Green argues that the 'bimetallic and tariff
campaigns reveal an alignment of interests that resists reduction to a straightforward "City versus industry" or "production versus services" conflict',[6] and
he seems to imply that our concept of gentlemanly capitalism involves this
degree of reductionism. He then suggests that there are 'more subtle' arguments

4 Martin Daunton, 'Home and colonial', *Twentieth-Century British History*, 6 (1995), p. 353.
5 There has certainly been a revival of interest in the role of the state in recent years, as witness
the excellent summary of much of the debate in J.A. Hall and J.G. Ikenberry, *The State* (1989):
but the new work has little of interest to say about the role of the particular socio-economic
groups in the formation of states or in the execution of state policy. Insofar as it deals with the
state, the same might be said of the new institutional economics at least as represented in the
work of its foremost economic historian, Douglass North. See his *Institutions, Institutional Change
and Economic Performance* (Cambridge, 1990).
6 Green, 'Gentlemanly capitalism', this volume, p. 48.

that can be mobilized in favour of a gentlemanly capitalist approach.[7] In response to this criticism, we would claim that the concept was never deployed as simplistically as Green suggests. Volume I of *British Imperialism* recognized the complexity of the bimetallic and the tariff reform movements, stressing the fact that not only manufacturers but also some figures in the City were in favour of both.[8] Green then proceeds to analyse, with authority and skill, the contemporary debate about whether Britain's future lay with industry or finance, and what the outcome of the choice might be.[9] Yet, again, we can reasonably claim that we made some of the essential points ourselves, especially in our discussion of the City's centrality as perceived by most of the political elite shortly before 1914.[10] When Green goes on to suggest that, given the City's geographical position and centrality to government finance, most senior politicians, administrators and bankers 'inhabited the same mental world', he provides authoritative confirmation of one of our own strongest contentions.

Green's belief that he is in disagreement with us on these points arises from his rather narrow definition of what constitutes a 'gentlemanly capitalist'. He appears to limit the term to elements within the City (though these elements are not closely defined) and to the high political elite, especially the aristocratic remnant. He then uses the argument that the City had no monolithic view of the really important issues to discredit the judgement that the concept of gentlemanly capitalism has much explanatory force in relation to the major debates of the time. Hence, he argues that some members of the aristocracy were under political as well as economic attack and were becoming dependent on the City, and that policy outcomes resulted from the vagaries of party politics as well as from the pressure of interest groups. Green's account of political outcomes presents the official administrative class as being an important factor in maintaining orthodoxy in economic policy, while also implying that it falls outside our own definition of gentlemanly capitalism. The result is to make the idea of gentlemanly capitalism appear too limited and contradictory to be useful without the amendments and the additions he proposes. Since this argument reduces the scope of gentlemanly capitalism to a smaller compass than we originally intended, it is important to restate our meaning of the term.

We certainly believe that the landed aristocracy was the original centre of gentlemanly capitalist groupings, maintaining traditional lines of authority and control while accepting the market as the arbiter of economic affairs. But we also recognize that the aristocracy was in relative economic and social decline by the late nineteenth century, and that the erosion of its position was

7 Ibid., p. 22.
8 P.J. Cain and A.G. Hopkins, *British Imperialism: Innovation and Expansion, 1688–1914* (London, 1993), ch. 7. Referred to hereafter as C&H, I.
9 See his impressive full-scale study, *The Crisis of Conservatism: The Economics, Politics and Ideology of the Conservative Party* (1995).
10 C&H, I, ch. 7 and pp. 151–3, 199–201.

slowed down by shifting resources into overseas investments via the City.[11] Green's struggling peers, Carnarvon and Portsmouth, are good examples of traditional figures of authority for whom a City connection offered a chance of survival once free trade had undermined agriculture. But gentlemanly capitalism was also developing in novel ways in the late nineteenth century, and some members of the landed elite flourished rather than merely survived under the new regimen of cosmopolitan finance. Davis's detailed research, referred to in this volume, bears out the importance of 'peers and gentlemen' in overseas investment and links them to the superior information flows that London was able to command.[12] At this stage, it was the impressive expansion of the service sector that was the key both to the change in the nature of gentlemanly capitalism and to the widening range of 'acceptable' forms of earning a living that it endorsed. This development gave rise to a complex of affiliations that helped to adapt, but also to maintain, the continuity of traditional authority structures within a rapidly changing economy and polity. This complex ranged from successful and less successful aristocrats on the one hand to a network of professional, religious, administrative, commercial and financial groups on the other. It included the higher grades of civil servants, neatly characterized by Robinson and Gallagher as the 'official mind',[13] who Green believes fall outside our definition of gentlemanly capitalists.

The City lay at the heart of this complex both because of its intimate links with landed society and because it was the economic hub of the great wheel of elite service occupations and interests, focused on London and the south-east, that were transforming and expanding the gentlemanly capitalist core. Within the City itself, only a very small, rich and privileged minority – recently brilliantly anatomized by Cassis[14] – was admitted to these exalted circles. But the rest of the congregation noted above can also be described as being gentlemanly capitalists either because they were directly connected with the privileged City, through business or personal ties, or because, in their eyes, the City represented the key element in the British economy. They had no experience of any more important locus of economic power: agriculture was in decline, and industry was a remote and not very tempting world at the edge of their everyday perceptions. This does not mean that the political and professional elites accepted everything the City said and did uncritically.[15] But they

---

11 Ibid., pp. 184–5. For a splendid survey of aristocratic fortunes – which in stressing decline may also obscure the success stories – see David Cannadine, *The Decline and Fall of the British Aristocracy* (New Haven, Conn., 1990).
12 See above, pp. 104–6, and Lance E. Davis and Robert A. Huttenback, *Mammon and the Pursuit of Empire: The Political Economy of British Imperialism, 1860–1912* (Cambridge, 1987), pp. 195–6, 206, 209, and Tables 7.33, 7.5 and 7.7.
13 See R.E. Robinson and J. Gallagher, *Africa and the Victorians*.
14 Y. Cassis, *City Bankers, 1890–1914* (Cambridge, 1994).
15 See, for example, Harcourt's row with the Bank of England when he was Chancellor of the Exchequer: D. Kynaston, 'The Bank of England and the government', in R. Roberts and D. Kynaston (eds), *The Bank of England: Money, Power and Influence, 1694–1994* (Oxford, 1995), pp. 23–5.

did accord it the status of being a prime mover, and ascribed it a galvanic significance within the economy that they attributed to no other set of institutions.

This form of gentlemanly capitalism inevitably frayed at the edges, and joined, imperfectly, different branches of capitalist culture, whether industrial or agricultural, and other service occupations that were unable to pass the test of elite acceptability. However, the main point is that gentlemanly capitalism, despite accounting for only a tiny portion of the total population of Britain, was itself composed of an intricate set of interlocking sub-groups. It disposed of much more influence in London than the non-gentlemanly capitalist economy could muster, and deployed effective means of social closure to keep unacceptable forms of capitalism at bay. Why the development of provincial industry failed to produce leaders who were capable of penetrating the gentlemanly capitalist web of interests and affiliations more effectively, and hence create an economic elite that was more representative of the nation as a whole, is an interesting question, though not one that can be answered at present.[16] The fact that no German type of finance capitalism, merging banks and industry and thus thrusting manufacturing into the middle of the gentlemanly capitalist network, appeared in Britain is a key issue that needs to be resolved. To some extent, the disjunction between finance and industry can be attributed to conservatism in the City and its hostility towards the world of manufacturing.[17] But it was also the case that British industrialists often remained resolutely local and resisted outside finance in the interests of preserving family capitalism.[18] Whatever the cause, industrial capitalists remained the core economic element of a separate elite, which was powerful in local affairs (when locality mattered far more than it does today) but lacked the institutional and socio-cultural connections that would have enabled its representatives to enter central decision-making circles in London.[19]

We hope that this restatement will persuade readers that the concept of gentlemanly capitalism not only has greater coherence than Green allows, but also encompasses many of the interests he invokes in his own explanation of events. There remains, however, the question of influence. Green highlights the importance of electoral politics rather than elite interests and ideologies in determining economic policy. In the case of the tariff reform movement, he is quite right to remind us that the decision to endorse free trade was decided on the hustings in 1906 rather than by interest groups.[20] Besides being a subject of popular debate, the tariff was also an issue that divided every section of

16 For a fascinating discussion of the failure of industrial radicals to achieve their initial objectives after the repeal of the Corn Laws, see G. Searle, *Entrepreneurial Politics in Mid-Victorian Britain* (Oxford, 1993).

17 D. Kynaston, *The Guardian*, 10 June 1995.

18 For a good example, see the firm of Edgar Allen & Co. as portrayed in R. Lloyd-Jones and M.J. Lewis, 'Personal capitalism and British industrial decline: the personally-managed firm and business strategy in Sheffield, 1880–1920', *Business History Review*, 68 (1994), pp. 364–411.

19 The remoteness of provincial industrialists from central sources of power has recently been stressed by A. Marrison, *British Business and Protection, 1903–1932* (Oxford, 1996).

20 The depth of popular support for free trade is demonstrated by E.F. Biagini, *Liberty, Retrenchment and Reform: Popular Liberalism in the Age of Gladstone, 1860–1880* (Cambridge, 1992).

business – including the City.[21] It was quite clearly a problem that could be dealt with only through the noisy process of democratic politics.

The discussion of the gold standard was a very different affair. Money was an arcane subject: there was some agitation for bimetallism in a number of industrial areas in the 1890s, but in general the question of the monetary standard aroused little public attention. Money was the business of the experts at the Bank of England and their City connections. Because the City was (with very few exceptions) adamant in support of a gold standard, monetary management failed to emerge as an overtly 'political' problem.[22] Governments deferred to City opinion in this matter because it was seen as having a 'national' perspective, whereas bimetallists reflected merely 'local' concerns.[23]

Green, however, judges that the debate over bimetallism was less important than the tariff controversy. This is true, if measured by the sound and fury of electoral politics, but the City's own perception was very different. The City was far more interested in monetary management than it was in free trade,[24] and the low public profile of the former issue was admirably suited to its purpose. Moreover, standing behind the placid acceptance of the City's expertise was the firm belief that the Duke of Devonshire's view of wealth, as being primarily a function of finance, should take precedence over Chamberlain's vision of it, as being rooted in manufacturing industry and labour.[25] It was in discreet discussion among experts, rather than in raucous public debate of the kind that marked the tariff controversies, that the thought patterns of gentlemanly capitalism were imprinted on the national sub-conscious:[26] the patent on the 'mind-forged manacles'[27] Churchill struggled vainly to shake off during the gold standard controversy of 1925 was registered in the previous century. In shaping the structure of the British economy, monetary rather than fiscal measures were the first choice of policy-makers.

POWER AND IMPERIALISM IN INTERNATIONAL RELATIONS

If Green's essay raises fundamental questions about the nature of gentlemanly capitalism, the other contributions are, in different ways, equally probing with regard to the meaning of that elusive term, imperialism, and are equally helpful

---

21 As attested by Cassis, *City Bankers*, pp. 301–7, and D. Kynaston, *The City of London: The Golden Years, 1890–1914* (1995), ch. 19.
22 See the debate between E. Green and M.J. Daunton in Y. Cassis (ed.), *Finance and Financiers in European History* (Cambridge, 1992), pp. 193–218, 283–92. Our view of relations between the Bank and the government in the later nineteenth century is very different from that implied in A.C. Howe, 'From "old corruption" to "new probity": the Bank of England and its directors in the age of reform', *Financial History Review*, 1 (1994), pp. 23–41.
23 A.G. Gardiner, *The Life of Sir William Harcourt*, vol. II (Paris, 1923), p. 614.
24 Kynaston argues that the City's interest in the controversy was brief. If forced to choose, the City also preferred tariffs to higher taxes: *The City of London*, pp. 384, 501.
25 P. Marsh, *Joseph Chamberlain: Entrepreneur in Politics* (New Haven, Conn., 1994), pp. 571–2.
26 For a good example of how the City was favoured in monetary matters, see J. Peters, 'The British government and the City–industry divide: the case of the 1914 financial crisis', *Twentieth Century History*, 4 (1993), pp. 126–48.
27 The phrase is from the poem 'London' by William Blake.

in prompting us to amplify the brief definition given in *British Imperialism* (C&H, I, pp. 42–6). We argued there that the 'distinguishing feature' of imperialism was that it

> involves an incursion, or an attempted incursion, into the sovereignty of another state. Whether the impulse is resisted or welcomed or whether it produces costs and benefits are important but separate questions. What matters for purposes of definition is that one power has the will, and, if it is to succeed, the capacity to shape the affairs of another by imposing upon it. The relations established by imperialism are therefore based on inequality and not upon mutual compromises of the kind which characterise states of interdependence.
>
> (C&H, I, pp. 42–3)

This definition implies, and *British Imperialism* tried to demonstrate, that imperialism existed not only when there was that deliberate exercise of political and military authority we call 'formal' empire, but also where power was expressed through 'informal' means. The concept of informal empire is, in our view, a powerful one.[28] Some historians, admittedly, deny its existence; but it is worth pausing to consider what would happen to the study of imperialism if all notions of informal or 'invisible' empire were abandoned. The subject would immediately revert to its earlier narrow, constitutional confines; the central question of power in international relations would be reduced to formal, and predominantly political, relationships; whole continents would be excised from the current historiography.

However, the concept of informal empire is also an extremely fluid one, and presents severe difficulties for historians in search of economic imperialism. When it is used both to describe Britain's relations with a white-settler capitalist society like Argentina, and with ancient indigenous economies such as China and Siam, historians can be forgiven for thinking that the concept lacks the requisite precision. One result of this fluidity is that, even among those sympathetic to the idea of informal economic imperialism, there is little agreement about where it begins and ends: Akita's dissent from our view of the extent of British economic influence in China in the 1930s is a good example of the general problem. Again, although Gallagher and Robinson recognized the possibility of movement from informal to formal status (and vice versa), the fact that relations with a country can exhibit both formal and informal features simultaneously (as was the case in China) adds a degree of complexity rarely addressed in the literature.

Yet formal empire offers no real refuge from this complexity. Behind the assertion of sovereignty lay a multitude of political relationships between Britain and her empire – from non-interventionist liberalism at one extreme to paternalist authority at the other. Similarly, the fact that the Union Jack flew

---

28 The classic formulation is by J. Gallagher and R.E. Robinson, 'The imperialism of free trade, 1815–1914', *Economic History Review*, 6 (1953), pp. 1–15.

over a territory implied nothing very specific about the nature and extent of its economic ties with Britain. The mother country's economic relations with the Dominions were far more like those with areas of informal influence, such as Argentina and Chile, than they were with other parts of the formal empire, such as India. Moreover, the links with India need to be further differentiated from those established with other parts of the dependent empire in Asia and in Africa.

Evidently, the concepts of formal and informal empire, though valuable, are not refined enough to deal with the problem of economic imperialism. Some of the contributors to this book implicitly accept this point. For Davis, Kubicek and Redish, the difference between formal and informal empire matters much less than the distinction between those areas of the globe that had open economic relations with Britain and others that were in some way exploited, and were thus subject to economic imperialism. Although we are willing to recognize that the distinction has its uses – tariff autonomy in the Dominions contrasts sharply with 'free trade imperialism' in India – we also feel that it fails to capture vital aspects of Britain's exercise of economic authority on a global scale.

With this in mind, we have recently attempted to look afresh at the concept of imperialism.[29] Since the general issue here is the nature of power in international relations, a useful analytical starting point is to distinguish between two forms of power in the international system.[30] One, structural power, refers to the way in which a dominant state shapes the framework of international relations and specifies the 'rules of the game' needed to uphold it. The other, relational power, deals with the negotiations, pressures and conflicts that determine the outcome of particular contests within this broad framework.[31] In the context of this essay, structural power, establishing the 'rules of the game', was fundamentally a manifestation of the core values and policy priorities of the British liberal state (backed directly or indirectly by military and naval force), with its preference for free trade, low taxation and sound money. Translated into global policy, these principles found expression in measures that were designed to produce congenial allies with a stake in the international economy dominated by Britain. The latter exercised structural power over smaller countries if they were subject to her military and naval might (or relied on it to preserve their independence), or if they were heavily dependent on British trade and credit. Such dependence implied that these countries were, in varying degrees, obliged to accommodate themselves to British political and economic liberalism, whether by opening their doors and agreeing to non-discriminatory tariff policies, by placing monetary and fiscal policy on

29 A beginning was made in A.G. Hopkins, 'Informal empire in Argentina: an alternative view', *Journal of Latin American Studies*, 26 (1994), pp. 469–84.
30 We are indebted here to Susan Strange, *States and Markets* (1988), ch. 2, though, of course, she bears no responsibility for the way in which we have developed her ideas.
31 Evidently, the two types of power are related. For further discussion see Hopkins, 'Informal empire in Argentina'.

a 'sound' footing,[32] by copying aspects of British constitutional procedures, or by adopting the cultural values of Britain's gentlemanly elite. The precise combination of attributes constituting structural power varied from country to country and with the passage of time in ways that form a central part of the history of imperialism. But, while the basic fact of dependence remained – even where it was entered into willingly – Britain continued to wield structural power on a scale that, through formal and informal means, shaped the world order between 1815 and 1945.

Defining imperialism as a particular form of power in international relations rather than as the expression of a purely constitutional arrangement thus requires us to reconsider a spectrum of possibilities ranging from informal influence to formal control. Where Britain's influence on the local economy and polity was profound, the host country was drawn into her orbit and its sovereignty was effectively diminished. The recipient became, in important ways, a satellite over which Britain exercised imperial power. But a subordinate relationship was compatible with a great deal of local political and economic autonomy for the smaller entities: at the level of relational power, particular elite groups in the host country could sometimes bargain successfully with the agents of the major power. In short, the distinction between structural and relational power enables us to see how degrees of local independence could be exercised within a broader framework of dependence, and thus to meet, in principle, the criticism made by Kubicek that the view from the metropole gives insufficient weight to local initiatives taken by Britain's numerous satellites.

In Britain itself, the principal controllers of structural power were gentlemanly capitalists. They were linked together through a web of occupations and activities that were directly connected to the exercise of economic imperialism. At the centre of the complex were the statesmen and officials who controlled what is known as 'high politics': foreign policy, defence, law and order, and macro-economic management, principally control over government spending and the money supply.[33] This official class overlapped, though it was not identical with, the class of 'peers and gents' who were the most prominent group of overseas investors[34] and who, through their City connections, helped to lay the foundations for the exercise of power abroad.

In this context, Gough's essay should be considered first because it provides an excellent illustration of an important aspect of British structural power, its naval strength, which made both formal and informal empire possible. Gough concentrates specifically upon a neglected aspect of one of the classic cases of nineteenth-century informal empire, Latin America, which figured prominently in Gallagher and Robinson's initial formulation of the concept and

---

32 This might also extend to adopting the gold standard (notably before 1914) or to adopting a more direct link with sterling (notably after 1931).

33 Here we have benefited greatly from reading J. Bulpitt, *Territory and Power in the United Kingdom: An Interpretation* (Manchester, 1983).

34 For the occupational structure of foreign investors in Britain, see L. Davis and R.A. Huttenback, *Mammon and the Pursuit of Empire: The Political Economy of British Imperialism, 1860–1912* (Cambridge, 1986).

subsequently in Platt's several criticisms of it.[35] In focusing on the role of the navy, Gough gives appropriate emphasis to an agent of empire that we were obliged (in one of many acts of over-compression) to take for granted. His chapter is particularly timely because military history is currently enjoying both a revival and a revision, and renewed attention is being paid to the coercive aspects of empire-building and management. Gough's analysis neatly divides the general from the particular, the structural from the relational. The navy's task was first to create and then to maintain the international order that Britain sought to bring into being after 1815. Piracy and the slave trade were to be put down; the 'roads of commerce' were to be opened up and British lives and property protected throughout the world. Exactly how this was to be done and with what degree of intervention was usually a matter for local judgement. The options ranged from a 'show of force' to negotiation. 'Gunboat diplomacy' caught the eye but it also increased the cost of operations and gave rise to international complications. Cost was an abiding concern, and it became a major preoccupation when the arms race began at the close of the nineteenth century because defence expenditure had serious budgetary implications that, in turn, had consequences for sterling. Senior naval officers were therefore diplomats as well as warriors, and their skills were put to good use, as Gough shows, in policing British interests in Latin America during the nineteenth century.

Gough's essay on the navy is also important because it draws a picture of one of the agents of the gentlemanly capitalist network that upheld British structural power in the world and made both formal and informal empire possible. His contribution offers a neat and hitherto scarcely known illustration of the intricate links between the military and economic arms of the gentlemanly elite. As he points out, the officer class of the defence services was firmly attached to the gentlemanly capitalist complex – and not only through its well-attested role of defending the realm and policing the empire. In a fascinating aside, Gough points to a little-known function of the Royal Navy in shipping bullion, bank notes, specie and bills of exchange, and notes how official business in this special type of freight, carried by the 'Securicor or Wells Fargo' of the age, could make capitalists of admirals.[36]

ECONOMIC IMPERIALISM IN THE EMERGING DOMINIONS BEFORE 1914

As we have already indicated, it is a mistake to suppose that the concept of imperialism becomes problematic only when applied to areas of informal influence. The degree of power exercised within the formal empire also varied greatly, both through time and across space. No better example can be found than in the 'white' empire, where emerging Dominion status conferred substantial local political autonomy but not, we argue, a commensurate degree of

---

35 The most convenient (and still very valuable) source for both references and discussion is Wm. Roger Louis (ed.), *Imperialism: The Gallagher and Robinson Controversy* (1976).
36 Gough, 'Profit and power', this volume, pp. 79–80.

economic independence. Davis and Redish both hold that imperialism necessarily involves some form of direct exploitation, though they disagree about
whether it was a significant feature of Canada's development before 1914.
Davis sees Canada's relations with Britain as being similar to Britain's relations with the United States, and therefore free from economic imperialism.
This interpretation is supported in general terms by Kubicek, who lays stress
on the economic autonomy of the white periphery. Redish, however, thinks
that Canada's economic freedom was compromised by her dependence on
loans from Britain in the period down to 1914. In our judgement, Redish is
nearer the truth here than either Davis or Kubicek. However, the point we
wish to emphasize, following our definition of the problem, is that exploitation is *not* the key issue in deciding whether imperialist relations existed between Britain and the white periphery.

The structural power exercised by Britain over the Dominions gave her
a degree of leverage that far exceeded the modest influence she disposed of
with respect to the United States. The analogy Davis draws between Britain's
relations with Canada and the United States is, in our judgement, mistaken
because it fails to compare like with like. In the case of Canada, and the
Dominions in general, Britain not only exercised military and naval control
but provided an indispensable market and enjoyed a marked predominance in
the supply of credit. Britain certainly invested as much in the United States as
in countries of white settlement within the empire, and the United States was
also the more important trading partner in absolute terms. But in the context
of the huge American economy, Britain's economic inputs were far too small
to give her significant leverage over either the economy or the polity of the
Great Republic. In the white colonies, by contrast, trade with Britain and
loans from the mother country weighed so heavily in the local economic
scales that Britain was able to exert a larger influence on their economic structures and political institutions. In estimating whether a relationship was an
imperialist one, it is essential to consider proportions as well as aggregates,
and it is precisely this dimension that Davis has overlooked.

The exercise of structural power was quite compatible with a great deal of
freedom for local economic agents in the Dominions, and undoubtedly gave
them opportunities that produced growth rates and living standards considerably in excess of those achieved in the mother country. It is in this context
that the local economic agents Kubicek refers to exercised their autonomy,
and it would certainly be straining words to describe their economic relations
with the metropole as those of exploitation. Nonetheless, the relationship
was an unequal one and remained so as long as the Dominions were reliant
on Britain militarily and economically. The weight of economic power was
scarcely felt in boom times, when trade was good and when access to credit in
London was easy, but it bore down at times of depression, when the need to
abide by the 'rules of the game' became fully apparent. At such moments,
fledgling settler societies on the periphery found their freedom to exercise
autonomy in economic policy significantly curtailed at both macro and micro

levels. It seems to us, for example, that Kubicek seriously underestimates the significance of the restraints imposed on Australian governments in the depression of the 1890s. Their inability to raise loans from the City had wide-ranging economic effects that were only marginally offset by the gold boom in Western Australia he describes. Nor does he recognize that, in the same decade, many British firms investing in Australia used the opportunity presented by the depression to centralize strategic management controls in London. The same process was at work in other territories of white settlement, including non-empire countries such as Argentina and Chile, which also depended heavily on British capital. Indeed, control of the Anglo-Australian banks after 1890 was so tight that the London directorate had to be consulted even on such mundane matters as the appropriate door locks for the bank's branches![37]

Within the white empire, gentlemanly capitalists conceded as much autonomy to local elites as was compatible with continued control of the levers of high politics. The strategy was similar to that adopted towards the regions of Britain itself, and sometimes meant conceding a good deal to local interests, both at home and abroad. Down to 1945, gentlemanly capitalist policymakers were generally successful in managing the tensions involved in trying to reconcile the priorities of high politics with demands from elites in various parts of the empire for greater local autonomy. In the Dominions, the broad aim of imperial policy from the outset was not exploitation in any crude sense: this would have been quite counter-productive in this context. Instead, power was exercised to guide the white settlements in economic and political directions that would add to the independence, prosperity and strength of Britain and its empire as perceived by the gentlemanly capitalist elite and its supporters. The aim was twofold: first, to ensure that the white colonies provided Britain with greater economic benefits than they would have received had they been independent or under the control of another power; second, to increase the strength of the mother country in the event of a major war, and hence to avert the possibility of them becoming an additional burden or even a hostile force in a crisis.[38] These aspirations were perfectly compatible with the spirited exercise of relational power by local elites and a rate of economic development that was higher on the white periphery than in the mother country. Yet policy involved the exercise of structural power that, in the language of our original definition, clearly involved 'the capacity to shape the affairs of another by imposing upon it'.

It is worth taking a closer look at Canada at this point because it was very much a marginal case and therefore presents a particularly severe test of our argument, as Davis, Kubicek and Redish all recognize. Canada was the only

37 G. Jones, *British Multinational Banking, 1830–1990* (Oxford, 1993), p. 81. For a more general argument on these lines see Charles Jones, *International Business in the Nineteenth Century* (1987), pp. 164–76.
38 See A. Offer, *The First World War: An Agrarian Interpretation* (Oxford, 1989), and *idem*, 'The British Empire, 1870–1914: a waste of money?', *Economic History Review*, 46 (1993), pp. 215–38.

part of the white empire that did not use sterling as its major international currency; there, too, Britain had to contend with the United States, which exerted an exceptionally strong countervailing influence because she possessed elements of structural power of her own. Yet it is our contention that Britain was able to exercise imperial authority in Canada in the nineteenth century in very significant ways.

The British North America Act of 1867, which created the Dominion of Canada, was a piece of high politics whose aim was to strengthen the empire by keeping the British presence alive in North America and by curbing the northward expansion of the United States. At one level, this was a matter of foreign policy, but it also had dramatic economic implications: by creating a united nation out of congeries of colonies, the Act was intended to establish confidence in Canada in the City of London so that capital could be raised for extensive transcontinental railways and other infrastructural needs. Finance on the scale required could not have been found elsewhere for this purpose at that time: without it Canada would not have been a viable economic entity. The overall concern was to add Canada to the strength of the empire; in this aim policy was successful. Britain conducted far more trade and invested far more capital in Canada than would have been the case had the colonies remained fragmented or been absorbed by their large southern neighbour. It is rash to imply, as Davis does, that Britain's trade and investment would simply have gone elsewhere had they not been attracted to Canada. Moreover, the creation of the Dominion ensured that Britain's broader influence remained strong; Canada was sufficiently British in orientation to swing her weight behind the mother country when war came in 1914. But for the 1867 Act, Canada might well have become a neutral force or part of the territory and resources of the United States which, it must be remembered, was regarded by Britain as being a potential enemy until after the turn of the century. Achieving this beneficial alignment through Confederation and other major policy initiatives[39] was a deliberate exercise of imperial power. It shaped the destiny of a dependent state; it set North America on a political and economic path that it would not otherwise have taken; and it did so in order to expand the wealth and the strength of Britain and her empire.

Redish argues that Canada was subject to exploitation because she was dependent on British finance in the late nineteenth and early twentieth centuries; the same argument could of course be applied to other areas of white settlement. However, as we have already suggested, exploitation is an inappropriate term to apply to a process that was mutually if not necessarily equally beneficial.[40] We prefer to argue that Britain exercised structural power in Canada and the other burgeoning Dominions to achieve the aims of 'high

39 Such as the Treaty of Washington, signed with the United States in 1871, which established definitively Canada's right to exist.
40 Unless it is argued that exploitation arises wherever market imperfections occur, in which case it is a universal condition and not, therefore, sufficiently refined to be helpful in the case under review.

politics', but shaped relational power to enable Canadians to benefit from the imperial connection, thus strengthening it. In the same way, to take an example cited by Kubicek, Britain's decision to go to war over the Transvaal in 1899 did not spring from a Hobsonian desire among British elites to exploit the gold mines (a view that at one point he appears, wrongly, to associate us with), even though many gentlemanly capitalists did very nicely out of 'Kaffirs'. Rather, the principal motive was the more general one of preventing a union of South Africa under the leadership of the Transvaal, creating what Lord Selborne called a 'United States of South Africa', which might have damaged Britain's economic interests in the region and harmed her broader geopolitical commitments.[41] Britain's policy towards southern Africa was copied from the Canadian example, though in this case Britain felt impelled to go to war to enforce it. If the outcome is judged by the subsequent trade and investment figures, and by South Africa's support for the war effort in 1914 and 1939 (despite the increasing influence of Afrikaner nationalism in domestic policy), the strategy was equally successful.

ECONOMIC IMPERIALISM BETWEEN THE WARS

Clearly, however, there comes a point at which economic imperialism of this nature diminishes to vanishing point. In *British Imperialism* we should, perhaps, have paid greater attention to the process whereby Britain's imperial authority dissolved in the twentieth century. The transition on the white periphery took place more rapidly in Canada than in the other Dominions. This was partly a result of the economic influence of the United States, which grew very rapidly after 1914, and partly because of the nature of Canada's own economic development, which led to the emergence of a sophisticated local money market by the 1930s. Redish is thus quite correct to point to Britain's diminishing imperial role in Canada between the wars. Even so, the influence built up over the years was still sufficient to ensure Canada's full backing when war broke out again in 1939.

Emancipation from London's influence took longer in the rest of the Dominions. Redish claims that Britain's inability to lend as much after 1914 as before was a key factor in the decline of imperial power over the white periphery between the wars. This view has merit as far as Canada is concerned because she had paid off most of her loans from Britain by 1930. Elsewhere, however, it does not provide a close fit with the evidence. The continued indebtedness of the other Dominions, and their desperate need to earn sterling to pay their annual interest charges, gave London considerable leverage by making membership of the Sterling Area compulsory.[42] There is no doubt

41 Selborne's phrase appears in a memorandum printed in Robinson and Gallagher, *Africa and the Victorians*, pp. 434–7. We believe that our interpretation is consistent with the findings of I.R. Smith, *The Origins of the South African War, 1899–1902* (1996).
42 For a summary of the problems see P.J. Cain, 'Colonies and capital: some aspects of Anglo-colonial financial relations after 1850', in F.M.L. Thompson (ed.), *Landowners, Capitalists and Entrepreneurs: Essays for Sir John Habakkuk* (Oxford, 1994), pp. 229–33.

that Britain viewed the Area, underpinned by the preferential trading system introduced after 1932, as an imperial economic bloc, a weighty manifestation of structural power that could be manipulated to claw back some of the ground lost to the United States in global finance after 1914. Indeed, given the tightening of sterling controls after 1939 and their extension into the early 1950s, it was not until then that the remaining Dominions were able to break free from Britain's financial grip, and slip out of her geopolitical net too.[43]

The rise of the Sterling Area is a reminder that Britain's economic policies in the 1930s were not seen as desperate attempts to keep the sinking imperial ship afloat but as part of a strategy to recover lost elements of structural power. The collapse of the United States' economy after 1929, and the relative success and stability of the empire and of the Sterling Area, led policy-makers to believe that Britain's days of glory as a global financial power were far from over. It is important to keep this in mind when evaluating British policy towards Canada in the 1930s. Redish criticizes our account of Britain's attempt to increase her financial influence in Canada by supporting the creation of a Canadian central bank, which began operations in 1935. The reconstruction offered in *British Imperialism* certainly exaggerated the role of the Bank of England in this process.[44] Redish is quite right to point out not only that the initiative for a central bank came from the Canadians, but also that the creation of the Bank of Canada made little difference to Canadian monetary policy, which continued to take its cue from New York rather than from London.[45] Nonetheless, the Bank of England did make a serious effort to ensure that the new central bank was created in its own image. The dependence of Canada on the British market was much increased in the early 1930s, as the economy of the United States floundered in the Depression. The Bank hoped that a pliable Canadian central bank would play its part in persuading the Canadian government to join the Sterling Area. Had that occurred, Canadian monetary policy would have been decided in London.[46]

Britain's continued pursuit of imperial advantage in the 1930s was also seen in China. Shigeru Akita takes us to task for exaggerating the impact of British economic imperialism there, preferring to accept the time-honoured argument that, here as elsewhere, Britain's influence was in retreat and that British

---

43 In the penultimate section of her essay, Redish casts doubt on our (admittedly attenuated) interpretation of the financial aspects of decolonization. Interesting though her comments are, they are not, in our judgement, convincing because their speculative nature is not borne out by the evidence that has recently become available. See, in particular, A.G. Hopkins, 'Macmillan's Audit of Empire, 1957', in P. Clarke and C. Trebilcock, eds, *Understanding Decline: Perceptions and Realities of British Economic Performance. Essays Presented to Barry Supple* (Cambridge, 1997), pp. 234–60; G. Krozewski, 'Sterling, the "minor" territories and the end of formal empire, 1939–58', *Economic History Review*, 46 (1993), pp. 239–65; and *idem*, 'Finance and empire: the dilemma facing Great Britain in the 1950s', *International History Review*, 18 (1996), pp. 48–68.
44 P.J. Cain and A.G. Hopkins, *British Imperialism: Crisis and Deconstruction, 1914–1990* (London, 1993), pp. 138–43. Referred to hereafter as C&H, II.
45 See also M.D. Bordo and A. Redish, 'Why did the Bank of Canada emerge in 1935?', *Journal of Economic History*, 47 (1987), pp. 405–17.
46 P.J. Cain, 'Gentlemanly imperialists at work: the Bank of England, Canada, and the Sterling Area, 1932–1936', *Economic History Review*, 49 (1996), pp. 336–57.

policy was concerned with managing decline. He downplays the significance of the Leith-Ross mission of 1935, which was sent to persuade the Chinese to set up a central bank on approved British lines and to join the Sterling Area, pointing out not only that it failed in its ultimate objectives but that the Treasury-inspired plan was opposed throughout by the Foreign Office, which was alarmed by the possibility of offending Japan. Instead, Akita highlights the importance of the United States, especially through massive silver purchases in 1934, which (he claims) were catalytic in persuading the Chinese to decide on monetary reform before Leith-Ross arrived in China.

In evaluating this criticism, it is important to remember that the silver purchases contracted by the United States were haphazard and were made almost entirely for domestic reasons.[47] In fact, it was the Chinese authorities who took the initiative to institute monetary reform before the United States intervened: one important outcome of our debate with Akita is to prompt all of us to recognize the degree to which China's reforms were inspired internally and were not simply a response to external stimuli.[48] At the same time, the United States was, on the whole, more fearful of offending Japan in China than was Britain. The State Department's attitudes were broadly similar to those of the Foreign Office, but in Britain the Treasury, backed by the powerful figure of Neville Chamberlain, provided some counterweight to the Foreign Office in suggesting that a judicious mixture of economic reform in China, together with political concessions to Japan on China's northern border, would dissipate tension in the Far East, Although the Leith-Ross mission was unsuccessful in its ultimate aims[49] – an outcome that came as no surprise to the Bank of England, which was more cautious than the Treasury in this matter[50] – it did trigger a whole series of Sino-British initiatives that helped the revival of China's economy and also increased British influence down to 1937, when progress was abruptly halted by the Sino-Japanese War.[51]

The British were beginning to recognize that, as China began to develop on capitalist lines, their economic interests were more likely to be advanced by playing down the older, direct forms of imperial power, such as the enforcement of extraterritoriality, and by promoting greater cooperation between British and local capital. At the same time, there is little doubt that Britain's gentlemanly capitalist elites still had spacious plans for financial imperialism in China and that they were intent on replacing more obviously offensive forms of structural imperialism with a subtler relationship based on overall monetary

47 D. Borg, *The United States in the Far Eastern Crisis of 1933–1938* (Cambridge, Mass., 1963), ch. 4.
48 Recent research on China's internal economic development during this period has totally revised the conventional wisdom on the subject. A handful of the key references are given in C&H, II, ch. 10, especially notes 7, 8, 9, 12, 15, 31, 85 and 109.
49 For a recent evaluation, see Gill Bennett, 'British policy in the Far East, 1933–1936: Treasury and Foreign Office', *Modern Asian Studies*, 26 (1992), pp. 545–68.
50 This is made plain in 'Provisional Answers to Questionnaire on China', 17 July 1935. Bank of England Archive, G1/300/2525/2, file 13.
51 For a summary of this argument, see P.J. Cain, 'British economic imperialism in China in the 1930s: the Leith-Ross mission', *Bulletin of Asia-Pacific Studies*, 7 (1997), pp. 23–34.

control. Their initiatives in China, as in Canada, were part of a wider strategy of protecting and enlarging the Sterling Area. Maximizing Britain's international financial advantage was, in their view, the key to economic progress generally, and thus to social and political stability and Britain's survival as a great imperial and world power. It must be acknowledged that, in both Canada and China in the 1930s, British policy was, to some degree, an imperialism of hubris and unrealized hopes; but it was also based ultimately upon an appraisal of world power relations that made sense at the time, and it kills the myth that Britain was a power conscious of the inevitability of decline.

Indeed, the relationship between the Dominions and Britain in the 1930s is a sharp reminder of the fact, all too frequently forgotten, that for most of the inter-war period Britain remained the only truly global power: in relative terms, her position until the late 1930s was, at the least, no worse than it had been before 1914.[52] Germany had been defeated, France had been devastated, and Russia had largely withdrawn from the international scene. Britain's dominance had indeed been challenged by the United States after 1914. But, despite economic offensives in Europe in the 1920s, the power of the United States was neutralized to some extent by isolationism after 1921, and her economic decline after 1929 was far greater than Britain's. It is hardly surprising, then, that British elites should have retained the same global ambitions after 1914 as before and that, given Britain's relatively rapid recovery from the slump, they should also have felt confident about maintaining both Britain's role as a great power and their own dominant position in British society.[53] It was only in the late 1930s, when faced with the combined hostility of a revived Germany, Italy and Japan, that Britain's world position began to come under serious threat, because it was impossible then to construct plausible counter-alliances with a weak France, a Bolshevik Russia and an indifferent United States.

GENTLEMANLY CAPITALISM AND FORMAL EMPIRE:
INDIA AND THE DEPENDENCIES

China was one of the classic arenas for the exercise of informal empire; the white empire provides an important, if also neglected, example of informal economic influence within the formal empire. The remaining constituents of the formal empire appear to offer a more straightforward illustration of the exercise of imperial control because they enjoyed much more limited degrees of local self-government (where it existed at all). Yet the realities of power were scarcely less complex than in the Dominions, even though Britain

---

52 J.R. Ferris, '"The Greatest Power on Earth": Great Britain in the 1920s'; and J.B. McKercher, '"Our Most Dangerous Enemy": Britain pre-eminent in the 1930s', both in *International History Review*, 13 (1991), pp. 726–83.
53 W.D. Rubinstein, 'Britain's elites in the interwar period', *Contemporary British History*, xxx (1998), forthcoming. The realization of how much they stood to lose both globally and domestically persuaded the gentlemanly capitalist elite to pursue appeasement with Germany for as long as possible. See S. Newton, *Profits of Peace: The Political Economy of Anlgo-German Appeasement* (Oxford, 1996).

commanded more extensive formal rights in the dependent parts of the empire. It was not just that the constitutional standing of territories within the formal empire varied greatly, embracing colonies, protectorates, condominiums, a sub-empire (India) and (after 1914) mandates, or even that their endowments were vastly different, as a comparison between India and Gambia readily demonstrates. Independent of these weighty considerations was the fact that the fulfilment of the imperial purpose in the dependencies was often hampered by the very lack of the resources and institutions that made members of the white empire such congenial and effective partners, while the sheer size and diversity of colonial societies obliged officials to enter a maze of negotiation, direction and compulsion in their endeavour to apply policy. Yet coercion, though undoubtedly an instrument of colonial administration, could not be widely used on a routine basis. Just as imperial control was not simply a matter of issuing edicts and assuming that they would be implemented, so colonial government was not simply a matter of passing on orders and expecting them to be obeyed. The fundamental dilemma accompanying the exercise of power was therefore much the same in the colonies as it was in the Dominions, even though its manifestations differed significantly: how could a distant authority lacking a popular local mandate secure consent to policies that were designed, in the first instance, to promote its own interests? Accordingly, we propose to carry forward our analysis of structural and relational power and apply it to the dependent parts of the empire – and specifically to the two cases presented in the essays in this volume contributed by Misra and White.

We are grateful to both authors for accepting our argument on its own terms, rather than annexing it to an alternative agenda. From an Indianist perspective, it would have been very easy to expatiate on the consequences of British rule, whereas our concern, as Misra clearly sees, was primarily with its causes.[54] In dealing with Malaya, White helps, additionally, to fill one of several regional gaps in *British Imperialism*. In doing so, he generously excuses us from the 'collective amnesia' that has caused several generations of historians to overlook south-east Asia.[55] In focusing on the twentieth century, both Misra and White identify three main themes (even though they assign them a different order and emphasis): the degree of autonomy enjoyed by viceroys and governors; the relationship between gentlemen and capitalists on the periphery; and the extent to which policy was directed towards assisting industry as well as finance.

54 An example of this misreading can be found in Dharma Kumar, 'Native capitalists and laisser-faire bureaucrats? – India, 1858–1914', *Modern Asian Studies*, 30 (1996), pp. 725–36.
55 White, '"Gentlemanly capitalism" and Empire', this volume, p. 175. In fact, we had completed a considerable amount of work on south-east Asia, especially for the period between occupation and decolonization (1870s–1950s), but we ran out of time even before we had used up all the space in what we then thought was a one-volume study. The other major omissions are Burma and the Caribbean. An important dissertation on Burma is now available: Thant Myint-U, 'The crisis of the Burmese state and the foundations of British colonial rule in Upper Burma, 1853–1900' (PhD thesis, Cambridge University, 1996) presents an argument that is supportive of our own interpretation of renewed imperialist rivalries in the late nineteenth century.

Although Misra and White are critical of our handling of these themes, we hope it is fair to say that their disagreement arises within the context of a broad acceptance of the direction taken by our general interpretation. Both authors provide admirable summaries of our principal thesis, note points of agreement, and then proceed to question the weight that should be given to it in their particular area of expertise. Misra, it seems to us, is particularly clear that the problem lies mainly in deciding how much emphasis should be given to our argument in relation to other possibilities. White's essay contrasts assent and dissent rather more sharply, concluding that the notion of gentlemanly capitalism poses more problems than it solves, at least for his region and period. Such criticism is not to be conjured away. But it does raise some interesting methodological problems that White has not fully resolved, perhaps for reasons for space. In contrasting generality with particularity, for example, he does not show unequivocally that the latter destroys rather than qualifies or elaborates the former. It is scarcely surprising to find that details of time and place do not replicate, perfectly, the broad principles governing a worldwide empire. But they do demonstrate that delegated authority did not allow the fundamental priorities of imperial policy to be abandoned.[56] As they stand, the two contrasting parts of White's essay are not fully reconciled. It seems to us that there is a strong possibility, at the least, that his essay (like those of Misra and Kubicek) is a case of viewing an agreed object through different ends of the telescope. If this is so, the debate between us is less about truth and falsity than about what philosophers call 'relative objectivity': we may all be offering faithful descriptions of the same object or event, but doing so from different standpoints.

We begin by looking at the degree of autonomy enjoyed by viceroys and governors because it is here that our distinction between types of power may help further to clarify the connection between the general and the particular, and, in this case, between the centre and the periphery. As we noted earlier,[57] the elements of structural power had to be adapted to particular circumstances at points where they impinged upon distant and different societies. Governing the empire required far-reaching adjustments to the maxims of liberalism, especially in limiting individual freedom and expanding the power of the state. This paradox was resolved, if only to the satisfaction of those who created it, by arguing that, while all states were set on the same evolutionary course, those at an earlier stage of progress required means of government that were appropriate to their condition.

Adjustments to core principles were seen to be inevitable in the colonies; hence the justification for paternal, interventionist government.[58] This attitude

---

56 India is probably the best example: the Government of India raised import duties to balance the budget, and so damaged British manufactured exports, but it conformed rigidly to London's requirements in monetary, as well as fiscal, matters. See C&H, II, ch. 8, and the further references given there.

57 Above, pp. 204–5.

58 An interventionism, incidentally, that continued in the immediate post-colonial era and was supported by the authority of the first generation of development economists.

helps to explain the Government of India's involvement, referred to by Misra, in promoting local manufacturing. But, as we pointed out in *British Imperialism*, this policy, though important in contribution to India's development, also served a higher purpose: local manufactures economized on imports (including Manchester textiles), helped to balance the budget and thus enabled India to service its large external debt. Misra generously acknowledges our argument here, but seeks to qualify it by suggesting that official concern with promoting industry 'predates the crisis in state revenues'.[59] It is not clear how far back Misra wishes to take the story; we ourselves had already drawn attention to the government's interest in developing local manufacturing as early as the 1870s as a means of dealing with the fiscal crisis arising from the Indian Mutiny (C&H, I, pp. 342–3), and there is no evidence that the issue was one of practical politics before then.

With regard to the colonial representatives of gentlemanly capitalism, Misra and White both argue powerfully that there was little social solidarity between government and business and a good deal of disagreement about policy too. Their observations on this theme are especially valuable because they direct attention to an important but neglected research topic: the social history and political role of expatriate business in the empire.[60] Whether they expose a flaw in the concept of gentlemanly capitalism, however, is another matter. As we have sought to make clear above, the gentlemanly capitalist complex spread beyond the confines of large landowners and leading City bankers to include, among others, senior figures in the civil and defence services. What it did not do, either at home or abroad, was to extend very far down the social scale. Tradesmen provided a valued service but were still looked down on, which is why they had their own entrances and exits. It is therefore not surprising to find that the discrimination that existed at home reproduced itself abroad. Even so, the relationship between administration and commerce is likely to have been more subtle in the colonies, where 'the white man' (and, increasingly, 'the white woman') felt threatened by 'the natives'. Social distance was less easily preserved where geographical circumstances favoured ethnic solidarity.[61]

The break point in the definition of social class occurs at the margin, that is to say not with those who are clearly in or out but with those who, in this case, were among the handful of successful, very wealthy, titled entrepreneurs at the top of the business hierarchy. Misra cites the example of Lord Inchcape,

---

59 Misra, 'Gentlemanly capitalism and the Raj', this volume, p. 168. Misra is correct in suggesting that the need to press ahead with Indian industry was also given impetus by the needs of the First World War, but this motive is to be seen as lending urgency to a policy that had already been formulated for the reasons given in *British Imperialism* and referred to here.

60 Economic history has been better served. For one of a number of good examples relating to the present discussion, see R.P.T. Davenport-Hines and Geoffrey Jones (eds), *British Business in Asia Since 1860* (Cambridge, 1989).

61 Neither Misra nor White has the space to explore this aspect of their commentaries. It might also be added that White is too quick to dismiss the significance of the link established between the Civil Service and business at the point where officials in both Whitehall and the empire accepted boardroom appointments on retiring from careers in the public sector. However, it has to be said that this is a matter that still awaits systematic investigation.

the shipping magnate; White refers (among others) to Sir Sydney Palmer, the prominent rubber planter. Misra regards Inchcape as being an exception; White considers Palmer to be an ungentlemanly capitalist. Both are correct, but neither conclusion damages the concept of gentlemanly capitalism. New money could not immediately compensate for lack of 'birth' or education, or for an ill-judged choice of occupation. Snobbery was a code that knew no frontiers: a gentleman was trained to sniff out upstarts and pretenders, whether they were found in London or Kuala Lumpur. But outstanding success in business held out the prospect of provisional membership of the elite, especially as the entrepreneur distanced himself from his working origins by becoming a board-room figure.[62] Membership could be confirmed after the passage of time had coated new money with tradition and enabled later generations of a family to acquire more suitable occupations. At that point, their inheritance, like their future, was assured: the *parvenu* had ceased to be, as Alan Clark observed disparagingly of Michael Heseltine, the sort of person who had to buy his own furniture.

White is therefore mistaken[63] in supposing that our argument assumes that government and business were homogeneous institutions with clearly defined monolithic goals. Our purpose was indeed to identify a powerful and cohes-ive gentlemanly elite, but we also made it clear that the elite was obliged to deal with an array of competing groups, and that it promoted (and at times endured) considerable internal debate about the best means of attaining broadly agreed goals. Misra's suggestion that officials may have begun to abandon gentlemanly values in the period after the First World War does not, in our view, fit the available evidence. The fact that recruitment to the Indian Civil Service placed increasing emphasis on intellectual merit is entirely consistent with the proposition that intellectual merit was placed at the service of gentle-manly values. The latest research suggests that this was indeed the case – after 1914 as before.[64]

It should also be remembered in this connection that Misra and White are both dealing with 'late' colonialism, when, as we too pointed out, some fundamental tenets of imperial policy were being rethought. The 1930s were particularly important in this respect. It was during that decade, and not simply as a result of the upheaval brought by the Second World War, that policy-makers recognized the necessity of striking a 'new deal' with national-ism. From China (as we saw above) to Argentina and including, en route,

---

62 We recognized the fact that the leaders of large industrial corporations did move closer to centres of power in Britain after 1914: C&H, II, p. 28.

63 Twice: see also his article, 'Government and business divided: Malaya, 1945–57', *Journal of Imperial & Commonwealth History*, 22 (1994), pp. 251–74, esp. p. 252.

64 Reba N. Soffer, *Discipline and Power: The University, History and the Making of an English Elite, 1870–1930* (Stanford, Ca., 1994); Peter Mandler and Susan Pederson, 'The British intelligentsia after the Victorians', in *idem* (eds), *After the Victorians: Private Conscience and Public Duty in Modern Britain* (1994), pp. 1–28. On India, see especially Gerald Studdert-Kennedy, *British Christians, Indian Nationalists and the Raj* (Delhi, 1991), and David C. Potter, *India's Political Administrators* (Oxford, 1986).

India, there were unmistakable signs that the old import–export economy was being modified to accommodate new joint ventures in manufacturing, property and services.[65] We welcome the emphasis given by Misra and White to these important developments, which we see as confirming rather than as qualifying our interpretation of the period. As Misra and White observe, there were strong disagreements between officials and businessmen about the new direction taken by policy (in the 1930s in the case of India and in the 1950s in Malaya). In both instances governments, which did not have to take the commercial risk, seem to have been more inclined than business to promote economic and political change, believing that the empire needed to adapt to survive. It is scarcely surprising, as White correctly points out, that disagreements between them were particularly acute in the hectic period shortly before independence.

This observation would present a difficulty for our interpretation of decolonization only if it required the two groups to be in substantial, if not perfect, harmony. The truth is that, while governments were of course committed to upholding Britain's strategic and economic interests in Malaya, as in other parts of the empire, the means of doing so were a matter of debate, and at a time of rapid change (and therefore great uncertainty) the argument between going forward and holding back was voiced with particular fervour. These remarks are not intended to minimize in any way the contributions made by Misra and White to our understanding of relations between government and business during this period. On the contrary, in going far beyond our own schematic remarks, their more substantial work has helped to open up a new area of enquiry.[66] It seems, on the whole, that colonial business did not dominate colonial government. Were there parts of the empire where that was not the case, and, if so, why? It also appears that colonial governments forced the pace of economic change, particularly with regard to local manufacturing. Does this generalization hold for parts of the empire other than India and Malaya? If not, in what circumstances were expatriate businessmen frustrated by the reluctance of governments to cooperate with moves to transform old-style colonial export economies? In answering these questions, the distinction to be borne in mind, as we have suggested, is between the principle of up-holding Britain's interest throughout the world and the means of doing so.

Although Misra and White argue that colonial governments were not manipulated by expatriate firms, they also think that we have underestimated the influence of British industry on the formulation of imperial policy. This is, perhaps, a matter of interpretation and emphasis. Our argument was not that industrial interests were of no account (as Misra at one point inadvertently suggests);[67] it

---

65 The trend was even clearer in the Dominions, which had reached a more advanced stage of development.

66 See Maria Misra's forthcoming study, *Enterprise and Empire: Business, Race and Politics in British India* (Oxford, 1998), and N.J. White's recently published book, *Business and Government in the Era of Decolonisation: Malaya, 1942–57* (Oxford, 1997).

67 Misra, 'Gentlemanly capitalism and the Raj', this volume, pp. 162–3.

was rather that the financial and service sector carried greater weight. Gentlemen had no natural affinity with industry, but they recognized its importance in generating employment and foreign exchange, and its role in contributing to the national interest that they were charged to uphold. However, when hard choices had to be made in key areas of policy and important parts of the world, priority was given to finance rather than to industry. Given the high level of unemployment in the British textile industry in the 1930s, and the conscious effort to find solutions in imperial markets, the concessions made to Lancashire (as noted by Misra) demonstrate, not the strength of the industrial lobby, but its weakness.[68] They certainly did nothing to arrest the decline of Manchester cottons in India. The fascinating example cited by White shows how industrial interests backing synthetics unseated the 'rubber barons' of Malaya in the 1950s. In White's view, the episode demonstrates that 'industrialists had considerable influence over policies which affected Malaya'.[69] This may indeed have been the case, but the important point to emerge from the contest between old and new interests is that it occurred right at the end of the period of British rule. At this moment, the government was bent on reorganizing Britain's international economic policy to take account of new opportunities in trade with other advanced economies (symbolized by the application to join the European Economic Community in 1961). From the late 1950s the aim was to move beyond the confines of the defensive imperial economic bloc that had come into being during the slump of the 1930s and had served the needs of wartime emergency and peace-time reconstruction so admirably. The real significance of the shift from natural to synthetic rubber in the late 1950s is not that it demonstrates that industry could influence policy, but that it symbolizes the declining value of empire.[70]

NEW HORIZONS OF EMPIRE

Perhaps the most important message to emerge from this volume is not that scholars disagree about major issues, for that is scarcely novel, but that the subject itself – the history of imperialism and empires – is beginning to enjoy a revival after a generation of relative neglect. This is partly because sensitivities about the imperial record are less acute than they were at the time of decolonization, and partly because the problems of the post-imperial world around us have revived interest in the era of empires that preceded it and in the legacy of their dissolution.[71]

68 It is perhaps worth noting that Basudev Chatterji's valuable recent study, cited by Misra, was first presented as a PhD thesis in 1978. Although revised and updated, it bears the marks of the widespread assumption of the time that economic interests were synonymous with industrial interests and that these had an important influence on policy. See Chatterji, *Trade, Tariffs and Empire: Lancashire and British Policy in India, 1919–1939* (New Delhi, 1992).
69 White, 'Gentlemanly capitalism', this volume, p. 192.
70 As argued, albeit in a compressed manner, in C&H, II, pp. 269–91.
71 Some of these issues are discussed in A.G. Hopkins, *The Future of the Imperial Past* (Cambridge, 1997).

Whatever view is taken of the interpretation put forward in *British Imperialism*, we hope that our work will contribute to the process of historical re-evaluation that is now under way. The prospects for future research are generous and inviting. The editor has drawn attention to a number of promising opportunities in his Introduction to this volume. Others include, at a more general level: the concept and course of modernization during the last three centuries; the domestic roots of international policy; the relationship between the centre and its satellites; the justification for conventional chronological divisions in the treatment of the subject; the causes and timing of the processes of decline and decolonization; and the enduring methodological problem of weighing material, cultural and all other elements in a complex story without being either reductionist or tautological. For those who find the prospect of considering these issues within the British context too insular, an agenda for exploring comparative history lies readily to hand, whether in studying the imperial experience of other European states, like France, or in looking into the process of modernization and expansion elsewhere, as, for example, in the case of Japan. Accordingly, as the age of empires recedes, we should not be surprised to find that its scholarly significance will grow, and that it will attract a new generation of researchers in the century that is about to begin.

A short bibliography

The following books and articles discuss, criticize or otherwise refer significantly to gentlemanly capitalism in two contexts: the interpretation of modern British history, and the controversy over Britain's role as an imperial power. The selection is intended to be an introduction to the debate, and not a list of all relevant studies, which would, of course, be very extensive. It is worth noting that items published before 1993 refer to the two articles by Cain and Hopkins that appeared in the *Economic History Review* in 1986, and should now be read in the light of the fuller statement made in the two volumes of *British Imperialism*.

Place of publication is London (unless otherwise stated).

GENERAL STUDIES

B.W.E. Alford, *Britain in the World Economy since 1880* (1996).

Huw V. Bowen, *Elites, Enterprise, and the Making of the British Overseas Empire, 1688–1775* (1996).

Stanley Chapman, *Merchant Enterprise in Britain: From the Industrial Revolution to World War One* (Cambridge, 1992).

P. Hudson, *The Industrial Revolution* (1992).

Will Hutton, *The State We're In* (1995).

David Kynaston, *The City of London: Golden Years, 1890–1914* (1995).

F. McDonough, *The British Empire, 1815–1914* (1994).

David Marquand, 'Travails of an Ancien Regime' in idem., *The New Reckoning: Capitalism, States and Citizens* (Cambridge, 1997), pp. 186–203.

Andrew Porter, *European Imperialism, 1860–1914* (Basingstoke, 1994).

W.D. Rubinstein, *Capitalism, Culture and Decline in Britain, 1750–1990* (1993).

J.F. Wilson, *British Business History, 1720–1994* (Manchester, 1995).

REVIEW ESSAYS OF *BRITISH IMPERIALISM*

H. Bowen, 'The British Empire – I', *History*, 79 (Basingstoke, 1994), pp. 263–6.

D. Cannadine, 'The empire strikes back', *Past & Present*, 147 (1995), pp. 180–94.

M. Chamberlain, 'The causes of British imperialism: battle rejoined', *The Historian*, 39 (1993), pp. 10–12.

M.J. Daunton, 'Home and colonial', *Twentieth-Century British History*, 6 (1995), pp. 344–58.

D.K. Fieldhouse, 'Gentlemen, capitalists, and the British Empire', *Journal of Imperial and Commonwealth History*, 22 (1994), pp. 531–41.

G. Ingham, 'British capitalism: empire, merchants and decline', *Social History*, 20 (1995), pp. 339–54.

M. Kuitenbrouwer, 'Capitalism and imperialism: Britain and the Netherlands', *Itinerario*, 18 (1994), pp. 105–15.

G. Krozewski, 'Rethinking British imperialism', *Journal of European Economic History*, 23 (1994), pp. 619–30.

D. Kumar, 'Native capitalists and laisser-faire bureaucrats? – India, 1858–1914', *Modern Asian Studies*, 30 (1996), pp. 725–36.

Hugues Legros, 'Comptes rendus: P.J. Cain and A.G. Hopkins, British Imperialism', *Revue Belge de Philologie et d'Histoire*, 74 (1996), pp. 905–9.

A. Porter, 'Birmingham, Westminster and the City of London: visions of empire compared', *Journal of Historical Geography*, 21 (1995), pp. 83–7.

J. Osterhammel, 'Gentleman-Kapitalismus und Gentleman-Charakter: Neues zum Britischen Imperialismus', *Neues Politisches Literatur*, 39 (1994), pp. 5–13.

K. Sugihara, 'British imperialism, the City of London and global industrialisation: some comments on Cain and Hopkins, *British Imperialism*', *Economic History Review of Japan*, 49 (1998), pp. 277–81.

SPECIALIZED AND INTERPRETIVE STUDIES

Britain

Huw Bowen, 'Investment in empire in the later eighteenth century: East India stockholding, 1756–1791', *Economic History Review*, 42 (1989), pp. 186–206.

R.A. Bryer, 'The Mercantile Laws Commission of 1854 and the political economy of limited liability', *Economic History Review*, 50 (1997), pp. 37–56.

Ann M. Carlos and Jill L. Van Stone, 'Stock transfer patterns in the Hudson's Bay Company: a study of the English capital market in operation, 1670–1730', *Business History*, 38 (1995), pp. 15–39.

Y. Cassis, *City Bankers, 1880–1914* (Cambridge, 1994).

P.J. Cain and A.G. Hopkins, 'Gentlemanly capitalism and British expansion overseas, I: the old colonial system, 1688–1850', *Economic History Review*, 39 (1986), pp. 501–25.

P.J. Cain and A.G. Hopkins, 'Gentlemanly capitalism and British expansion overseas, II: new imperialism, 1850–1945', *Economic History Review*, 40 (1987), pp. 1–26.

P.J. Cain and A.G. Hopkins, 'Reconstructing British imperialism: the autobiography of a research project', *Itinerario*, 18 (1994), pp. 95–104.

P.J. Corfield, 'The rivals: landed and other gentlemen', in N. Harte and R. Quinault (eds), *Land and Society in Britain: Essays in Honour of F.M.L. Thompson* (Manchester, 1996), pp. 1–33.

M.J. Daunton, 'The entrepreneurial state, 1700–1914', *History Today*, 44 (1944), pp. 11–16.

M.J. Daunton, 'Gentlemanly capitalism and British industry, 1820–1914', *Past & Present*, 122 (1989), pp. 119–58.

E.H.H. Green, *The Crisis of Conservatism: The Economics, Politics and Ideology of the Conservative Party* (1995).

A.C. Howe, 'Free trade and the City of London, *c.*1820–1870', *History*, 77 (1992), pp. 391–410.

A.C. Howe, 'From "old corruption" to "new probity": the Bank of England and its directors in the age of reform', *Financial History Review*, 1 (1994), pp. 23–41.

Scott Newton, *The Profits of Peace: The Political Economy of Anglo-German Appeasement* (Oxford, 1996).

R. Pearson, 'Towards an historical model of service innovation: the case of the insurance industry, 1700–1914', *Economic History Review*, 50 (1997), pp. 235–56.

W.D. Rubinstein, '"Gentlemanly capitalism", British finance and industry, 1820–1914: a response', *Past & Present*, 132 (1991), pp. 150–70.

W.D. Rubinstein, 'The structure of wealth-holding in Britain, 1809–39: a preliminary anatomy', *Historical Research*, 65 (1992), pp. 74–89.

Paul Thompson, 'The Pyrrhic victory of gentlemanly capitalism: the financial elite of the City of London, 1945–90', *Journal of Contemporary History*, 32 (1997), pp. 283–304.

Paul Thompson, 'The Pyrrhic victory of gentlemanly capitalism: the financial elite of the City of London, 1945–90', Pt 2, *Journal of Contemporary History*, 32 (1997), pp. 427–40.

Overseas

Shigeru Akita, '"Gentlemanly capitalism", intra-Asian trade and Japanese industrialisation at the turn of the last century', *Japan Forum*, 8 (1996), pp. 51–65.

P.J. Cain, 'British economic imperialism, 1919–39: towards a new interpretation', *Bulletin of Asian Studies*, IV (1994), pp. 233–54.

P.J. Cain, 'Gentlemanly imperialists at work: the Bank of England, Canada and the Sterling Area, 1932–36', *Economic History Review*, 49 (1996), pp. 336–57.

P.J. Cain, 'British economic imperialism in China in the 1930s: the Leith-Ross mission', *Bulletin of Asia-Pacific Studies*, 7 (1997), pp. 23–34.

P.J. Cain, 'Was it worth having? The British Empire, 1850–1950', *Revista de Historia Economica*, 16 (1998), pp. 351–76.

Juan R.I. Cole, *Colonialism and Revolution in the Middle East: Social and Cultural Origins of Egypt's 'Urabi' Movement* (Princeton, 1993).

J. Darwin, 'Imperialism and the Victorians: the dynamics of territorial expansion', *English Historical Review*, 112 (1997), pp. 614–42.

P. Henderson, 'Cocoa, finance and the state in Ecuador, 1895–1914', *Bulletin of Latin American Research*, 16 (1997), pp. 169–86.

A.G. Hopkins, 'Informal empire in Argentina: an alternative view', *Journal of Latin American Studies*, 26 (1994), pp. 469–84.

A.G. Hopkins, *The Future of the Imperial Past* (Cambridge, 1997).

A.G. Hopkins, 'Macmillan's audit of empire, 1957', in Peter Clarke and Clive Trebilcock (eds), *Understanding Decline: Perceptions and Realities of British Economic Performance. Essays Presented to Barry Supple* (Cambridge, 1997), pp. 234–60.

Dane Kennedy, 'Imperial history and post-colonial theory', *Journal of Imperial and Commonwealth History*, 24 (1996), pp. 345–63.

G. Krozewski, 'Sterling, the "minor" territories and the end of formal empire, 1939–58', *Economic History Review*, 46 (1993), pp. 239–65.

Gerold Krozewski, 'Finance and empire: the dilemma facing Great Britain in the 1950s', *International History Review*, 18 (1996), pp. 48–68.

J.T. Lindblad, 'Economic aspects of Dutch expansion in Indonesia, 1870–1914', *Modern Asian Studies*, 23 (1989), pp. 1–23.

J. Lunn, *Capital and Labour on the Rhodesian Railway System, 1888–1947* (Basingstoke, 1997).

Rory Miller, *Britain and Latin America in the Nineteenth and Twentieth Centuries* (1993).

I.R. Phimister, 'The Chrome Trust: the creation of an international cartel, 1909–38', *Business History*, 38 (1996), pp. 77–89.

I.R. Phimister, 'Africa partioned', *Review* (Fernand Braudel Centre), 18 (1995), pp. 35–81.

Andrew Porter, 'Gentlemanly capitalism and imperialism: the British experience since 1750?', *Journal of Imperial and Commonwealth History*, 18 (1990), pp. 265–95.

Andrew Porter, 'The South African War (1899–1902): context and motive reconsidered', *Journal of African History*, 31 (1990), pp. 43–57.

J. Tann and J. Aitken, 'The diffusion of the stationary steam engine from Britain to India, 1790–1830', *Indian Economic and Social History Review*, 29 (1992), pp. 199–214.

David Torrance, *The Strange Death of Liberal Empire: Lord Selborne in South Africa* (Liverpool, 1996).

Luke Trainor, *British Imperialism and Australian Nationalism: Manipulation, Conflict and Compromise in the Late Nineteenth Century* (Cambridge, 1994).

J. Ward, 'The Industrial Revolution and British imperialism, 1750–1850', *Economic History Review*, 47 (1994), pp. 44–65.

A.J. Webster, *Gentlemen Capitalists: British Imperialism in Southeast Asia, 1770–1890* (1998).

Index